PENGUIN BOOKS

ANOTHER WAY HOME

John Thorndike is the author of two acclaimed novels, *The Potato Baron* and *Anna Delaney's Child*. He lives in Santa Fe, New Mexico.

Another Way Home

A Family's Journey Through Mental Illness

JOHN THORNDIKE

PENGUIN BOOKS

PENGUIN BOOKS
Published by the Penguin Group
Penguin Books USA Inc., 375 Hudson Street,
New York, New York 10014, U.S.A.
Penguin Books Ltd, 27 Wrights Lane, London W8 5TZ, England
Penguin Books Australia Ltd, Ringwood, Victoria, Australia
Penguin Books Canada Ltd, 10 Alcorn Avenue,
Toronto, Ontario, Canada M4V 3B2
Penguin Books (N.Z.) Ltd, 182–190 Wairau Road,
Auckland 10, New Zealand

Penguin Books Ltd, Registered Offices:
Harmondsworth, Middlesex, England

First published in the United States of America
by Crown Publishers, Inc. 1996
Reprinted by arrangement with Crown Publishers, Inc.
Published in Penguin Books 1997

1 3 5 7 9 10 8 6 4 2

The names of several characters in this book have been changed.
Grateful acknowledgment is made for permission to reprint an excerpt from
the composition *Goodnight, Irene*. Words and music by Huddie Ledbetter and
John A. Lomax. TRO copyright © 1936 (renewed), 1950 (renewed)
Ludlow Music, Inc., New York, New York. Used by permission.

ISBN 0-517-70542-7 (hc.)
ISBN 0 14 02.6570 8 (pbk.)
(CIP data available)

Printed in the United States of America
Set in New Baskerville

For AT, who loves being a father

Many people bring a book to life.

Thanks to Natalie Goldberg, who convinced me I should write down these stories—and who also warned me, "This book will break your bones." She was right.

Thanks to Janir Thorndike and Joseph J. Thorndike.

Thanks to my agent Kathy Anderson and my editor Elaine Pfefferblit.

Thanks to Sandy Weymouth and Lois Gilbert.

Thanks to Charles Flowers, Biddle Duke, David Wade Smith, Juliet Wittman, Eddie Lewis, Anne Pedersen, Henry Shukman, Rod Barker, Janet Bailey, Doug Preston, Hadley Harper, Deborah Parks, Kristin Cook, and Lady Borton. Thanks to Dave Reichert, Michelle Ajamian, Patty Coughlan, Linda Sonna, Felicia Bond, Granville Greene, Rob Wilder, Judith Hurley, Pam Shepherd, and Sandy Brown.

And special thanks to Elspeth Bobbs, gardener extraordinaire and patron of the arts.

"Of them all, it was the true love. Of them all, it was the best. That other, that sumptuous love which made one drunk, which one longed for, envied, believed in, that was not life. It was what life was seeking; it was a suspension of life. But to be close to a child, for whom one spent everything, whose life was protected and nourished by one's own, to have that child beside one, at peace, was the real, the deepest, the only joy."

—James Salter, *Light Years*

JANIR AND I WALK SIDE BY SIDE DOWN THE CHAPEL'S carpeted aisle. The room is silent and richly appointed, the walls a pale rose. Janir looks handsome in his blazer, white shirt and tie, but he moves as stiffly as I do, and his face looks the way I feel: cautious, intent, dismayed. His mother lies in a shallow box on a gurney in front of us. We pause to let the others catch up, then approach the box and peer in. It's Clarisa, but I hardly recognize her. One side of her face has been covered with a white cloth, and on the other side her flesh is dense and dark. Five days ago she fell from the fire escape of her hotel here in San Francisco. She may have jumped, no one knows for sure. She was forty-seven.

She has no expression. Her mouth seems firm, as if someone has closed it for her. The funeral home brought her directly from the morgue this morning, and she may still be cold. She looks it. Though admonished not to by the funeral director, I want to touch her.

Her mother must have the same idea. Paquita fusses with the white cloth, twitching it back and forth, minutely rearranging its folds. As she does so, the back of her hand grazes her daughter's hair.

When I finally step back, Janir does too. For a while we stand to one side, then sit down in the second row of benches. The dark wood is so burnished it's slippery. We have a whole pew to ourselves, but sit with our arms and shoulders touching as if huddled in a tight space. Janir is twenty-three. He's had his muscled arms and broad shoulders for years—yet they still surprise me. For ten minutes we don't say anything. With Clarisa's death our world has shifted on an axis so deep, so hidden, we've forgotten how much our lives still revolve around her.

Paquita sits down on the bench in front of us, flanked by her son Victor and Janir's half brother, John Leslie. He's a handsome kid with slicked-back hair, five years younger than Janir. The two of them met as adults only yesterday, and so far have spoken little about their mother. I think Janir resembles her more, with his dark skin, curly hair and strong features.

From our pews we stare at the carton she lies in. No one has said anything about it. A second white cloth is draped over most of it, but no one can ignore that the box is made of corrugated paper.

Planning Clarisa's funeral from out of state, none of us thought we should install her in an elaborate casket for this one-hour viewing before her cremation. But I never imagined they would move her around in a cardboard box. I didn't think it through, I must have seen her just lying on a table. Now I feel delinquent and ashamed. I search for something to say, something to refute this vision of a bargain service and a broken body.

"She was so brave," I tell Janir. I want to explain, in the few words I can manage, how unafraid his mother had been. "When she had you she was completely devoted. Her best year was right after you were born. That was the happiest I ever saw her."

That's so sad I break into tears. Janir wraps his arms around me, puts his face next to mine and holds me tight until I calm down. Even then he doesn't let go.

"I cried already," he says.

This almost makes me start again. "You don't have to cry," I tell him. "You don't have to do anything."

He leans against me.

•   •   •

After the viewing, Clarisa's mother, her brother, her two sons and I—the five who were closest to her—drive downtown to Turk Street and the Winston Arms, the hotel where she died. We park the car in a commercial lot and walk the last couple of blocks past streets smelling of fry oil and urine. Winos hang out on stoops, and the homeless, dressed in coats and sweaters in the September heat, push shopping carts piled high with plastic bags, clothes and water jugs. I had never imagined Clarisa living in such a rundown neighborhood. For years she had stayed in orderly halfway houses or sheltered hotels, closer to the part of San Francisco she liked most, the Haight and Golden Gate Park. Every month the state sent her a

Supplemental Security Income check, and she roamed the city on her transit pass, visiting the Presidio, Point Lobos and Ocean Beach.

Over the years Victor, Paquita and I all gave her money. Once I sent her an emergency thousand dollars, along with some hopeful advice on how to make it last. She used it to put a new engine into a twenty-year-old station wagon, and two weeks later bumped the car into a light pole. She got into a hassle with the police, and when I next heard from her she didn't know where the car was. Maybe they'd towed it. It was gone.

The sidewalks on Turk Street are greasy and discolored. We stand in front of the Winston Arms, staring up at the fire escape, then back at the sidewalk. Is this where she landed? After a morning fog the day has grown warm and I'm starting to sweat. People shuffle past, giving us a wide berth. Dressed for church, we are outsiders here among the shabby buildings and alcoholic faces. Even in the bright sunlight the air feels thick and soiled. What friends could Clarisa have had here?

I watch Janir. I want to protect him, but I can't. He stands apart, unmoving, his white collar tight around his neck. An unshaven old man in a stained jacket comes to a stop beside us. He studies the fire escape and the sidewalk, then turns to the two boys, almost as if he knows who they are.

"A beautiful girl fell to her death here last Sunday," he says, then shuffles away down the sidewalk.

"*Qué dijo?*" Paquita asks. What did he say?

I repeat it to her in Spanish. Though she gives the old man a suspicious look, I'm filled with a strange gratitude, for he has said exactly what I feel. It is not my tired and embattled ex-wife who has died here, but the Clarisa I knew years ago: the smiling young woman who pulled me headlong into life and decided to have a child with me.

Paquita has been here before, and leads us into the lobby. One of the ceiling lights is buzzing, the walls are battleship gray and the only piece of furniture is a crumbling sofa.

They haven't touched Clarisa's room, the manager explains. He's young, Malaysian, neatly dressed in a pressed shirt, slacks, white socks and rubber thongs. He's been waiting, he tells us, for someone to come for her things. We follow him up the carpeted stairs to the third floor, and with every step my alarm grows. I don't want to see this room. Halfway down the corridor he unlocks a door, pushes it open and turns on the light.

We take a couple of steps inside. The bed is unmade, the mattress bare and filthy. The lone window, half covered by a blanket, faces a brick wall only four feet off. There's a small television, no magazines or books. Piles of damp clothes lie on the floor next to old pairs of shoes, empty vodka bottles and scraps of paper. The air is stale and acrid, and a cluster of black flies hovers over the bed.

Victor looks stiff and formal. He folds his arms over his chest and appraises the chaos. All morning he has seemed to be in complete control—but I know from his wife that after his sister's death he came home from the office, lay down on his bed and wept for hours.

Paquita goes to work. She finds a paper shopping bag and folds some clothes into it. She moves erratically, picking up and dropping things, and her choice of articles seems random: a blouse, a flowered towel, a pair of slacks. Though she cried all through the mass this morning, and again at the viewing, I've never seen Paquita fall apart. Now she seems on the edge.

Janir probes. He opens a dresser drawer and picks out a cheap hairbrush, then a pharmacy bottle containing a single capsule of Prozac. He inspects them. He picks up an empty can of hair spray, shakes it, then holds it stiffly in front of him as if it might explode. His face, his whole body looks tight.

I look in the closet. I push aside the clothes that have fallen to the floor and pick up a lone moccasin. I get down on my hands and knees and peer under the bed. I don't know what I'm looking for, but I have to see everything. I have to crush myself with the worst details. I step into the tiny bathroom. There's nothing on the cabinet shelves, not even a toothbrush, but on the floor may be a reason for the flies. Even after decades in the U.S., Clarisa has dealt with toilet paper the Latin-American way. In El Salvador, so as not to clog the plumbing, you put it in a basket and someone cleans it up. Here she has dropped the used paper into an overflowing black plastic bag, and no one has cleaned up anything.

Slowly we come to a stop. There is nothing more to examine.

Paquita's shopping bag is full. *"Cayó en una depresión enorme,"* she says. Clarisa fell into an enormous depression. "She wouldn't eat anything. She gave up hope. She wouldn't clean up or take care of herself." Paquita's arms hang limp beside her. "I didn't know what to do."

I'm convinced now that she jumped.

Could I have done anything myself? If I'd heard how Clarisa was doing, would I have come and tried to help? Probably not. We were divorced almost twenty years ago, and I'd grown used to her tumultuous life. I could never have imagined a room like this. Clarisa had always had mood swings, but I'd never seen her suffer from the kind of depression embodied here.

Underlying my remorse is a bitter truth: I haven't seen Clarisa in five years. When Janir went off to college I moved as well and didn't tell her where. I was tired of her five-A.M. phone calls and unannounced visits. I wanted to keep her at a distance.

Janir looks hurt and puzzled. I step over some clothes and stand beside him as his eyes settle on the demeaning mattress. "I thought she was doing better," he says.

She was. For most of the last six months she had seemed to be on an upswing. She had asked him for my address and sent me several coherent letters—the best in a decade—and only ten days ago I'd sent her a newsy letter about Janir. I had begun to dream, for the first time in years, that he might wind up with a mother he could talk to.

"She wrote me at work," he says. "She told me she had a job."

Victor knows about this. "She answered the phone in her old hotel," he says. "It was just two afternoons a week."

"It was something," Janir says.

I hear the pain in his voice, the deception, even anger. I'm starting to feel it myself. The dead always let us down. Janir stares out the window at the sooty brick wall.

I edge closer to him. For the last twenty years I've loved him better and taken better care of him than I ever did his mother. We don't say anything, we just stand beside each other with our arms touching.

ONE

CLARISA WAS NINETEEN WHEN I MET HER. SHE HAD A quiet look, dark hair and Mayan, almost oriental eyes. It was October of 1967, the end of the rainy season in El Salvador, where I was a Peace Corps volunteer teaching English at the National University. I'd come out that night to practice my Spanish with some friends, and the open-air café was full of teachers and students talking politics. Clarisa sat two tables off but never looked my way. Her skin was as smooth as a child's, and her thick hair, pulled back with two barrettes, fell on a cream-colored jacket with cloth buttons.

I stared at her. I ignored the conversation at my table. As a Peace Corps volunteer I wasn't supposed to get involved in politics anyway. I was twenty-four, I'd been in Central America for ten months now and still worked on my Spanish every night. I talked with friends or saw a movie or sat at home reading the newspaper with a dictionary on my lap.

Someone at her table signaled for the bill. When they stood up I did too. I'd been struggling to invent some comment, some way to introduce myself, but hadn't come up with anything. I followed her anyway. Below her elegant jacket she wore a short pleated skirt and a pair of plastic sandals. I reached her before she got to the sidewalk.

"Hola," I said, as I came up beside her. *"Qué tal? Cómo te llamas?"* Hi, how was she doing? What was her name? I felt like an idiot, but the Spanish made it easier. I could pretend I was just practicing.

Her mouth showed the trace of a smile, and she extended a cool hand. *"Clarisa Rubio Betancourt,"* she said as we shook. It was one of those father-and-mother surnames I could never remember both halves of. *"Y tú?"* she asked.

My name is difficult in Spanish, so I enunciated it as clearly as possible: *"Juan Torn-di-que."*

"Tanto gusto," she said, and the tiny smile lingered.

I was doing well, I thought. I plunged ahead. I asked if she came here often, and commented on the rainy season. But my Spanish seemed to have taken a plane back to Connecticut. I muffed a subjunctive and forgot the word for lightning: *relámpago*. It was impossible to look at her and talk at the same time.

I was rescued momentarily by the first drops of rain, pinging on the tin roof above us. Motorbikes scooted for cover on the street, and a moment later the downpour began. Drops splashed in from the sidewalk, but Clarisa did not move back from the deluge. She just let her feet get wet in their sensible plastic sandals. She held her notebooks to her chest as I stared at her sleek wet toes.

"Tú eres estudiante?" I asked.

"No," she said coolly, *"soy profesora."*

She seemed too young to be a teacher. Of what, I asked: *"Profesora de qué?"*

For a moment she didn't say anything. Then, in flawless English, "Are you in the Peace Corps?"

"You're American," I said. I was stunned.

"No," she said, "I'm from here. I went to school in San Francisco."

I couldn't get over it. "Your English is perfect. You don't have any accent at all."

"I was there for five years. And I was only fourteen when I went."

No wonder she had smiled when I introduced myself. "And how long," I asked, "were you going to let me stumble around in Spanish?"

"Not very long. And you're doing pretty well. That's how you learn, isn't it? That's how I learned English."

Her skin was dark and smooth, and her lips full. She looked more Indian than anyone in the café, yet from her mouth came an American girl-next-door voice. She had only come back a month ago, and already she missed California and was thinking of returning. She still had her U.S. residence, and she could stay with her brother in San Francisco. On the other hand she had a good job here, teaching English at the U.S. Center.

After twenty minutes the rain let up. The air smelled of wet leaves, garbage and woodsmoke, and the streets were washed clean.

"I have to go," she said.

"Do you?"

"It's different, living with your mother."

We shook hands a second time. Then she stepped out onto the sidewalk and crossed the street, heading for the bus stop. Until she disappeared around a corner I watched her swaying skirt and shining calves.

•   •   •

Two nights later I went looking for her at the Center and invited her out for an ice cream. After another couple of nights she took me home and introduced me to her mother, her sister and her younger brother. I thought her mother, Paquita, would be suspicious—perhaps because the last time I went out with a young Salvadoran woman we had been escorted to the movies by an uncle who owned a taxi, and picked up by him when the show let out. But I found Paquita relaxed. Her only rule for me, no matter what night of the week, was to get Clarisa home by eleven.

We started kissing on the wooden benches of the city's parks. Then in cafés, in the backs of buses and on the flat roof of Clarisa's house. I always feared someone would pop up the stairs and discover us, but she never seemed to give it a thought.

After a month we went to bed in my airy upstairs apartment, and started spending most Sundays there, talking, painting, reading and making love on my narrow bed. Though raised a Catholic she seemed completely unashamed and relaxed about sex. Afterward she padded naked around the room, unconcerned that someone might see her through the window.

Sunday afternoons were good because we could claim we had gone to the soccer game at the national stadium, only six blocks from my house. I liked having an alibi. Even so, as roars from the game filtered in over the rooftops and we lay naked through the sweltering afternoon, I sometimes worried. I was afraid Paquita would see through our story. I thought she could just look at us and know we were having sex.

"Don't worry about it," Clarisa said. "She'll never find out."

"We better ask who won the game."

"Relax, John. She likes you."

"I always get caught," I said.

She laughed. "Not me. I never get caught."

•   •   •

In the United States my mother was a doctor, and my father a former managing editor of *Life* and one of the founders of *American Heritage* magazine. I'd gone to boarding school, Harvard and Columbia, and my family had some money.

Paquita, after her husband's suicide in 1954, had raised her four children on a teacher's salary, and managed to send two of them to school in California. But money was scarce for the Rubios, and Clarisa, when I met her, lived at home in a tiny room with a bed, a dresser and an overhead light. Her house that year had bare walls, a broken television, no telephone and no hot water—but none of that mattered to me. I liked her big family and was entranced by Clarisa. Though five years younger than I, she had twice the raw confidence and was far more at ease in her skin.

One Saturday morning we lay on the coarse grass of Cuscatlán Park, kissing and laughing and enduring the fat relentless ants. Finally we stood up, scraped them off our arms and ankles and headed for my apartment. We were halfway there, walking down the middle of a quiet street, arm in arm and lit up with sex, when a car approached. We stepped aside but it stopped, and Ricardo Ruiz leaned across the front seat. He was a family friend, kind of a godfather to Clarisa.

"Hola, compadres," he said. He was smiling broadly. *"Pa'donde van?"*

I panicked. I was sure he knew where we were going. "To Paquita's house," I lied.

"Hey, that's where I'm going. Get in, I'll give you a ride."

He was headed the wrong direction for Paquita's. He knew I was lying, and I knew he was. But now we were trapped.

"No thanks," Clarisa said. "We can walk."

"Don't be silly," he said. "Get in, get in."

She held back. But he didn't look at Clarisa, he looked at me. I was flustered, I didn't know how to refuse him. Finally I took a step forward and opened the door.

"Clarisa," he said, "come."

She got in without a word, but her face looked like a Mayan stone carving. Ricardo smiled and chattered beside me. I hated his phony good spirits and sat upright between the two of them, gripping the seat with my hands and trying not to let my shoulders touch either one of them.

At Paquita's I plotted our escape. I figured we could get away after thirty minutes and recover that divine state we had been in.

But Paquita roped the three of us in for lunch. Clarisa was no help at all. She hardly said a word. She didn't care what they thought. I tried to carry our end of the conversation, but as soon as she finished eating she got up and left the room.

Ten minutes later I found her on the roof, her back to me, staring out over the neighborhood's pastel houses.

"Clarisa . . ." I said.

She spun around. "Coward."

That was it precisely. "I didn't want him to get the wrong idea," I said.

"What wrong idea?"

"We could go to my place now. We could tell them we're going to a matinee."

She watched me with disdain. "I wanted to go then, not now."

I tried to put my arms around her, but she shook me off. "Go home," she said coldly. "Leave me alone."

•   •   •

Twice the next week I stopped by her house, but both times she left for the corner store and didn't return. When no one was looking, I stepped outside and walked home, my hands stuffed into my pockets. How long would she keep this up? Saturday I went again, but she shut herself in her room. I hung around anyway. I talked to her sister, Eva Luz. I talked to the maids and to Paquita. Everyone pretended Clarisa was simply taking a siesta.

My best bet was Max, her fourteen-year-old brother. I played cards with him at the kitchen table and invited him to tomorrow's soccer game—the same game I had supposedly been going to every Sunday with his sister.

The ploy was so obvious I was afraid Clarisa wouldn't be home when we got back from the game. But she was, sitting in the parlor and drawing freehand on a large tablet. I gave Max some money and sent him to the store for Cokes.

Clarisa kept drawing. Her charcoal stick rasped faintly on the soft paper. "Who won?" she asked, with a slight hint of mockery.

"San Miguel."

"Good for them."

She had no interest in sports. We had always told her mother that I was the aficionado. Max came back with three Cokes in cold bottles. He described the game's two dramatic scores.

"Sit down," Clarisa told him, and started to draw his face.

"We could go to next week's game," I suggested to her.

"I don't think so. Max, don't move."

"Or we could go to the beach."

"Let's do that!" Max said.

Clarisa glanced at me. She still looked aloof. "Perhaps the beach. Eva Luz might like to come."

I had to lure her back, bring her presents, ingratiate myself with everyone in the family. We all went to the beach, but it was another few weeks before I got her back to my house. And by then a precedent had been set. In some ways, even long after we married, I would always be courting her.

Clarisa at 19

T W O

JANUARY 1970. SNOW FELL IN THE NARROW STREET, A WET
New York snow that stuck to trees and cars and the tops of hats, but
not to the pavement. We'd been married for almost a year. We sat
by the window of our one-room sublet beside the clanking radiator,
watching the skies darken under a swarm of big flakes. Without a
word Clarisa stood up and drew me across the room onto the bed.
There she lifted her skirts and let them float down over my knees.
When I wanted sex I set the stage and plotted to get her in the
mood. When she wanted it she reached out and took it. We kissed,
we lay down on the worn chenille bedspread and slowly got out of
our clothes. Finally I stood up to get a condom.

"Don't," she said.

"Don't what?"

"Don't use one."

"Of course I'm going to use one."

I headed for the bathroom. We had argued about this before. I
didn't want to be tied down with a child. I wanted us to travel, to be
adventurous and free, to have dinner at midnight and sex in the
midst of snowstorms.

But I did love being married: sharing meals, sleeping together,
lying in the bathroom tub by candlelight and washing each other's
hair. Clarisa's eyes were closed when I came back from the bathroom, and her limbs splayed. She lay motionless as I crouched above
her, kissing her breasts and trailing my fingertips over her skin the
way she liked: the faintest touch. Slowly she responded, arching her
back and spreading her legs, yielding, whispering *"Sí, Juanito."*
When making love we often spoke Spanish. It reminded us of our
sultry Sunday afternoons in El Salvador.

Now, after waiting until I was inside her, she came alive. She

1 3

gripped me with her legs and held me close, her fingernails digging into my back. After sliding into a half-dozen positions she wound up above me, riding me in fierce gyrations and grinding herself against me. I had never seen her so acrobatic, so inflamed by sex. Her frenzy impelled my own, until an orgasm swept over me and I sank back onto the mattress.

For a moment she crouched above me, then lifted herself off and stretched out beside me on the bed. I felt something amiss, and looked down to find the condom split into three useless flaps. She had shredded the thing with her hips. She settled down beside me, her body still unwinding, and rested her head on my shoulder. But the afterglow of sex was extinguished for me. It was the worst time of the month for this to happen.

"Don't be afraid," Clarisa said.

Already she seemed to know. How compact she looked, how un-ruffled, as she slid one leg over mine. I wasn't in a panic, because there was nothing for me to decide. She would do as she pleased, I knew, and I would watch the tide rise.

•   •   •

We had been living a transient life since I got out of the Peace Corps. We were married in San Francisco in the spring of 1969, drove to New York to spend some time with my parents, then took a long backpacking honeymoon through Ecuador and Peru. In September I enrolled in a Ph.D. program in English at NYU, but al-ready, after a single semester, I'd had my fill of droning professors. I'd spent most of the fall on a bench in Washington Square anyway, reading Thoreau's *Walden,* Krishnamurti, Carlos Castaneda and Gary Snyder. It was a quiet revolution compared to the changes sweeping the nation in the fall of 1969, but a major one for me, for I had long assumed I would become a professor myself.

Clarisa didn't care for New York, she wanted to live in the country. So when my old friend Bruce invited us out to Boulder, Colorado, where he was planning to build a house, I dropped out of NYU. Clarisa and I gave back our New York sublet, found a driveaway car and headed west.

Boulder lay at the foot of the Rockies, a handsome town but too tame for Clarisa. We bought an old pickup and scouted the winding mountain roads. There were houses and cabins, but either they were occupied or boarded up.

"Let's live in a tipi," she suggested.

"Clarisa, it's the middle of winter."

"It's been sunny every day. We could set it up in one of those meadows near Bruce's land."

"And what if you're pregnant?"

"What difference does that make?"

In those days there were no home tests, and she was not about to have a lab kill a rabbit just to prove she was pregnant. If she didn't get her period and her breasts started to swell, that would be evidence enough for her. The word *abortion* never crossed our lips.

Instead of a tipi we found a ten-man army-surplus tent and a small sheepherder's stove and set them up at the end of an old mining road at 7,500 feet. We were lucky, it was the mildest winter in years. During the week I found work in town painting houses, laying carpets and delivering telephone books. Clarisa stayed up in the hills. She gathered firewood, took a hike every day and painted watercolors of magpies, mule deer and the bobcats that screamed at night outside our tent.

She didn't want to work and didn't have to, for we had money in the bank from my parents. When spring came Bruce and I built a cistern for his house and a giant lean-to out of recycled lumber so Clarisa and I could move out of the tent. Clarisa had her own projects. She planted a garden and bought goats, chickens and a two-year-old, half-Arabian filly she broke and rode bareback across the hills. By then she was five months pregnant. She hiked the steep Melvina Mine road and swam the chutes in Dream Canyon. Twice the filly threw her, and both times she climbed back on.

I loved Clarisa's courage, but I couldn't believe how nonchalant she was about her pregnancy.

"Don't you think you should see an obstetrician?" I asked one night. We lay on our mattress, propped against the back wall of the lean-to. A couple of candles burned on a milk crate, and the moon lit up the meadow below us. Clarisa, though approaching her third trimester, hadn't read anything about pregnancy or birth, hadn't talked to anyone, hadn't prepared in any way.

"I'm healthy," she said. She pulled up her nightgown and drummed her fingers on her swollen belly. Her breasts were almost as taut. I massaged them lightly, put my ear to her stomach, listened but didn't hear anything.

"I called my mother when I was in town," I said. "She suggested we could take a birth class together. Maybe a Lamaze class where they teach you breathing and stuff."

I thought this was remarkable advice from my mother—an M.D. who considered practitioners like osteopaths and chiropractors to be on the far fringe of medicine. But Clarisa dismissed the idea. She pulled her nightgown down to her knees. "You think I don't know how to breathe? Or how to have a baby? I don't need to go to school for that."

"It's not school, it's just a class. We could meet some other couples who are going through the same thing."

"Going through what? We won't be here anyway, we'll be in Chile."

"If we get the visas."

"We'll get them."

On our trip through the Andes we had been drawn to the simple life of the campesino, and now, like thousands of others in the early seventies, we had decided to go back to the land. Of course we might have bought a farm in Maine or Nebraska, but such a domestic move would not have been dramatic enough for us. Even the counterculture had a competitive side, and we wanted to go farther into the hinterlands than anyone else, live a more primitive life.

After years as a student and teacher I was seeking a new vocation. I wanted to build things and work with my hands. I wanted to be independent, and to study what Thoreau called "the true necessaries" of life. Immersed in the iconoclastic sixties, I found most occupations either useless or nefarious, and in the end chose agriculture as one of the few indispensable trades.

Still a researcher, I read up on South America. Clarisa and I had liked both Ecuador and Peru, but those countries had too little arable land, and we didn't want to take land away from those who needed it. After a couple of slide shows at the library we settled on Chile for its stable democracy, good weather and expanses of rich farmland.

We leaned back against the irregular planks of the lean-to. Out in the pasture we could hear the whir of the nighthawks as they pulled out of their headlong dives. One of the goats, as pregnant as Clarisa, wandered in and tried to open the wooden food box with its nose. Clarisa threw a slipper at it. After a while it tiptoed back into the meadow.

"I still think we should wait," I said, "and have the baby here. What if we run into trouble?"

"What trouble?"

"I don't know. You hear about complications."

"Where do you hear that?"

I thought for a minute, then had to admit, "Novels, I guess."

"You've read too many of those."

"What about the pain?"

She seized my hand and nipped my palm with her front teeth, somewhat more than playfully. "Who's going to have this baby, you or me?"

"What if we went to El Salvador and stayed at your mom's? You could have the baby there and then we'd go on to Chile."

"I can have the baby anywhere. We want a farm, so let's go get one."

It was the summer of 1970, and the world was doing cartwheels. We were stopping the war in Vietnam, we were choosing new livelihoods, we would live close to nature and our true selves. And Clarisa, without seeming to try, was on a frontier of her own.

•   •   •

In July the Chilean embassy in Washington turned down our residence visa applications, informing us that only a few highly trained and technical workers were ever honored with such a permit. I was secretly relieved. Now, I thought, we would be obliged to stay in Colorado for the coming birth. But Clarisa barely glanced at the letter. "Where's their nearest consul?" she asked—and five days later we were on a Trailways bus bound for Galveston, Texas.

There the consul received us politely in his office near the port. He was an elderly man dressed in an ancient broadcloth suit and polished shoes. I myself wore the blue suit I'd been married in, and Clarisa her most sedate maternity dress. We exchanged the usual polite greetings in both Spanish and English, and then I presented my case. I wanted to raise chickens, I told the consul. I implied a large operation, something that would benefit the Chilean economy, and related a spurious background of chicken husbandry in both Arkansas and Colorado. I'd been reading books on aviculture.

The old gentleman nodded. He held his pale chin in his thin hands. The longer he waited, the more convinced I was he'd seen through my bogus vita. Finally he turned to Clarisa, now seven months pregnant.

"And your baby?" he asked. "Where will it be born?"

"In Chile," she said. *"Dios quiere."*

It was the consul, of course, who had to be willing. His face immediately softened. He leaned forward and extended a hand toward her stomach. "May I?" he asked.

"Go ahead," she said.

This surprised me, for several times already I had seen Clarisa brush away both men and women who had presumed to reach out and touch her like that. The consul grazed her belly with a delicate hand, then sat back and looked from one of us to the other, rocking faintly in his chair.

"I've been told Chile is beautiful," Clarisa said.

The old man glanced away, a look of pain on his face. He stared out the window at the bleak vista of warehouses and shabby office buildings near the port.

"Wait until you see my country," he said. "The mountains and farms, and the vineyards in the spring. And the music. And the poets."

"Pablo Neruda," said Clarisa, who'd been reading him: his hymns to salt and bread and cooking oil.

"And Gabriela Mistral," the consul said. "And Nicanor Parra." He sighed. "I miss the *empanadas* and the wine in big jugs."

Clarisa sat before him like a fertile queen, with her great belly and thick cascading hair. He stared at her. He had stopped looking at me altogether.

"What about you?" Clarisa asked him. "Why don't you live there?"

His eyes dropped to his hands. "Because I fell in love and got married here," he said. "I was a young man then, a sailor off a boat. That was thirty-eight years ago, and in all this time I've only gone back twice. I have a wife and family, children and grandchildren. They're all Americans."

Clarisa reached out and took his hands in hers. The consul looked at her so gratefully I think he forgot I was in the room. And I saw, in this white-haired septuagenarian, the same response I'd felt myself soon after I met her: joy, relief, the gratitude of winning her favor.

That night, our visas in hand, Clarisa and I lay down on a friend's fold-out couch in Houston. I was unexpectedly aroused. The night was humid and both of us damp with perspiration. I lay close beside her. I couldn't stop kissing her. She looked like one of Gauguin's Polynesian women, dark, luxuriant and imperturbable. Perhaps it was the consul's attentions that spurred me on, or Clarisa's affection for him: her unfeigned compassion for an old man who had lost his country and his youth. She hadn't just been working the consul, as I had. She hardly seemed to think about the visas at all, and she wanted to hear about the old man's life. She was true to herself, and I loved her for that.

* * *

One train a day made the long trip south from Santiago to Temuco, Chile. Clarisa, vastly pregnant, rocked and dozed beside me, her arm looped through mine and her feet propped up on the seat in front of us. Through the window I watched the sunlit countryside flow past: long rows of trellised grapevines, dirt roads lined with peeling eucalyptus trees, isolated farmhouses with tile roofs and swept, hard-packed yards. The farmers here, like the porters at the airport, all looked like down-at-the-heels gentlemen in their single-breasted black wool jackets. They drove their horse carts into the small towns, where election posters for Salvador Allende still dotted the walls and telephone poles. Allende had been elected president the day Clarisa and I left the United States, but while we welcomed his socialist victory, our trip had little to do with politics. We were immersed in our own adventure.

I had not left behind all my worries. Clarisa's due date was less than four weeks off, and we were headed for a town we'd seen once in a slide show, and in which we knew not a single person.

The train rattled on. "First we should rent a house," I said, "and then check out the hospital."

When I got anxious I made plans and lists. Clarisa knew this and ignored me. After a while she said, "Rub my feet, would you? The blood isn't getting down there."

The train, which had been crowded setting out from Santiago, emptied slowly with each stop. The farmhouses turned from adobe to wood, and the villages grew poorer as we rolled on into colder country. By afternoon all the roofs were bluish zinc, or just tarred corrugated paper. In Mulchén we swapped our diesel locomotive for an old coal-burner. The skies grew cloudy and it started to rain, a persistent drizzle. I swayed in my seat, unable to shake my anxiety as coal dust drifted past the windows and an early dusk settled over the fields and forests.

"Here," Clarisa said. "Let me rub yours."

I took off my shoes and rested my feet on her thighs as she massaged them. She stopped to press them against her belly.

"Do you feel that?" she said.

"What?"

She peeled off a sock and pressed the ball of my foot against her stomach, holding it there until I felt the underwater movement, the press of little feet.

"He's strong," she said.

"He?" I had no idea if it was a boy or a girl.

"Es varón," she said categorically. It was a boy.

•   •   •

By the time our creaking railway car pulled into Temuco it was eight at night. The train squealed to a stop, and we stepped down onto the wet platform. Four single bulbs under tin covers lit the entire station, and the air smelled of coal and damp earth. After a few minutes the locomotive whistled, the cars jolted and the train pulled out for Puerto Montt. The red light at the center of the caboose grew smaller and dimmer, until there was nothing to do but leave the station and find a hotel.

Our room in the Hotel de Ferrocarril was icy, for the building's only source of heat was a squat sawdust stove in the lobby. We dropped off our knapsacks, went out to a restaurant and ordered a salad. It came piled on a white plate: a hill of young romaine lettuce served with a sliced lemon. We ate a potato soup as well, then went back to the hotel to lie on one of the single beds, huddling for warmth under our down sleeping bags.

After three days in the hotel I found a small new house on the outskirts of town. An electrician named Antonio had built it for his brother, and offered it to us for the next two months. The house had three rooms, a small propane stove, a table and a bed, but no other furniture. We moved in with what we carried in our knapsacks. A pair of wooden trunks would arrive by ship in another six weeks.

On our second night in the house Clarisa gripped my wrist and woke me out of a deep sleep. "Get up," she said. She was sitting with her back propped against the headboard and her sleeping bag pulled down to her knees. "The baby's coming."

I leapt up. "How do you know?"

"I know."

I tried to stay calm as I dressed and got my shoes on. She was three weeks early. I didn't even know where the hospital was. I woke Antonio next door. He found a taxi and came with us, escorting us into the hospital. There he was all smiles.

"These are two North Americans," he explained to the nurses at the desk. "They have come to live in Cautín Province!"

This brought exclamations, friendly nods and questions—but not about the baby. No one seemed in any hurry to address the question of birth. Clarisa stood beside the reception desk, leaning on it, looking tired.

"Por favor," I said finally.

Two of the nurses, thickset women in white shoes and starched uniforms, took her by the elbows and led her toward the stairs. I followed along until they turned and stared at me.

"Can't I go with her?"

"She is going to have a *baby*," one of them said. Then they guided her up the stairs. Clarisa, flanked and supported by the two older women, glanced back over her shoulder. For the first time she looked afraid.

"You can do it," I told her in English. "You'll be fine."

I tried to sound assured, but her expression unnerved me. I had always imagined holding her through labor, talking with her and somehow sharing in the pain. The physical details were vague, for I knew little about the actual procedure. And now it was too late. She was going to give birth upstairs in the Temuco Municipal Hospital, and I wasn't going to be allowed any part in it. My legs had begun to shake.

I would wait here, I thought. There was nothing else I could do. The high-ceilinged lobby was lined with chairs and benches, but it was chilly. The nurses all wore sweaters, and a tiny electric heater glowed behind the reception desk. I was confused. Was this the waiting room? My suppositions about what came next were all taken straight from the movies, old black-and-white films in which nervous fathers wait through the long night—it is always night—drinking coffee and pacing back and forth in a drab white room stocked with magazines and ashtrays.

Antonio put his hand on my arm. "The taxi," he said.

I'd forgotten about the taxi. I pulled out some escudos to pay for it, and told him to take it home.

He looked confused. "What are you going to do?"

"I'm going to wait here," I said. "Until the baby comes."

"No, no." He smiled and patted my arm. "There's nothing you can do about that. It's going to take a while. You can come back in the morning."

One of the nurses chimed in. "There's nowhere for you to sleep here," she warned me, and lifted her hand to indicate the stiff furniture against the walls.

I stood at the base of the stairs, gazing up. I was in a foreign country. The women's faces were faintly curious, but confident of what came next. There was an established way. Finally I let Antonio lead me outside, down the steps and into the taxi. I felt like a traitor. At this crucial moment, at Clarisa's great trial, I had abandoned her.

The taxi took us home. "Don't worry," Antonio said. He leaned back against the seat. "Soon you will have a strong little son."

"How do you know it's going to be a son?"

"A son," he assured me. "With his birth you will enter a new station in life, and your seed will continue on the earth." It sounded like he was quoting the Bible, but in Spanish I couldn't be sure.

Son or daughter, I had no preference. I was too swept up by having a child to worry about its gender. At home I sat on the mattress and thought, I'll just wait here, I'll keep my vigil here instead of at the hospital.

The next thing I knew it was nine A.M. and the sun was pouring through the curtainless window onto my legs. I bolted outside, couldn't find a taxi, fretted through a slow bus ride and ran up the hospital steps three at a time.

There was no news and I couldn't go up.

Back at ten and still no news.

Back at eleven, and the nurse telephoned upstairs. She smiled. "You have a son," she reported. "He's fine, and so is his mother."

I pumped her hand, I leaned across the desk and embraced her. "Can I go up now?"

"Oh no," she said, shaking her head. She studied the clock on the wall. "Come back at two."

I stepped out the front doors and bounded down into the park in front of the hospital. I had a son! It was a miracle. I strode through the swept and watered streets, past buildings bathed in sunlight, saying *"Buenos dias!"* to everyone I met. How vivid and alive their faces looked. Every one of them had been born! It seemed an astounding revelation.

Clarisa had been right, she could have had the baby anywhere. I kept walking the streets. I couldn't sit down or eat—but my worries had evaporated. I knew this baby was going to be an amazing and extravagant child. With Clarisa as a mother, how could it be otherwise?

•   •   •

At two I went back to the hospital and they let me upstairs. Clarisa was sitting up in bed, propped against a pillow and holding the baby. She looked like she'd been through a war. Her hair was matted and tangled, her nightgown ripped over both shoulders and flecked with spots of blood. Three other mothers lay in their beds, and a couple of babies were crying. Not ours. Ours was nursing lustily. I knelt beside him, astonished and speechless. Though he paid me no mind, he seemed right at home in the world, a casual traveler whose unfocused eyes rolled freely as his two red fists worked the air. He looked bald and blotched and misshapen by his passage—not at all the darling baby of a diaper advertisement—but also strong and determined.

"They told me not to feed him yet," Clarisa said. "But he was hungry, so I did."

"They told you not to feed him?" What kind of advice was that? Clarisa just shrugged her shoulders. No wonder, I thought, she had steered clear of modern medicine.

"Was it bad?"

"He's perfect," she said. She ran her fingertips over his tiny bald head and caressed his rosy ears. "Yes, it was bad."

I put one hand on her shoulder and the other on the baby's arm, on his warm dry flesh that until this morning had lived in fluid. Our amphibian child. I poked my finger into his fist and felt him close his hand around it. He was strong for such a tiny person.

"You want to hold him?" she asked.

"God, no."

I meant I was afraid to, that I didn't know how, that I might hurt him. Besides, he was still nursing.

"Just lift him a little."

I slid my hands underneath him and cradled his chest.

"Go ahead."

I lifted him slightly off her stomach. He didn't complain, and went right on nursing. Clarisa laughed. "He's stuck on there."

She looked so worn I was glad to see her laugh. But I wasn't ready to detach the baby from her. I lowered him onto her stomach, then kissed his naked back.

"How bad?" I asked.

"They cut me."

"Where?"

"Down there. They do it so you won't tear. I tried to stop them but they did it anyway. They cut me too much."

I felt faint, and my testicles pulled up inside me. I'd never heard of such a thing.

"They think they know everything," Clarisa said.

Slowly, almost imperceptibly, the baby went to sleep in the midst of nursing. I lay my head beside him, touching one cheek to him and the other to Clarisa. The three of us, I was sure, were now joined forever.

"He has no name," I said.

Though we had talked about names, we hadn't decided on anything. Clarisa lay back on the pillow and closed her eyes. "You name him," she said. "I've done enough."

That afternoon I bought her some blouses, a new nightgown, some sheets for the bed at home and a half dozen diapers. Then I sat in the park outside the hospital and thought about names. It seemed to me this child of ours, who was sure to be a completely original being, should have a completely original name. And so, Janir, pronounced Ja-NEER: two syllables put together on a park bench on the day of his birth.

•   •   •

Home from the hospital, Clarisa recovered slowly. She spent her first days in bed with Janir beside her, both of them sleeping long hours as I cleaned, cooked and ran errands. When awake she was content to lie beside her son and stare at him, sometimes for hours on end—and I was content to watch them. We had nowhere to go, nothing to do, all our plans were suspended. We fussed over Janir, scrutinizing his every move and expression. One afternoon I stripped off my clothes and joined Clarisa under the covers. There we lay until dark, not talking at all, dozing from time to time, kissing Janir's little fingers and toes.

I think I felt closer to Clarisa that week than at any time in our marriage. She had performed a miracle, but the hard birth and painful episiotomy had set her back, and I was moved to see her in such a vulnerable state. In some way that allowed me to relax, and the feeling lifted that I was perpetually running behind her, never quick enough to be her emotional equal.

At night Janir woke constantly: four times, five times, I was never sure how many. I struggled awake to his cries and sat up in bed, trying somehow to share in the job as Clarisa fed him. She slipped him onto her breast, I watched for a minute or two, then tumbled back into sleep. In the mornings even Clarisa wasn't sure how many times he had woken and nursed.

They had only been home for a day and a half when I set out to wash the first diaper. Enlightened fathers, I knew, did diapers, and this would be the first of many. I heated up some water on the gas stove and poured it into an oval enamel pan. The diaper was soiled with a tarry, dark green glob, a tenacious packet of excrement. I soaked the cloth, scrubbed it with detergent, rinsed it and soaked it again. It was like cleaning up after an oil spill. I heated a second round of water, then a third as Clarisa slept on in the bedroom. I spent forty-five minutes on that one diaper, and in the end I got it clean but not white. Bleach, I thought desperately, I'll buy some bleach. My God, no wonder women complained about doing the laundry. It was horrifying, it was an occupation unto itself. There wasn't going to be time to do anything *except* wash diapers.

It was meconium. I learned about it the next morning from Antonio's wife, Rosa. It only happens once, she told me, as an infant evacuates the accumulated waste of nine months in the womb. And as I discovered after that first terrifying movement, the ones that follow are so mild they wash out easily in running water.

•   •   •

Buoyed by Clarisa's trust, only a few days after Janir's birth I was cradling him, supporting his head, lying back and letting him wriggle around on my chest. It was back to his mother's nipple, of course, when a rage came on, but I soon grew confident about picking him up and cleaning him and carrying him around the house.

When he was a week old I took him outside into the sunlight. I walked him down the street and back, shielding his eyes and showing him off to Rosa—who was scandalized to see him outdoors so soon. But Janir seemed content, even fascinated, to be under the open sky. I carried him past the neighborhood's last houses onto a knoll amid some grazing sheep. He didn't seem to notice them. His dark brown eyes were still soft and unfocused, and his smooth head completely bald. When he stared at the flickering new leaves of a poplar I sat down under the tree with him. I unfolded his blanket and inhaled his milky smell as he gazed up into the branches. I felt protective, I felt inspired, I felt something I couldn't name. It was as if my heart were being gently squeezed. I took his prehensile toes between my thumb and forefinger. This was his first time away from Clarisa, and I couldn't get over the feeling that I'd snuck him out of the house. I traced my finger over the fontanelle on top of his skull. How scary that soft gap felt, how exposed and fragile.

T H R E E

JANIR'S BIRTH OVERWHELMED US BRIEFLY, BUT WE DID not lose sight of why we had come to Chile. A couple of weeks after he was born I started scouting for land. Temuco, a town of eighty thousand, had no real-estate brokers, and most sales were made through word of mouth. Janir was only three weeks old when Clarisa and I took him on his first trip into the country. We followed up a half-dozen leads, and after a month found a farm we liked. It was forty miles east of Temuco at the foot of the Andes, an isolated backcountry farm that had been carved out of the forest only decades before. The topsoil was said to be a hundred feet deep, and the land was surrounded by fields, woodlots and clear streams that pitched down out of the cordillera. There was no telephone, no electricity, no running water, and the dirt road from the nearest small town was passable to vehicles only half the year. The price for a hundred fenced acres, a small house and a well with a hand pump was $1,200.

We moved in when Janir was ten weeks old. We furnished the house with a bed, a dresser, a cookstove, a sink that drained into a bucket, a slab of varnished wood for a table and a rattan crib Janir refused to sleep in. He would play in it, but he would only go to sleep in our bed.

We had almost none of the gear that makes it easier to look after a baby: no playpen, no stroller, no wind-up swinging chair, no unbreakable dishes or juice cups, not even a pacifier. Most of those devices allow a parent to keep an infant entertained at a distance, and that was never what Clarisa wanted. Instead she thought only of her son. When he cried she picked him up, and when he was hungry she fed him. She seldom got bored or irritated, and could lie around with Janir under the apple trees for three or four hours at a time, tickling him, talking to him, showing him the grass and the bugs that lived there. Sometimes she would laugh at something he did, he'd laugh back and they'd lie there face to face, the two of them enveloped in a giddy secret mirth.

She was never a cautious mother. She set Janir down in the garden where he groped around and tested the dirt with his mouth. One morning she lay him on top of a week-old calf in the middle of a sunny pasture, one soft and curious infant stretched out on another. The calf, as if hypnotized, never moved. Even its mother merely watched from a distance.

Inside the house Clarisa picked Janir up by one foot, held him upside down while she stoked the fire, then swung him up and draped him over her shoulder. She never dropped him. They spent all day together, and soon after dinner lay down in bed. After he nursed, the two of them fell asleep, their bodies in perpetual contact. This seemed exactly what he wanted.

I watched her and learned. I did my best with him, but I was never as confident as Clarisa was. I played with him, I carried him around the garden, I changed his diapers and bathed him in the sink. Yet he was rarely as interested in me as in his mother. Through nine months of pregnancy the two of them had been a single body, and his cells still seemed to cling to that fact.

•   •   •

After a month on the farm Clarisa hired a neighbor, sixteen-year-old Teresa Sandoval, to help out with Janir—but even then she kept him with her every minute of the day and night. When Teresa came the three of them lay in the orchard, giggling and chatting and playing with Janir's toes. Teresa had three younger siblings, knew all about infants and was soon to be married. But she also carried with her the customs of the neighborhood, and at first she could not believe we would let a naked baby lie out on a blanket on the grass in the humid air. That was not the Chilean way.

Then again, it was not just a blanket. It was a fur coat from Henri Bendel which my mother had given Clarisa in New York, before we left for Colorado.

"Don't do it," I told Mom in private. "We're going to live in the mountains."

Mom tossed the coat over a chair. "Let her have it. What do I need with a fur coat? It just hangs in my closet, I don't know why I ever bought the thing."

Clarisa never wore it herself, but when we moved to Chile we shipped it down in one of the wooden trunks along with some tools and kitchenware, and once we got to the farm she cut the lining out of it and used the fur as a spread for Janir. At first I resisted this. But it was not my coat, it was hers. And I did love the vision of Janir's bare bottom resting on a field of sumptuous mink, far out in the boondocks of Chile. When he puked or peed on it we rinsed it off under the pump. I don't know how much the coat had cost, but probably more than the farm.

• • •

"Hey, John."

Clarisa gave me a yell from the house. I was five feet down in a bank of pure loam, digging a root cellar and completely focused on the job. Her despairing tone snapped me out of it: "Give me a hand here, will you?"

It was a cold cloudy day, one of several in a row, and all afternoon she had been inside with Janir. He was seven months old now and crawling, though only backwards. He was also teething and colicky, and now he was wailing. He often cried in the late afternoons, and sometimes I stayed out of the house because of it. Clarisa was better at soothing him. She had more patience than I did, and she could breast-feed him.

But today her patience had worn thin. She stood in the doorway as I approached, holding him out like a package. "He doesn't want to eat, he doesn't want to sleep, I don't know what he wants."

He squirmed and cried in my arms, fighting to get back to her. As his legs pumped in outrage I put my nose to his pants and sniffed. "He's dry?" I asked.

"Of course he's dry."

In spite of the weather he wore neither shoes nor socks. "Maybe he's cold," I said.

Clarisa frowned and shook her head. It was an old argument between us, but she was probably right, for his bare feet were toasty. And he'd always been a healthy child. At seven months he had not once had a cold or fever. He'd never taken a cough medicine, an aspirin or an antibiotic. Clarisa had never so much as dusted his butt with baby powder. Her way was to raise him like a wolf.

"Take him for a walk," she said. "See what you can do."

This was a rare request, for in Janir's whole life she had yet to let him out of her sight for an hour. Before she could change her mind I slipped a pair of woolen socks on him, then a knit hat he promptly threw to the ground. The barrage of his sobs continued as I maneuvered him into our one child-care device, a prototype backpack carrier I had ordered out of *The Whole Earth Catalog*.

Normally Janir loved this carrier. He liked to ride up high as I packed him about the farm, feeding the chickens, pumping and carrying water, even hoeing potatoes in the garden. But today he would have none of it. When I lifted him up he twisted back to his mother, jerked up and down in his seat, grabbed my hair and yanked on it. He cried all the way out past the chicken coop, where a flock of Rhode Island Reds were fluffing and scratching in the yard. He didn't even glance at them. I stopped, lifted him out of the carrier and checked him once again, just in case. His pants and diaper were dry, the pins were safely closed away from his skin, and when I pressed his stomach he didn't flinch. He couldn't tell me what was bothering him, so I slipped him back into the carrier and tramped out over the pasture.

His bellowing soon got on my nerves. But I slogged on, there was nothing else to do. At the top of the meadow I reached back to run my hand over the few wispy hairs on his scalp. It was a caress he sometimes enjoyed—but not today.

Autumn was sliding into winter. We came to a stream and crossed it on a tree trunk someone had flattened with an adze. There was some danger of falling in, and Janir must have sensed it, for as we crossed he stopped crying. He started again briefly on the other side, but his desperate affliction had eased, and soon he stopped altogether. I walked on past the filbert bushes we had picked clean the week before, past a waterfall and up a steep dirt trail. When it leveled off I raised my hands so Janir could hold my thumbs in his fists.

I risked a question. *"Te sientes mejor, mi querido?"* Do you feel better, my darling? "We are going to see the volcanoes."

From the top of the hill the three coned peaks lay far to the south and east, all somber under a bank of high clouds. Janir stared at them intently.

"You know that first one," I told him. "That's Volcán Llaima. And that white at the top is snow. You're going to learn so many things. Next week you're going to ride in a truck up to the umbrella pines so we can pick piñones. And one day we're going to take you to the ocean, and one day you're going to start walking, and one day you're going to say *papá*."

I thought he'd fall asleep on our way home, but he didn't. Instead he leaned against me and circled my neck with his arms. Dusk was settling, and the colors fading from the landscape. Just as our house came into view, one of our horses trotted up to visit. As I stroked the horse's muzzle Janir's small hands grasped my ears, and his warm breath puffed against my neck.

For ten minutes we didn't move. We listened to the horse as he drifted off to eat, his teeth shearing the grass. The last light was going out of the trees. I stood in the middle of the dusky field and let Janir slump against my back. I understood how week after week he was all Clarisa needed.

The night came down around us, and it was dark by the time we reached the chicken coop. The hens had all roosted for the night, and a candle burned inside the house. Janir didn't move or make any noise, but held my hair as I walked. I circled the house at a distance, passed through the orchard into the garden and stood amid the rows of broccoli. I didn't want our time to end. Suddenly the door opened and Clarisa stepped out. She looked around the corner of the house toward the pasture I'd just crossed. I held still in the garden behind her. If she'd looked she might have seen me.

"Juan?" she called out in the other direction.

Janir didn't say anything, he didn't make a sound. How I loved him for that. The two of us, for once, were confederates.

Five minutes after Clarisa went back inside I approached the house, stomping and scraping my boots on the steps. She ran to the door and opened it.

"Where did you go?" she asked, but didn't wait for an answer. She spun me around, lifted Janir out of the carrier and immediately opened her shirt. Janir fastened onto her nipple as she rocked him in her arms.

I watched them, half resentful. How easy it was for Clarisa, and how quickly he went swimming back to her.

"He cried all the way past the stream," I told her.

"Did he?"

But she wasn't listening. She sat down with him next to the stove and cooed at him, singing and chanting bits of Spanish. She ran her hand over his light new hair as he nursed happily, his mouth on one nipple and his fingers on the other.

•   •   •

I threw myself into farm work, as absorbed by this job as I had once been by literature and teaching. A half-acre garden, I saw, was not big enough—not if, like all our neighbors, we were going to grow enough potatoes for an entire year. So I borrowed a yoke of oxen and plowed an adjoining field. There are few sounds as satisfying as the sustained low roar of a plow being tugged through the sod, ripping through grass roots and peeling back long crumbling slabs of earth. Meadowlarks swooped down behind me to poke for worms, and the two massive beasts plodded along in front of the plow, their yoke's leather straps creaking in the sunlight. I could have plowed the whole hundred acres.

We kept horses, cows and enough chickens for a small trade in eggs. Our goal was that back-to-the-land ideal, self-sufficiency, and I filled my letters home with the precise, sometimes fanatical details of our progress. Food and its provenance had become a mania, and I was once able to announce to parents and friends that over the previous eight months everything we had eaten had come from the farm, save for wheat, oil and salt.

Of course, our campesino life was different from that of our neighbors, because it was voluntary. The year I turned twenty-one my parents had given me some American Heritage stock: not a trust fund but an outright gift. I'd sold some shares to finish college and go to graduate school, but almost eigthy thousand dollars remained. During my two years in the Peace Corps I'd been strict about living on my allowance of $120 a month, and in general I was secretive about my money. I was embarrassed by it and seldom told anyone I had it. Though Clarisa knew it was there, her aim, like mine, was to live an elemental life.

While still in college I'd read that Bertrand Russell, in his idealistic youth, had given away all his inherited money. Briefly I'd considered doing the same. Instead, after considering how my parents would take such an act, I resolved never to spend the money carelessly. By refraining from all luxury, I thought, and by working like a mule, I would annul the money's corrupting influence.

During our first year on the farm Clarisa and I were equally involved in the local community. We hiked everywhere, made friends with other families and asked our neighbors a thousand questions about goats and gardening and how to make cider, how to treat a cow with mastitis, which mushrooms were safe and which herbs were good for a headache. We immersed ourselves in these pastoral details, even as we avoided that other world we lived in daily, our own marriage.

I missed the sex and affection we had shared before Janir's birth. Now, if I lay down beside Clarisa in the orchard, or after dinner as she nursed the baby, she remained faintly aloof. I could stand beside her as she fixed dinner, but if I brushed her shoulder she edged apart. Plainly she had all the contact she needed from her son, a perfect creature who slept beside her every night and whose life she sustained with her breasts.

It would have helped, I'm sure, if I'd understood what I later read, that a mother's reserve is often hormonal, a biological response designed by nature to tighten the bond between mother and child, and to delay the conception of the next child. But with no support group or friends to talk to, no Donahue or Oprah, no *Redbook* or *Mothering* magazine, I felt my way along on my own, as if I were the first father on the planet to go through this kind of estrangement. I could only assume that Clarisa loved me less. Though in some ways her pregnancy had tied her closer to me, now she had stepped with her son into a room too small for me to get into.

I'd heard of postpartum depression. But Clarisa wasn't depressed, she was simply wrapped up with her child. And perhaps, I allowed, there was a logic to the distance she maintained between us. Affection might lead to sex, sex might lead to childbirth, and childbirth had been hell.

Day to day I buried my urges in a round of vigorous chores. But after several months on the farm it seemed anything might excite me: a bareback ride on a horse, the sun on my skin, the cows giving milk, even the wind flowing over the grassy meadow. Once I hiked to a grove of trees above the Rio Codingue, took off all my clothes and walked barefoot through the flickering sunlight, brushing my hips past ferns and branches and straddling young saplings until I came.

One night I sat up alone by the stove, reading by candlelight after Clarisa and Janir went to sleep, when the howl of a mountain lion lifted me out of my seat and raised every hair on my body. I'd heard them before, but never so close. I stepped outside into the moonless night and waited for another cry. When it didn't come, something drove me to leave the safety of the house and walk out past the chicken coop into the pasture. Though I couldn't see more than twenty yards off, I could imagine the big cat stalking some prey or loping along through the night. A wave of desire swept over me. I dropped my pants to my ankles and stood in the dark pasture, aroused and erect, my entire body trembling.

I hoped things would change as Janir got older. But month after month Clarisa and I went on sleeping with our son between us. A couple of times while he napped we contrived a tame little coupling —but her heart wasn't in it, so neither was mine. I missed the sex between us, but I also began to worry that she could drift away from me and never look back.

F O U R

AT TWELVE MONTHS JANIR LEARNED TO WALK. ONE WEEK he couldn't and the next he could. At the same time his verbal skills took a leap. He was enchanted by the new blathering sounds he could make with his mouth and tongue, and occasionally he burped out something like a word. Even when silent he seemed to possess a new calculating intelligence. Sometimes I'd turn to find him staring at me with a long cool look, the kind of overt inspection adults rarely give each other.

"Janir," I said, "what are you looking at?"

In response only a deadpan scrutiny.

At other times a wild laughter would bubble up out of his body for no apparent reason. Then tears, then boredom, then anger, sometimes the whole gamut in an hour. It seemed a marvel how he could bathe in such feelings without drowning.

When it was warm Clarisa refused to put him in a diaper. At first I thought this peculiar, then I adjusted to the notion, then I joined her crusade. After all, if he peed or even crapped on the wooden floor the cleanup was simple. Without a diaper he got more sun and no rashes, and he was freer to move his legs.

We did have a few arguments about it. One cool March morning we hiked over to the Mendoza road and caught the twice-weekly bus to Temuco. Janir was sixteen months old by then, an agile kid who could walk anywhere, climb stairs and run down the aisle of the bus. Clarisa passed him over to me at the window seat so she could pull out a change of clothes. Off with his bulky long pants and on with a pair of navy blue shorts and a white shirt. That was all. He didn't own any underwear. It was warm in the bus and Clarisa took off her coat. She wore the red velvet dress she'd been married in. Last night she had washed her hair in the metal tub, and today it shone.

I stood Janir on my legs so he could look out the window. Usually he warned us about peeing, and probably he wouldn't let fly on the bus. But when he was ready to poop he just did it. He got a concentrated look on his face, then a little smile.

"Clarisa," I said, "let's put him in a diaper."

"How would you like to be wrapped up like that?"

"I'm holding a time bomb. You know he's going to go off."

"Not until later."

She was the expert, I had to admit. I was usually out working when he did his business each morning. So I held him up and hoped for the best.

The bus dropped us at the market in town, and we walked to a restaurant where the owners, a pair of older women, remembered Janir from other visits. How big he'd grown! How cute he was! He responded to their attention by marching across the floor with a sure step. His hair was thick and dark. His shirt had a navy insignia on it, and the women dubbed him "Sailor" as he scampered among the chair legs and under the tables, peering out at his fans. They couldn't get enough of him.

I sat down to consult the menu, and when I looked up Janir was standing perfectly still in the center of the room with that concentrated look on his face. I jumped up but couldn't get between him and the women before a brown turd the size of a meatball rolled out of his pants onto the floor. Then a second.

The women raked us with their cold stares as Clarisa rose, picked Janir up and carried him off. I took some napkins, removed the two turds and carried them to the rest room, where Clarisa was pinning Janir into a belated diaper. He looked subdued, but Clarisa was fuming. I slipped out to apologize to the owners.

They heard me out coolly—but when Clarisa emerged with Janir they looked away. This made her even angrier.

"*Viejas cabronas,*" she said: the old goats. It was an emphatic insult. As she stormed outside she added in English, "They think they're too good for my kid's shit. They're not good enough to *eat* his shit."

I caught up with her as she strode though the market. "They just don't remember about kids," I said.

"Don't talk to me. Don't start in with your fucking Harvard logic."

Stung by her words, I recoiled into silence. And the silence grew. We didn't start talking until we got back to the farm. By then, at least, I had an idea of how hard on Clarisa it was going to be to raise

Janir the way she wished. She was confident around me, but out in the world she was going to find it harder to act on every insight about what was right for her son, and what was foolish.

•   •   •

We had a cookstove on the farm, and Clarisa had warned Janir about it several times. But in the end she let him figure out about hot surfaces on his own, in the inevitable way. One night he stood beside the stove, lifted his fingers to it and lightly touched it, then screamed in outrage and pain. Clarisa picked him up and we poured cold water over his hand. She comforted him, nursed him, told him again how some things were too hot to touch—and that was the last time he ever burned himself.

One afternoon we walked down the hollow to a neighbor's barn and climbed up into the loft to play in the piles of hay. It was a ten-foot drop to the floor, and that sense of empty air below him was something Janir wanted to explore. Clarisa let him crawl to the edge and look down. He knelt there, completely attentive, and she never moved. Neither did I—though I was on my toes and coiled.

As we walked home I asked, "Did you know he wouldn't fall?"

"He isn't stupid. He just wanted to look."

"He could have slipped," I said.

"He knew it was dangerous. That's why he didn't walk over there, he crawled. Babies are born intelligent. This one, anyway."

No one I knew raised her child the way Clarisa did. Sometimes we argued about it, and sometimes I worried, but I was sure there was no better mother.

•   •   •

I was working in the garden one morning when I heard Clarisa scream. I jumped up and ran for the orchard. She stood with Janir in her arms, naked, his limbs splayed and his head tilted back. *"He can't breathe,"* she shrieked.

His lips were blue. I took him from her, lay him on the fur coat and pressed his chest with my palms. Nothing happened. Clarisa stood beside me, howling. I blew into his mouth but he didn't react. He didn't move or breathe. I couldn't remember CPR, I couldn't think. Clarisa jumped up and down and gripped my arms and soon we were both screaming together, *"Janir, breathe. Oh God, please breathe."*

He didn't. His lips and eyelids turned a deeper blue. His chest was a stone. I pressed him but there was no response. I pushed up his eyelid and exposed an inert brown pupil. Clarisa kept wailing. He was dying in front of us.

Water, I thought. I picked him up and took off for the pump, his arms and legs knocking against me as I clasped him to my chest. Clarisa followed. *"Pump,"* I roared, and she flung herself against the handle.

I held him under the spigot and squeezed his chest as the icy water ran over him. It was so cold it could have stopped a child from breathing. Yet only seconds after the first splash hit him I felt a tiny movement in his torso. I cradled him away from the stream and felt his body in the grip of tiny spasms. Finally he took a desperate gulp of air, then another, then broke into an enormous sob. We held him between us, enfolding him with our arms as he cried. What a gorgeous sound that was. He breathed between bawls, and as we carried him back to the fur coat a flush broke out over his lips, then his entire body. We set him on the coat, lay down on either side and sobbed along with him.

We never discovered the reason for that convulsion, and he never had another.

•   •   •

Our second winter was coming, and the next time we went to Temuco it rained most of the trip. We spent the night at the Hotel de Ferrocarril and in the morning, as we set out to do the last of our shopping, it was still sprinkling.

There were so few gringos in Cautín Province in 1971 that we'd heard about all of them, even if we hadn't met them. Peter Dutton was one, a Peace Corps volunteer who worked in reforestation with the Mapuche Indians, and that morning in town we finally ran into him. He shook hands with me, with Clarisa and even with Janir in his carrier, which immediately won my favor. Peter and I were dressed identically in rubber boots, long woolen ponchos and wide-brimmed black felt hats: the customary local garb for rain. Peter's Spanish was as fluent as mine, and that's what we spoke.

"Qué niño más bello," he told Clarisa: what a beautiful boy.

"Claro," she said: of course. The Chileans commented so often on Janir's beauty she had come to take it for granted. If someone *didn't* remark on it she looked at them askance.

Though cheerful and friendly, Peter was unable to hide his amazement at how Clarisa was dressed. She wore a long skirt and a baggy maroon V-neck sweater, one of mine she had appropriated and almost worn out. Her hair was damp in the drizzling rain, and she was barefoot. Though the temperature was about forty degrees, she had left her shoes, poncho and hat at the hotel.

Peter, finally, could not contain himself. He stared at her feet. *"No tiene frío?"* he asked. Wasn't she cold?

"I don't like to hide from the weather," she said.

He smiled. He almost laughed. He had heard about us as well, but he probably hadn't imagined anything quite as curious as this.

·   ·   ·

Though I didn't look forward to winter, on the whole I was happy with Chile. I had made some friends on nearby farms, my hens were laying eggs like little machines, and I still had much to learn about gardening and the peasant life.

Clarisa was less content. The oppressive local customs she had once found comical now angered her: how tightly the women were tethered to their houses and stoves. She mocked the local culture and fell into dark moods. Sometimes she was depressed and sometimes she broke into a rage. One night she flung our iron frying pan onto a stack of dishes in the sink and broke half of our earthenware plates and bowls. I think the sight of them had enraged her. It was near the end of her week to do the dishes, and perhaps I'd been too insistent on waiting for my week to start before I pitched in. We had split up all the household chores that way: a week on and a week off. For a while that had seemed to resolve our squabbles over housework, but something larger was now amiss. Clarisa, I think, had finally burned out on doing so much child care.

As Janir got older he and I were having more fun. We played hide-and-seek or I took him fishing a mile away, at the big Codingue River. But as I grew more responsive to him, his mother grew less so. Gone were the days when she could lie around with him for hours at a time looking at bugs in the grass. She was worn out, and I understood it.

One afternoon Doña Tencha, one of the few neighbors Clarisa still got along with, came over to visit with her daughter, a girl six months younger than Janir. Clarisa served tea as Janir played on the chilly floor, dressed in only a T-shirt.

"Doesn't your boy need some more clothes?" Dōna Tencha suggested.

Clarisa gave her a hard look. Yet only a few minutes later she seemed to have forgiven her, for she picked up Doña Tencha's baby and walked her around the house, cradling her in one arm. When the girl burst out crying she passed her back.

"She's only happy with me," said Dōna Tencha, opening her blouse with a satisfied look.

Twenty minutes later Clarisa gave the baby another try. She sat her on the counter beside the sink and combed back her thin hair. I was stoking the fire in the cookstove and chanced to look over just as Clarisa took the girl's fleshy arm and pinched it. Again she burst out crying. Clarisa watched her with an amused, almost gratified expression, then handed her back to her mother to be consoled again at the breast.

Clarisa was unrepentant after Doña Tencha left. "Meddling old woman," she said.

"So you pinch her baby?"

"Something's wrong with that baby anyway. I think it's feeble-minded. I just wanted to see how fat it was."

"If someone pinched Janir you'd kill her."

"These women should stay home where they belong, not come around and tell me what to do."

Pinching that baby, I think, was Clarisa's way of resisting the conventions of a society that treated its infants like dolls, swaddling them in shawls and immobilizing them in bulky sweaters. I didn't worry about the baby, but about Clarisa, who seemed oblivious to every consequence, and who had now kissed off one of her last friends in the neighborhood, as if she would never need another. Yet even then, as whenever she broke the rules, I had to admit to a tiny bubble of delight. No one was going to tame Clarisa. It was why I'd fallen in love with her in the first place.

•   •   •

By the time Janir turned eighteen months Clarisa had nursed him long enough. They were already down to once or twice a day, but when she tried to wean him entirely he complained long and loud. Finally I offered to help. "Take off for three days," I told her. "Go to Temuco, stay in a hotel and see some movies."

I figured while she was gone Janir and I would get closer, and then he might be willing to make the break. And perhaps, finally, Clarisa might find sex more appealing. I was still waiting for that.

I tried to share in his deprivation by fasting while his mother was gone. I cooked for him—he'd been eating solid foods for almost a year—but drank only tea myself. I milked the cow and made a cheese each morning, then gave up work for the day. We went for a long walk to the Codingue, where we lay on the bank and I informed him of a hundred rules and regulations he would have to follow in life—all so he could dismiss them with his ever more powerful *No!* He loved this game.

"When you grow up," I told him, "you'll have to milk the cow."
"No!" he cried.
"You'll have to cook and clean the dishes."
"No!"
"You'll have to become a doctor or a lawyer or an Indian chief."
"No!"
"You'll have to stop pooping on restaurant floors."
"No!"

At night he missed his mother. I worried about her, alone in town and apart from her child. But I did love curling up in bed with Janir after dinner, as the two of them had done every night of his life, and lying beside him until he dropped off to sleep.

On the third day I carried him up the road to visit my friend Don Fernando Lopez and his wife. I was weak by then after three days of fasting, and worn out by Janir. It wasn't my body that had given out, but my mind. My mind wanted to wander. It wanted to float down its own stream and land where it pleased—but Janir wanted me to follow wherever *his* mind led.

No wonder Clarisa had been falling into dark moods. Over the years I'd worked as a carpenter, a stonemason, a house cleaner and a high-school teacher—but nothing had worn me out like taking care of a young boy for three days. The fact that women had been doing this for thousands of years didn't make it any easier.

At least I was no longer hungry. That had passed after thirty-six hours. I sat peacefully at the Lopezes' kitchen table as they fed Janir some applesauce and bread sopped in milk. Later, walking home, I missed Clarisa. I didn't even know for sure where she was or when she'd come back. For the first time since her pregnancy I felt a tinge of worry about other men.

Janir rode in his carrier on our way home, chattering away in a language of his own invention. When we got to our house the door was ajar, but Clarisa wasn't there. I stepped outside, still carrying Janir, and called out for her. No answer. Then I saw her, standing in the orchard in her long white dress. I walked toward her past the fruit-laden trees. She looked thinner than when she'd left. She didn't say anything and didn't reach out for her son. Her dark stare was unnerving: the apathy of it, her lack of joy or even friendliness at seeing us again. I hugged her but she didn't respond. Janir squirmed to get out of the carrier, and I set him at her feet. He reached up to her, but she lifted her arms and crossed them over her breasts.

"No more sucking," she told him.

Winter fell on us with its cold and rainy days, and Clarisa turned her back on our neighbors. I felt alone and isolated, and our family seemed a small island in the hinterlands of Chile. One night we fell into talk about San Salvador: the warm nights in the city, the neighborhood kids playing soccer in the street, the balm of tropical weather.

"Janir has cousins there," Clarisa said. Her face looked softer than it had in weeks.

I stood up and fed the fire. I checked on Janir, asleep in our bed, then brought in some more wood. I sat down in front of Clarisa.

"Let's go back," I said. "Let's sell the farm and go back."

For a few seconds she stared into the firebox. She nodded. "Okay," she said. And that fast it was decided.

Yet I felt it as a defeat. We had never talked about how long we might stay in Chile—but certainly longer than two years. I sold my chickens to Don Fernando, sold the cows, sold the horses, sold the farm itself. I found a guy with a flatbed to come out one chilly morning and load up our trunks. Clarisa rode inside the cab with Janir, but I stood in back so I could savor the land as we left it: the trees I had planted, the wooden fences, the rich loam of the garden, the potatoes still lying under long hilled rows. Neighbors were coming to dig them up. We'd given them away.

I knew I would farm again. I had to believe that.

•   •   •

San Salvador, after our tranquil life in the country, seemed to burst with noise and crowds. In the evenings, after the daily rainstorm, women kindled fires in steel barrels or outdoor adobe hearths and cooked *pupusas,* thick tortillas folded around cheese or sausage. It was warm enough, day or night, to go without clothes. Downtown, under business awnings and overhangs, homeless mothers and their children lived on sheets of cardboard. A recent war with Honduras had driven hundreds of thousands of Salvadorans back into the country, but there was no land for them, and many wound up living on the streets of the capital.

Clarisa and I rented a small house not far from her mother's, on an alley lined with avocado trees. The avocados fell with a crash at night and we ate them for lunch the next day. A few times we left Janir at his grandmother's, went out to dinner and a movie, then took a taxi home and had gentle, almost solemn sex.

I was blind enough to imagine this was what we both wanted. But one evening as we lay in bed half dressed and on the edge of intercourse, I lost my erection. I was alarmed and embarrassed.

"That's all right," Clarisa said. She looked calm, almost relieved, as she buttoned up her shirt. And I saw then what I must have already registered unconsciously: that she wasn't aroused at all, but had simply gone along with my desire. That was so unlike her it had knocked my erection out from under me.

We lay beside each other in silence. Like most people—like our own families—we left a lot unsaid. My marriage was coming apart in my hands, but I was afraid to talk about it. I had never learned how. Instead of dragging everything into the open and putting up a fight, I held on in silence.

• • •

Janir spent most of his time at his grandmother Paquita's house, surrounded by women. Paquita worked but came home for lunch and a siesta. Clarisa's younger sister Eva Luz lived there as well, along with her brother Max, a married cousin and a couple of servants. In those days you could hire a live-in girl or young woman to cook, clean and look after kids for thirty dollars a month. Everyone in the house was crazy about Janir: they passed him from arm to arm, kissed him, held him and rattled away at him in Spanish.

In that house of women I was unsure what my role should be with Clarisa. Paquita thought I should exert my authority over her, but I found that difficult. In the subtle dynamic of power I always felt that Clarisa had more control—if only because she desired me less. I wanted her affection, but that was nothing I could command.

She was moody, she argued with me and her mother and everyone in the house. Sometimes she stormed out into the street. She took to wandering around the city on her own, visiting old friends: men or women, she wouldn't say. Sometimes I smelled marijuana on her clothes and hair. Sometimes I imagined she had fallen in love with someone else. There was no hard evidence for this, only her distance and the cold looks she gave me when I tried to pry.

One afternoon I found Janir and Clarisa in the living room of Paquita's house. Clarisa was sitting on the couch, leaning forward as she played a boxy wooden harp. Janir leaned against her back, toyed with her hair, crawled into her lap and played with the nearest harp strings. He wriggled around in her arms, then turned and butted his head against her shoulder, lightly but repeatedly. She neither acknowledged him nor stopped what she was doing.

The harp was a Chilean folk instrument she'd bought in Santiago the day we left. It was four feet tall, ungainly and untuned, and Clarisa was no musician. She just sat and strummed it.

"Are you going to learn to play that thing?" I asked.

She didn't look at me or respond at all. There was a new passivity to her that drove both me and Janir crazy. And today there was something else, for she had lifted her skirts and pulled the harp up between her legs, gripping it with her thighs. Her bare toes rested on the tiles beneath the couch, and she held the harp as if it were a lover: as she had not held me for weeks or months. I felt like starting an argument. I'd grown used to her apathy, but now her posture suggested that her sensual nature was in fact still awake, perhaps whetted.

"It's ridiculous," I said. "You can't play the simplest tune."

"So?"

"What do you want to do with your life? Do you want to stay in the city?"

"*Janir, véte a tu papá.*" She pushed him out of her lap, but he hung around her legs, grabbing the strings of the harp. "I don't see you doing anything," she said.

I picked Janir up. He seemed content but I knew it wouldn't last. Soon he'd get antsy and go back to pestering his mother, trying to keep a hold on her attention.

"I still want to farm," I told her. "But I've been thinking of going up to the States for a few weeks."

She pushed the harp away.

"I want to see Alan and my parents," I explained. I hadn't seen my brother for the four years he was in the coast guard, and my mother was about to leave on a trip to India. "You can come if you want," I said.

"You want us to?"

I didn't. I was afraid she'd embarrass me. I didn't want my parents to see how she looked these days, with her unkempt hair and inert expression. I didn't want them to see how distant she was. But, "Sure," I said.

She stood up and took Janir from me, held him in one arm and smoothed his hair. He went still. It was the attention he'd been looking for.

"Your father's a liar," she told him in Spanish. Without another glance at me she headed for the kitchen with him, her bare feet padding across the tiles. "I wouldn't trust him," she said.

•   •   •

Over the years an odd dynamic had transformed my relationship with Paquita. We had begun not as enemies, but with an inherent tension between us: I wanted to get her daughter into bed, and Paquita wanted to make sure nothing unlucky happened to her there. Paquita and I had always liked each other, but I knew she would have preferred me to be more conventional. Somehow, in spite of my educated background, I'd been swept up by the sixties, grown my hair and embraced some maverick ideas about agriculture and the peasant life. But I was never as unpredictable as Clarisa, and eventually that had driven me and Paquita into the same camp. Now, when it came to looking after Janir, we were co-conspirators, and she agreed to keep a close eye on him while I was in the States.

The entire family accompanied me to the old open-to-the-weather airport at Ilopango. There I picked Janir up and carried him around the terminal. I told him I was leaving, but soon I'd be back. The "soon" was kind of a lie, but he hardly listened. I lowered his feet onto mine and walked him across the floor, swaying like an elephant and chanting, *"Dun, dun-dun, dun, dun-dun."*

He was approaching the age at which I could remember bits of my own childhood. I'd always loved it when my father played the elephant with me—but I must have been older then. Janir, not quite two, wasn't interested. He only wanted to lead me on laughing chases around the terminal, his hair flying and his shirt flapping out of his shorts. We had a great time, but there was no way I could prepare him for what was coming: I was about to drop out of his life for six weeks.

I flew to New York and took the airport limo out to Westport, Connecticut, the town I'd grown up in. Though my parents were divorced, my father still lived there with his second wife. It felt soothing to be around him. Though I'd married a woman from El Salvador, dropped out of graduate school and moved to Chile to raise chickens, he had never tried to steer me in any other direction. At the same time he didn't have much advice about Clarisa: he hoped we could work things out, and he wanted to meet his grandson.

I visited my brother Alan in Vermont, and Nana in New York. Nana was our housekeeper and nanny—my second mother, really —who had come to work for my parents when I was six months old. She had lived with us for almost twenty years, and she remained an intimate part of the family.

My mother had recently quit her job as in-house doctor at Blue Cross to go on a month-long yoga tour to India. She was in poor shape physically, and was apprehensive about the trip's demanding itinerary and the backpack she would have to carry. For much of the last ten years—after the cataclysm of divorce in her late forties— she'd been depressed. She drank, she took too many sedatives, she found and lost one job after another. She'd had several psychiatrists, and on two occasions had signed herself into a private clinic. But no one in the family could help her. We had our own lives to lead, and none of us knew anything about clinical depression. "Get out and jog," my brother told her. "Meet some new people," was my hopeful advice.

* * *

In Clarisa I had chosen an entirely different woman from my mother. Or so I believed. Mom was a doctor who had long been ambitious, and who was commonly drawn to dynamic men and women. Clarisa cared nothing for any of that. She was impulsive, self-absorbed and careless about the future. Though they were both troubled women, I thought of Clarisa as moody and capricious, and of my mother as depressed—as if those traits had nothing in common.

In those days I would have laughed at the suggestion that I had married my mother. Yet now I see what an unerring path I followed to Clarisa. I chose a woman who was all emotion, someone who would nourish the frail connection I had to my own feelings. When younger I'd depended on my mother for this. Then, as men often do, I found a woman who could fill her shoes, and married her.

When I was a teenager, a stiff kid submerged in a repressive New England boarding school, Mom had found ways to remind me there was always a life of feelings beneath the veneer of the one we led. When I came home for Christmas or summer vacation she invariably left some book on my bedside table: Anne Morrow Lindbergh's *Gift from The Sea*, Virginia Woolf's *A Room of One's Own* or Lawrence Durrell's *Justine*. Over the family dinner table there was not much talk about emotions, but the books my mother gave me spoke of little else.

Later, after my parents' divorce, I wanted my mother to be the same cheerful and self-reliant parent I'd had as a child. Those days had passed, and I found it hard to accept how she had changed. Yet somehow we stumbled along and became better friends. We talked more as two adults, and after my first year in the Peace Corps she flew down to Central America and we rented a car and drove through Guatemala for a week, telling stories and talking the whole way.

We stayed in a German hotel overlooking Lake Atitlán, a lodging so clean and orderly I felt as if we'd been transported directly to northern Europe. There was a piano, and after dinner I sat in an antimacassared armchair as Mom played from her favorite piece, Schubert's *Trout Quintet*. As a child I'd often gone to sleep as she played the piano downstairs, directly beneath my bed.

The next night, in a more primitive hotel in Chichicastenango, we turned off the lights in our small whitewashed room, propped ourselves up in our beds and watched the fire burn in a corner hearth. Mom told me how, at seventeen, she had won the Ohio diving championship—and lost her two front teeth on the bottom of a Columbus swimming pool. No one had offered her so much as an aspirin for the pain, and years later the memory of that accident helped decide her field of medicine, anesthesia.

She told me how at nineteen, fearful she would never get another offer, she had married a trucker named Larry Tidball. Larry moved her to Beaumont, Texas, where his jealousy and possessive ways slowly ground her down. Finally she packed two small suitcases with her best clothes, her shoes and a few books, and left to visit her parents in Brooklyn, where her father was teaching music. It was 1937, and my mother twenty-two.

"I took my diaphragm with me," she added. "Of course I didn't tell my parents that. But after a week I broke down and admitted I didn't want to go back to Larry or Texas. Pop put his arm around me. He really surprised me. 'Ginny,' he said, 'there's nothing you have to do, as long as you're willing to pay the price.' "

Our talk died down in the whitewashed room. We were unaccustomed to such intimate moments, and just lying in two beds, side by side in the same room, was a novelty. In the silence that followed her stories I remembered a night the two of us had spent together in a tiny roadside wooden cabin somewhere in Vermont or New Hampshire, on our way home from a family vacation. I might have been seven or eight. After unpacking our bags we lit a fire in the woodstove and then, in the last of the violet dusk, went for a cold swim in the pond behind the cabins.

Afterward, inside but still shivering, Mom turned her back, slipped out of her bathing suit and wrapped herself in a towel. I did the same, and we crouched together before the open door of the stove, soaking up the heat from the flames. I was acutely aware of her body and my own, both naked beneath the towels, in a room lit only by the fire.

By then my mother had stopped holding me. Indeed, perhaps that's what made it possible to crouch there in our towels. Mom had been physical and affectionate with me as a young child—I know that from early photos—but that was now done. And I'm sure I found it perfectly normal, for no boy I knew ever lay around in his parents' arms. All the same, whether Mom was planting tomatoes in the backyard, making swan dives into some swimming pool or just curled up on Sunday mornings in a white bathrobe on the living-room couch, I was tuned to her body, to her strong physical presence. From an early age it was clear that she and I were the two sensuous members of our family—and the two whose emotions were closest to the surface. I couldn't have put that into words back then, yet I knew it.

Now I think back. I try to remember the last time she held me. I'm not sure. Can I have been as young as five or six, that time I got lost on Jimmy's Island? This was in fact a small wooded promontory that stuck into the salt marsh behind our house in Connecticut, and late one autumn afternoon, while playing with a friend, I left my red sweater there, hanging on a branch. At dusk I went back alone and found it—but then, just out of sight of my house, I got lost. The night came down fast, seagulls were flapping into the trees overhead and I couldn't find the path. I stood in one spot and cried without stop, until Mom came out with a flashlight and found me. She knelt beside me on the leafy ground, held me close and rocked me. That's what I remember now: how she held and held me, as long as I wanted.

* * *

There are memories we keep without ever mentioning them or writing them down. A small scene, perhaps, but for some reason too vivid to be forgotten. Here's one I've never told anyone, yet remembered for forty years:

I'm nine. Mom is driving Alan and me up to Maine in our '48 Mercury convertible. It's summer, the top is down, and as we pass a road construction site the driver of a steamroller glances down into our car just as my mother's skirts fly up in the wind, briefly exposing her thighs. She pushes down her dress but is not at all embarrassed. Indeed, she laughs and seems to enjoy it. After a tiny hesitation the man laughs back, and we drive on through the site.

* * *

Now, staying with her in her New York apartment, I questioned her decision to leave a good job at Blue Cross for a one-month trip to India. Though she had taken some classes from Jerry, the leader of the tour, she was hardly a yoga devotee.

"I've already quit," she told me. "I can't go back. Besides, this is a tremendous opportunity. I don't want to pass it up."

I went along with this unlikely explanation—only to discover a few years later that in fact she had been fired by Blue Cross, then used the tour as her excuse for having "quit."

On the day of her flight I drove her out to JFK in her old Chevy. It was a hot October afternoon, and perspiration dotted her forehead. After a long silence she asked, "Are you still in love with her?"

I moved out of the left lane, drove a bit slower. "I guess so. Sometimes I don't want to be, but I am."

"How is she with Janir?"

"They fight a lot, sometimes like two little kids. But other times she's sweet with him. It comes and goes."

Mom stared out at the battered landscape of Queens. "Her father killed himself, didn't he?"

I nodded. "When she was seven."

"Why?"

Clarisa had told me her father was upset because someone had cheated him on a business deal. That was another explanation I'd gone along with, and now, as I repeated it, I could hear how inadequate it sounded. I added at the end, "I don't really know why."

"Maybe she should talk to someone. A psychiatrist."

I resisted this. It was a delicate point between us that I'd never had much faith in Mom's psychiatrists. Today I credit one of them, at least, with keeping her alive through hard times. But in those days I viewed the whole profession skeptically.

"I doubt if she'd sit still for it," I said. "When she was pregnant she wouldn't even see an obstetrician."

We drove toward the airport over the broken highways. "Are you going to keep farming?"

"I want to."

"Can you make a living at it?"

"Maybe a small living," I said.

Mom rolled down her window. She wasn't feeling well, I could see. "I guess that's what most of us get," she said. "No matter how much money there is."

By now we were close to the airport, and the traffic was stop-and-go. She'd been anxious all day and now leaned forward in her seat. She didn't look good at all.

"You okay?" I asked.

She reached into a small clutch purse, pulled out a plastic bag and threw up into it. Afterward she knotted the top of the bag and set it on the floor behind her seat.

For a while neither of us spoke. Then she said, "I'm just nervous about flying."

I knew it was more than that, but didn't say so. She was afraid of leaving her safe city apartment and flying halfway around the world with a group of people she didn't know. I wondered if she had taken along a stash of her prescription drugs—and if she was on something now.

At the airport we found Jerry and the other tour members. They all looked young and trim and ready for an adventure—and none of them save Jerry took the least notice of my fifty-seven-year-old mother. She was invisible to them. Jerry came over to say hello, but he was busy with trip logistics and didn't stay long. My heart went out to her. Suddenly Virginia Thorndike, who had always been an attractive and resourceful woman, who had worked for *Vogue* and *Life*, who had gone back to college at thirty-four and graduated Phi Beta Kappa from Barnard, then gone on to medical school, become an anesthesiologist and practiced in the city for fifteen years, was now the geek no one wanted to sit next to on the school bus. While the other tour members chatted and compared equipment Mom stood to one side, her face pale under the fluorescent lights. I was afraid she'd get sick again. I didn't want her to disgrace me. It's terrible to recall this now: I wanted her to get on the plane and not fall apart on me in front of all those people.

•   •   •

In her apartment that morning, while she packed, I had taken one of her photo albums off the shelf and leafed through it. There, in old black-and-white, eight-by-ten photos, was the evidence of her better days:

In 1938, the year before she met my father, she stands in one of Philip Johnson's glass-walled houses facing the Japanese-American sculptor Isamu Noguchi. Mom is young, slender and alert. Noguchi is shorter, older and more at ease. He gazes at her placidly. I know little about their relationship, but the photo is suggestive. "I loved how he smelled," she once told me, "of sandalwood."

In 1949 my father snaps her with his Leica on a snowy street in Lech, Austria. I'm seven, and the three of us have gone there to ski. Mom stands upright, her skis over her shoulder, a pair of climbing skins wrapped jauntily about her waist. She has just won the slalom race for tourists.

A year later she ices Christmas cookies with me and my brother: the same gingerbread cookies her great-grandmother made in the 1800s. Mom wears an apron and a smile, looking fully ensconced in family life.

The next summer, on either side of her, Alan and I lie on the lawn in our bathing suits beside the seawall of our house in Connecticut. We are wasted by what we call "the disease," a waterlogged reaction to spending five straight hours in Long Island Sound. Mom wears a skirted two-piece bathing suit that bridges the gap between sensible mother and sensual woman. Dark-haired, cheerful and slender, she looks like most of the women I've been attracted to in my life.

•   •   •

In the airport she practiced with her knapsack, trying to slide it on and off. It was a simple move I could do one-handed, that I could manage in the dark or when dangling from a crowded bus. But Mom couldn't get the hang of it. She lifted the knapsack by both straps, slipped an arm through one of them—but then the pack, loaded with too much gear and clothing, swung away from her groping hand and tipped to the floor.

I hated myself for being so impatient. She was old and fat and ungainly. I tried to suppress my intolerance but couldn't. I wanted her to fly off to India and get better among this crowd of healthy young people. I put my faith in these strangers.

Mom shook off my help and tried the knapsack once again. When she couldn't get it she lowered it to the floor and sat down on one of the chairs. "I'll figure it out later," she said.

Jerry, I hoped, would look after her in India. She was a doctor, after all, and surely he'd be glad to have her along on his trip— even if now she seemed to need more help than anyone else.

"They're all so young," she said, glancing around at the other travelers.

It softened me to see her worry. "You don't have to go," I said. I was afraid she wouldn't, but said it anyway.

"No, I want to. It'll be good for me. Listen, don't wait. The flight doesn't leave for a couple of hours."

"That's okay. I'm in no hurry."

"Don't, John, it's silly. I'll be fine. Really, I will."

We talked it over, then embraced and said good-bye. I felt awkward hugging her in public. Probably even if we'd been alone I would have felt self-conscious about putting my arms around the bulk of her shoulders. Neither of us, I think, had ever gotten used to the changes in her body.

"You're a lovely son," she said.

The words embarrassed me—though only an hour later, as I lay close to tears on the sofa in her apartment, I clung to them, even whispered them out loud.

After our embrace in the airport I turned and left. I rounded the corner, then stopped, waited a moment and peeked back into the lobby. She was already introducing herself to the young couple next to her. They shook hands and began to talk. The young man and woman wore polo shirts and shorts. Mom was dressed in an oversized athletic warm-up suit, and her head wagged slightly as she spoke, which made her look older. But the couple seemed interested, they weren't just being polite. By now she was probably telling them she was an anesthesiologist. That was one of her calling cards, and she wasn't afraid to use it.

As an intern and resident she had done hundreds, perhaps thousands, of operations, and occasionally came home and told my brother and me electrifying tales: the time she was pumping anaesthetic and the surgeon put his thumb through the wall of a patient's heart. The room was filled with fine sprays of blood until he got it sewed up.

She had a stock of good stories. On December 7, 1941, she and my father were eating dinner at Henry and Clare Boothe Luce's. Henry was the founder of Time, Inc. and my Dad's boss at *Life*. Clare was a playwright, later ambassador to Italy. Halfway through the meal a butler appeared, carrying a folded slip of paper on a silver tray. It was the news about Pearl Harbor—and he took it straight to Clare, not Henry. My mother loved that.

Her next tale might be about the gangster she'd gone out with recently, a Sicilian who lived in her building, dressed all in black and had taken her twice to the dog track in Jersey. He carried his cash, a wad of Franklins, in his right front pocket, where it created what Mom called "an unseemly bulge."

How she had clung to life in the last ten years. It wrenched me to watch her: still meeting people, still showing her best side, still fighting despair.

Finally I turned and left. I never saw her again.

•   •   •

From New York I hitched to Boulder. It was 1972, the revolution was in full flower, and I got one ride after another in painted vans, old hearses and a bus full of the Missouri disciples of a guy called Michael World Peace.

I stayed with Bruce in Boulder and helped him frame a house. In the evenings we talked long hours about Clarisa, marriage and heartache. I kept putting off my departure, for I had been too long without a friend to talk to: an old friend from my own world.

After two weeks Mom surprised me with a call from New York. She had gotten sick in India and come home early. She'd caught a flight from New Delhi to Cairo and managed to change planes there on her own, but by the time she got to JFK she was out cold. An ambulance took her to Presbyterian Hospital and now she sounded fine. She always did when she called from a hospital bed or clinic lounge, for there she was always sober.

That same night I called Clarisa in San Salvador. She was out, but Paquita put Janir on. I heard him talking before he took the phone —but then he clammed up. I told him it was his dad and I'd be back soon, but still he didn't say anything. Paquita told me he was doing fine, that he and his cousin Frankie were having a great time. We avoided the topic of Clarisa and what she was doing. My heart ached enough as it was, thinking of Janir.

A week later, on my thirtieth birthday, Mom called again, this time from her apartment. The minute she said hello I could hear the slur in her voice. She had sent a present, she told me—but I cut her off.

"You're drunk," I said.

"I'm not. I can't, I'm on Antabuse."

"Then it's pills. Look, Mom, I can hear it. I always know. Why do you call me up like this?"

"It's your birthday," she said.

I didn't care. I didn't want to hear it. For a long time neither one of us spoke. Finally she said, "I know I've made some mistakes, but having you and Alan was the best thing I ever did."

Even to that I closed my heart. I didn't want any maudlin talk. So what if she told me, as she often had, that she loved me, that I was a handsome young man, that Alan and I were both wonderful sons. She'd been drunk and stoned too often for me to give in easily. I wanted her to do all the work, to thaw me out, to prove she loved me after creating so much havoc.

Two days later Nana called me after I got home from work.

"John," she said, "your mother died last night."

I sagged back against the kitchen counter. I closed my eyes. I'd been afraid of this, and Nana and I had discussed it several times: how alcohol and sedatives were a lethal combination, and how one day it could happen. But I had never really believed it. Mom and I had recently talked: only two days before, we had talked as if there would always be time, as if we had years left.

"John?" Nana said.

"Yeah, I'm here. I'm okay." I wasn't hurt yet, just stunned.

"You sure?" she asked.

"Tell me," I said.

A friend had found her on her living room floor. She had passed out there—or perhaps just lain down and drifted into sleep. Her body had looked composed and there was no note, no indication that she'd done it on purpose.

I paced around the kitchen in Boulder, trailing the phone cord. After all she had suffered in the last ten years, Nana suggested, in some ways this was best. I knew that was true. And I didn't cry that night, or the next. I only felt the shock, and a guilty sense of relief. The heartache would come later: the years I missed her every day.

The autopsy would eventually show that Mom had taken three different prescription drugs. But I don't believe she set out to kill herself. She just wanted to be unconscious. She had played with that line before and probably, as a doctor, thought she knew how far she could go. But she misjudged and slipped over the edge. Her bathroom closet, when my brother cleaned it out, was filled with five-hundred-count bottles of Seconal, Valium, Librium and other tranquilizers. She had hoarded these defenses against misery and depression, and had ridden the brink so long between consciousness and oblivion that she must have lost track of the danger.

·   ·   ·

I flew back to New York, met up with Dad and Alan, and we picked up her ashes at Campbell's Funeral Chapel. Though Campbell's was a decorous mortuary on Manhattan's East Side, they gave us the ashes in an unadorned container with a pry-open lid, much like a paint can without a label. Dad carried it out into the street and we stood in the city's weak sunlight, unsure what to do next. We went out to eat but didn't say much. Each of us, I think, worried about the other two.

The can's weight surprised me, and when Al and I were alone with it we sat down on some steps on Park Avenue and opened the lid with a quarter. They weren't ashes at all, but dense calcium fragments of bones and teeth. I slipped my fingers into them, lifted out a few pieces and let them clink back into the can. Al looked at them soberly, blankly. I pressed the lid back into place and we walked on down the sidewalk as a string of cabs thumped by on the street. What a strange thing to be carrying through Manhattan. And what, I suggested, if a mugger made off with the can? We joked about it, even laughed. Help, he stole our mother! It was farcical, it was ridiculous. It was easier than crying.

Three days later we held a service on the beach at Sagaponack near the eastern end of Long Island. Nothing religious, for none of us were churchgoers. It was more like a Quaker meeting, in which those who were moved to say something did. I waited until the end, then told how my mother had loved this beach above all others, how we'd been coming here since 1949, how our annual picnics with friends from nearby Sag Harbor were a benchmark for my own happiness. It was November but warm. The mourners stood in a circle on the sand, three hundred yards down from the parking lot. I'd made them all walk down to her favorite inlet.

What I wanted to say, but couldn't, was that my mother had gone through hell. No one had talked about that or even mentioned it. The smoothing and polishing of her history had already begun, and the torment of her last years seemed unspeakable: her loneliness and depression, the shock of growing old and her fear that she would never know romance again.

Al and I opened the paint can and started throwing the chips into the ocean. They disappeared with only a rustle on the surface of the water. We walked down close to the waves as we had done as kids, jumping back when one surged toward us. And then I stopped jumping. I wanted to be broken, and I let the sea do it. I clutched the can and walked into the waves, my shoes sinking into the sand as the water smacked against my knees. I stood at the edge of the gray empty ocean, finally sobbing, throwing out the last of the ashes and letting the waves soak me. I didn't move until Dad came out into the water, put his arm around my shoulders and led me back to shore.

One thought had started the tears: She never met Janir.

I FLEW BACK TO BOULDER AND BOUGHT A PICKUP TO drive to El Salvador. I hadn't figured out what I was going to do there, but I wanted to get back to my family.

A few days before I left Colorado Paquita called to tell me she had put Clarisa in a private psychiatric hospital. "I had to do it," she said. "She was acting crazy. It's only a ten-day treatment and I think she's better already."

"What do you mean, crazy?"

"You know Clarisa. Her thoughts are ungoverned."

I wasn't sure that was reason to lock her up. "And Janir?" I asked.

"Feliz," Paquita said tersely. Happy. But from her tone I wasn't so sure.

Since returning from New York I'd been moving slowly. The world looked the same, but my mother wasn't in it. I joined Bruce's framing crew but made too many mistakes. One day at lunch I said good-bye to Bruce, drove back to his house, threw my bags in the pickup and took off for Central America. I left without food, water or maps, crossed the border at El Paso and drove day and night down the long sweep of Mexico, eating at roadside taco stands and sleeping in the truck bed on a pair of old blankets. The potholed roads battered the big Chevy, and the truth crushed me: I would never see my mother again.

And what if something happened to Janir?

•   •   •

Little had changed on the narrow streets of the Colonia Cucuma-cayán. When I pulled up in front of Paquita's house the first person I saw was Clarisa, standing in the doorway, peeling and eating an orange.

"Hi, Clarisa." I parked and jumped out.

"Qué tal?" she said coolly, as if I'd been away for a couple of days instead of two months. She threw some peels into the street and ate another section of her orange. I came around the truck and gave her a hug.

"And Janir?" I asked.

"Janir," she said matter-of-factly over her shoulder. *"Ven, aquí está tu papá."*

He skipped into sight in his bare feet. He had grown. But at the sight of me he stopped. He took hold of Clarisa's skirt, hid behind her and peered around at me. When I got down on one knee he backed up a step. He was scared of me.

"Janir," I told him, *"soy tu papá."* His hair was long and silky and light from the sun, and his face had grown firmer. He was a young boy now, two and a quarter. He pulled on his mother's skirts.

"Mamá," he said, *"vamos a la tienda."*

Amazing! When I left he'd barely spoken words, and now it was sentences. He wanted to go to the store. "He likes the pastries there," Clarisa explained.

"Come on," I said, and held out my hand to him. "We'll get some."

But he wouldn't leave his mother. She swung him up on her hip, and we walked down the street to a store in the front room of someone's house. Janir pointed to a roll and I bought it for him. I wanted to take him in my arms, to hold him and smell his hair and see how much he weighed. Forget it: he wouldn't even take the pastry from my hand. I had to give it to Clarisa, who gave it to him. He ate it slowly, watching me from her arms. He looked not just shy, but resentful. I'd been away too long.

"Hey, buddy," I told him, "I'm your dad. I'm going to be around from now on!"

We walked back to my truck, where Clarisa set him down in the bed. He seemed more relaxed there, and explored my two old suitcases.

"So how have you been?" I asked Clarisa. "I hear you were in the hospital."

"My mother's idea. She's trying to get Janir for herself. She wants to raise him her way so he'll be like everyone else."

Though I didn't say so, I'd begun to think that wouldn't be such a bad idea. I asked if she had talked to any psychiatrists at the hospital.

She ignored the question. She leaned back against the truck and stared at me. "Did your mother kill herself?"

I felt like she'd slapped me in the face. I stared at her but she didn't budge, she just waited for an answer.

"They haven't done the autopsy yet," I said. "They froze some tissue. There was no note. I think she died in her sleep."

"My father was a great man," Clarisa said. She put her hands on her hips and gave me a fierce look. "Don't you ever fucking judge him."

I knew what she was driving at: now we both had a dead parent, and both were suicides.

Janir watched us from the truck. He didn't understand English but he could see we were arguing, and he called to Clarisa to pick him up. I reached into the cab and pulled out the first of several presents I'd brought him, an old-fashioned jack-in-the-box. I cranked it for him a couple of times, then he made Clarisa do it, and finally he did it himself. He was careful with the toy, solemn, as if he'd forgotten how to play.

The rest of his presents I meted out over the next few days: trucks, bulldozers and backhoes, the toys I'd loved myself as a boy. He lined them up on Paquita's living room floor and rolled them back and forth a little, but he was never enthusiastic about them. Probably he was too young for them. In the end I found a local toy store and bought him a couple of stuffed animals and a big mushy beanbag he liked to jump on. I was buying back his trust, I knew. But the fact was, at least to a degree, it could be bought.

•   •   •

After supper on my first night back, Clarisa took Janir to bed and never came out of her room. Paquita and I went for a walk, strolling in silence down the first few streets past the immediate neighbors. It was warm, and everyone's door was open. Two old men played chess under a streetlight, ignoring the flapping moths, and the *sereno* passed, the private policeman who patrolled on an old bicycle, blowing a high soft whistle to let both thieves and residents know he was on the job.

"Did they give her drugs?" I asked.

"Yes. To tranquilize her."

"But no electric shock?"

"No, no, it was just to give her mind a rest."

"From what?" I asked.

"From all her crazy notions. She is contrary about everything. She can do nothing like a normal mother. She has no instinct for that."

I reminded Paquita of how attentive Clarisa had been with Janir when he was younger. Paquita heard me out, but her mind was made up. At the avenue she took my arm. "If you and Clarisa rent a place together," she said, "I don't think you should take Janir with you. He'd do better at my house where there's always someone around to keep an eye on him."

I couldn't tell if there was any real danger. When I hesitated, unwilling to promise Paquita I'd leave Janir with her, she let slip some other hints. She had been unable to control her daughter, she said . . . and perhaps there were other men involved.

Perhaps, I thought, that was why Clarisa had given me such a cold reception. But instead of feeling jealous I felt numb and exhausted. I was still overwhelmed by my mother's death, and by Janir, who seemed afraid of me.

●   ●   ●

I spent a few nights on the stiff couch in Paquita's living room. It was ridiculous, I thought: I was married but couldn't sleep with my wife. I could hardly touch her, and each night she closed herself off with Janir. I wanted to hold her, I wanted to talk to her about my mother and the funeral. She wasn't interested.

But did I have any idea what *she* wanted to talk about? No. How different things look in hindsight, and how my own flaws stand out in relief.

After three days I rented an apartment in a drab part of town. The place seemed adequate when I rented it at noon, but that evening, after I carried in my luggage and a cotton mattress, everything looked shabby. I unrolled the mattress on the dusty tile floor, flopped down on it and lay there close to tears. I thought about my mother: Thank God she couldn't see me now. Of course, maybe she could.

Clarisa didn't seem to care where I lived, or how often I came around. She wanted money to buy a car. When I resisted this idea she asked to borrow the truck. The Chevrolet was a stiff-handling, three-quarter-ton pickup, and I didn't trust her with it. Her California license had expired, so I told her to get a Salvadoran license and then I'd see about lending it to her. This infuriated her—because we both knew getting a license in El Salvador was not as simple as it was in the United States. I was putting her off, and she knew it.

I picked up a couple of English classes at night, teaching without a work permit, and hauled some fruit with my friend Julio Torres. At dawn we drove out to his uncle's farm, filled the pickup with oranges, grapefruits or melons and trucked them back to the city's wholesale market. It was a risky job—the truck had Colorado plates and anyone could have turned me in to immigration—but I loved the hustle and bargaining, and the chance to prove I could make some money.

I also liked working the market because we finished by eleven and every day at noon I picked Janir up at his preschool. Paquita had chosen the school for its propriety and decorum—qualities she hoped would offset Clarisa's "irregularities" as a mother. Just before noon each day a bevy of maids gathered outside the stately old house to retrieve their charges, while those of us with cars double-parked on the street. I had trimmed my hair and beard, and took a clean shirt every day to change into after sweeping out the truck. Soon all the girls who worked at the school knew the gringo father with the big white pickup. They all made a fuss over Janir, and I wasn't the only one who thought he was the cutest kid around.

Paquita dropped him off each morning on the way to her classes, having dressed him in a clean pressed shirt with a little handkerchief pinned to his lapel. The first couple of times I picked him up he hardly looked at me as we drove home. But after a few days he started to warm up, and before long he was shaking off the girl who escorted him to the street and scrambling into the truck by himself. As we drove home he chattered in Spanish, and by the second week he was leaning against me and helping me shift the gears. Child seats were unheard of in El Salvador in those days, and no one bothered with seat belts for a mere trip across town.

Dinner was served as soon as we got to Paquita's. Sometimes Clarisa was there, often not. If she was absent no one mentioned her. After the meal Janir and I lay around on the parlor floor—the tiles were mopped twice a day—and played with some blocks I'd made him out of Nicaraguan cedar. Or I carried him up onto the roof to watch the pigeons clap from house to house. He threw his arms around my neck and hung there.

When I asked Clarisa where she spent her days, she answered vaguely. And I didn't press her. I was afraid of what I might hear. It was easier to resent her distance, and to pour myself into work and childcare.

Janir and I spent our afternoons together. At one, in the stifling heat, we took a siesta. Then a shower to wake up, then an expedition in the high-riding Chevy. Janir loved that truck. We drove across town to a public swimming pool, out to the lake at Ilopango or up to the verdant peaks at Devil's Door. Sometimes coming home he was tired and cranky. He wanted his mother, and some elemental consolation I couldn't give him. Other times he curled up in my lap, or lay with his head against my thigh and his brown legs stretched out on the seat.

On one of our outings we ran across a string of elephants lumbering through the streets of the city, each clasping the tail of the one before it. Their walk advertised a circus whose posters had adorned walls and lampposts for the past week. I drove as close as I could, then parked and lifted Janir into the truck bed to watch the great beasts tramp by. Janir could not contain himself. He leapt up and down in desperate happiness. *"Elefante-camello!"* he cried. *"Elefante-camello!"*

Somehow, out of one of his books, he had combined two animals into one: an elephant-camel. He jumped into my arms and squeezed my neck deliriously: *"Mira, papi, qué chulo los elefante-camellos!"* His thrill at seeing them was too great for me to correct him, so on Saturday afternoon when I took him to the circus he was still chanting, like some kind of mantra, *"Elefante-camello, elefante-camello, elefante-camello!"*

•   •   •

Clarisa, once so attentive to Janir, now came and went without much regard for him. He still slept in her bed most nights, but usually she had left the house by the time I brought him home from school, and often she didn't return until after I left in the evening to teach my classes.

I asked her again what she was up to. What did she do all day? Where did she go?

"I'm taking a class from Ricardo Aguilar," she said.

"In painting?"

She folded her arms over her chest. "We have a group, we paint every day."

"And smoke dope?"

She just looked at me.

"We're still married," I said. "You ever think of that?"

"If we're married how come you're so stingy? Why won't you buy me a car? You've got one."

"I use that truck for work."

"You play with it."

"I take Janir places."

"You've got the money," she said. "What are you so damn cheap for?"

I could easily have bought her a car, it was true. But I was afraid to. I thought she'd go wild if she had one, drive all over the place, just take off and disappear.

"Clarisa," I said, "let's figure out what we're doing first."

"You figure it out. I want a car."

My money was in a bank in New York. Our money. The justice of her demand for a vehicle was clear, but on this one issue I controlled her, and I was afraid to give that up. Paquita was on my side and steadily urged me not to buy Clarisa a car. She forecast disaster if I ever let her get behind a steering wheel.

•   •   •

Janir, at two and a half, still clung tightly to his mother. When she came home he dropped everything and everybody, including me, and ran to her. But she was less and less responsive to him. She let him crawl over her, but looked away as he hung from her neck, played with her hair and poked his fingers into her ears. Her passivity only made him more frantic.

Steadily I disappointed Paquita, who believed it was my job to lay down the law with Clarisa. I couldn't do that. I could refuse to buy her a car, but I could not insist that she feel some affection for me. And after a while I was too proud to ask. I still wanted her, but damned if I'd make any overtures. Let her make the offers, I thought. After being so cold she owed me that.

If I hadn't been blinded by my own insecurity, I might have seen that Clarisa needed help more than I did. Instead I retreated into a shell of injured pride. I had done the same when my mother hurt me, in the midst of her depression and drug abuse.

Clarisa came home late for supper one night wearing an old blouse and a long gypsy skirt, smelling of dope and avoiding my eyes and Paquita's. Janir got down from his chair and ran to her, but Paquita barred her way to the kitchen.

"You're not sitting at my table like that," she said. "You look like a tramp."

"Wear your own damn clothes," Clarisa said. "You can't tell me how to dress."

"As long as you live in my house I can. And as long as I take care of your son."

"Then I'll take him *somewhere else*," she screamed. "You're trying to steal him from me." She wheeled toward me. "Just give me the money. I'll find my own place."

Paquita waved her finger at me. "Don't do it," she said.

Janir tugged at his mother's skirts, crying and clinging to her. Finally Clarisa picked him up and disappeared into her room. After a while, when he had quieted down, we could hear her singing to him, faint lullabies in both Spanish and English.

Paquita and I sat awkwardly at the kitchen table, her shoe tapping nervously on the tile floor. We looked at each other and then away. Clarisa still had a mother's claim, and neither of us was ready to defy it.

•   •   •

A week later I was giving Janir a bath in the raised tub in the laundry room. The corners of the tub were tiled but square, and I kept a grip on him to make sure he didn't fall. Since my return he'd been short on cheerful spirits and laughter, but now he had them in spades. He squealed as I poured water on him, jumped up and down while I shampooed his hair.

"Water baby," I said.

"Soy muchacho," he cried, *"y tú eres niño."* He was the boy and I the baby. He grabbed my nose with a soapy hand and squirmed into my arms, soaking the front of my shirt. I had missed this rowdy child. I leaned forward and gave him a sloppy kiss on his belly: blub-blub-blub.

He went still. I thought he didn't like the kiss—but a shadow had come over his face. He stared at the door.

"I'll take him," Clarisa said, and stepped into the room. Obedi-ently Janir lifted his arms to her. She slid between us and picked him up.

"Let me rinse him off," I said. "His hair's full of shampoo."

She ignored me and carried him into the kitchen. "He doesn't need his hair washed, he needs to swim in the ocean." She stood him on the kitchen table, where he dripped soapy water onto the plastic tablecloth. He gave me a hesitant smile. He knew he was breaking the rules. In some ways he was just like his mother.

"Guineo," he demanded. He wanted a banana.

Clarisa peeled one and handed half of it to him. "Monkeys love bananas," she said.

He stuffed the whole half in his mouth, then crouched on the table and grunted, letting his arms hang next to his feet. Paquita would not be happy, I thought, if she walked in on this. And I wondered if she was right, if Clarisa was losing her last inclination to do things the ordinary way. Janir sat down on the tablecloth, then stretched out on the table and wriggled back and forth, as slippery as a fish but grunting like a chimp. I had a mad son and a mad wife. Was one all right and the other not?

I pulled up a chair and sat on it backwards. "Clarisa," I said. "I'm going up to Guatemala next week."

She gave Janir the second half of the banana. "To look for a farm," she said.

We had talked this over before. Though she had never shown any interest in the project, I'd talked about buying some land there, perhaps starting a communal farm with friends from the States. "I want to take Janir with me," I said.

She stared at me. Her thick hair fell forward over her face. She was wearing one of my mother's silk skirts and a white peasant blouse now damp from Janir. "No," she said.

"He needs to have some time with me. More than just a few hours. I need it, too."

"You don't like it that he loves me more."

"He can love us both," I said. "It's not a contest."

But the truth stung. No matter what Janir and I were doing, no matter how much fun we were having, all she had to do was hold out her arms to him, and he went.

"He shouldn't live on a farm," she said. "That's too quiet for him."

"What about you?" This was as close as we had ever come to talking about a separation. "Would it be too quiet for you?"

"What's wrong with the city?" she asked.

"Because I still want to farm."

"Not me."

Janir stood up on the table. He reached for me, took my shirt in one hand and Clarisa's in the other and pulled us closer together. We'd been speaking English, and I don't think he understood much of it, but he knew what was going on.

W<small>E</small> LEFT EARLY ONE MORNING, PASSED THE BORDER
before noon and drove on into Guatemala, slowly gaining altitude.
Janir took a long nap, woke up and felt the cooler air and looked
around suspiciously. Guatemala City was the usual logjam of trucks,
buses and exhaust, and before we got through it Janir began to
moan, *"Yo quiero a mi mamá. Yo quiero a mi mamá."* He wanted his
mother. I tried to explain that this was like the trips we'd taken
around San Salvador, only longer, but he would not be comforted.
He lay on the seat, banged his head against it, slumped onto the
floor and cried relentlessly. There was nowhere to stop, so I kept
driving. I was tense from the traffic, and my neck felt like steel cable.
Finally, halfway to Antigua, I pulled off at a wooden stand under
some pine trees and bought him a bowl of strawberries and cream.
This was a delicacy he loved, and rarely available in tropical El
Salvador. But now he wouldn't eat them. He stared rigidly at the
bowl in front of his face, looking as offended as an old man. I ate
my strawberries, then his, then picked him up and carried him back
to the truck. Still mute, he curled up on the seat and went to sleep
again. That was a relief, but I still felt miserable.

Two hours down the road he woke up, coming out of his nap
slowly and resentfully. He didn't want to hear my explanations of
where we were headed or when we'd be going home.

My marriage, my whole life was caving in on me. Maybe Clarisa
was tearing it apart, but I wasn't strong enough to resist. I was too
unsure of myself, too constrained and hesitant. There was so much
I hadn't learned yet: to touch people, and to talk openly when
problems arose between us. I'd made some progress with Clarisa—
and my next teacher would be my son.

After dinner he had another long cry as I arranged a bed for us in the back of the pickup. We were parked at the edge of a pine forest above Chichicastenango. Though the night was cold, I had a foam pad, a blanket and a down bag. Janir crawled in next to me, moaning softly but steadily, *"Yo quiero a mi mamá."* At least he clung to me and let me wrap my arms around him. I think that consoled me more than him.

I should have left him home with his grandmother, I thought, with his aunt and the maids and that whole busy household. What a crazy idea this had been, to rip him away from everyone he knew at once, and everything he was comfortable with.

But the next morning my resistance to looking after him disappeared, as we woke in the back of the truck. It was the first time in a year that I'd spent the night alone with him. Though the down bag was covered with frost, we were cozy inside our crinkling nest as we waited for the sun to rise over the eastern hills. Two Indians padded by carrying firewood, their loads braced by tumplines stretched over their foreheads. They barely gave me a nod when I poked my head up over the side of the truck. I flopped back down next to Janir. Even after the long night he smelled nutty and clean. I remembered the look I'd seen so often on Clarisa's face as the two of them lay close: This is better than anything.

When the sun hit the side of the truck we got up, stood on the wood-slatted bed and peed together onto the dirt. Already he could pee higher and farther than I could, and his pleasure at this was manifest. I put on my shoes, then his, washed our hands and faces with water from a plastic jug and drove us into town for breakfast.

• • •

I love Guatemala. Most tourists do. There's something reassuring about the native population, a solace one feels in their presence. Perhaps it's the simplicity of their daily lives we find appealing, or their resplendent clothes, or the deep keel of their traditions.

As an outsider I knew little about their culture. Most of my contact on previous visits had been with *ladinos:* mestizos or Indians acculturated to Latin ways. That remained true on this trip, but one thing changed. Earlier I'd met only men, and now the world of women opened up to me. Whenever I walked around town with Janir they came up and smiled at him, touched his hair, offered to hold him. Sometimes he let them and sometimes not. They all commented on how beautiful he was. They loved his golden skin and solemn look.

Grandmothers approached us, playful girls and young women with infants slung in cloths across their backs.

And his mother? they invariably asked.

At home, I told them. She needed a rest, and a child was so much work.

They nodded soberly. I couldn't tell if that struck a chord, or if they simply lumped my explanation with other baffling gringo notions.

Throughout the trip I was conscious of how rare it was in Central America for a man to travel with a young child. It made me stand out, and I liked the feeling: I fed off it. I would always be an outsider here—no matter that I spoke fluent Spanish, was married to Clarisa and had lived in El Salvador for years. But Janir opened some doors.

One chilly evening at a crossroads gas station I offered a ride to a young woman who had missed her bus. She was headed to Huehuetenango, and so was I. Never, were I alone, would I have offered her such a ride, nor would she have accepted. But she had seen me with Janir.

"I will pay you," she said.

"No, there's no reason. I'm headed to Huehue and the truck is empty."

"And his mother?" she asked.

"She's at home," I said. "She's . . . been sick."

We lifted the woman's three massive, cloth-wrapped bundles and set them into the bed of the pickup. They were filled with blankets, sweaters, coats and other clothing. She offered to sit in back with them, but I wouldn't let her, it was much too cold. She resisted, I urged her, and finally, timidly, she got into the cab and sat close to her window on the wide bench seat, her clothes and hair smelling of woodsmoke. She tucked her feet up under the heater, and when the truck warmed up she unzipped her parka, uncovering a traditional embroidered blouse. Her clothes were mixed, her Spanish fluent, her features pure Indian.

It took Janir some miles to warm up to her attentions. What did it, I think, was how she unwound her braided black hair and rewrapped it over her forehead. He watched her intently as she performed this habitual act—then climbed into her lap and let her hold him. For some time they had their own conversation on the far side of the truck. Then, gradually, he stretched out in her arms. The green light from the dash illuminated the two of them faintly, and as Janir drifted off to sleep she sang him a lullaby in Spanish, then another in her own language. He lay in her arms, rocking gently as we bumped over the uneven surface of the Pan-American Highway.

"What language do you speak?" I asked her.

"I speak Mam."

"And the words to your song . . . what do they say?"

"They say your son will grow up to be strong. He will plant and harvest corn. He will build a house and marry. He will be the father of many."

Her name was Otilia. She was married and had only one child, a girl who had died as an infant. Her husband drove a truck, ferrying cotton workers from the highlands down to the coast and back. He was often away, and she didn't get to see him enough. She and her mother ran a clothing store in Huehuetenango.

When we got there I helped her lift the bundles out, and again she tried to pay me for the ride. I wouldn't let her. "A thousand thanks," I told her, "for singing to my son. It's been hard for him without his mother."

She stepped toward me, so close that for a startling instant I thought she was going to kiss me. Instead she said, "You are lucky to have him. Now you will never be lonely."

•   •   •

Over the next week Janir and I drove hundreds of miles through the high country north of Huehuetenango, then east to Nebaj and Cobán. We stayed in hotels, sharing single beds in small dark rooms. In the cold early mornings, as soon as the sun rose, I dressed us both and we went out to the open market for breakfast. Wood fires smoked, dogs scrounged for the least scrap of abandoned food around the stalls, and kids only a few years older than Janir swept the packed dirt under the wooden tables and benches. The brilliant sunlight, pouring down on our backs, was as welcome as the tortillas, black beans, scrambled eggs and steaming hot chocolate.

During the last two and a half years I had changed Janir's diapers, carried him on my back, taken him to the beach and the circus and the puppet show. But I had always been the adjunct parent. In Guatemala that changed completely. For ten days we ate together, slept together, never spent two minutes apart. In the truck he sat on my lap, helping me steer. At bedtime, under the worn sheets and raspy woolen blankets of some primitive hotel, he held on to my

T-shirt and lay his head against my chest. Neither of us, night after night, could get too much of that.

Sometimes, after he slept, I lay beside him and thought about Clarisa, remembering the small-town hotels we had stayed in while looking for land in Chile after Janir's birth. Once, when dusk caught us miles out in the country, an old couple took us in for the night. They gave us dinner—potato soup, and potatoes on a plate—and we slept in a bed so narrow we had to lie head-to-toe with Janir between us, barely a month old. Afraid of crushing him, I woke every twenty minutes and was exhausted in the morning. Yet now a nostalgia swept over me for those days, when my dreams and Clarisa's had been the same.

During the day Janir and I often stopped to take a walk or eat lunch by a river, and occasionally we discovered men digging on the steep slopes above us, preparing their fields for the next corn crop. I loved watching them work: the flash of their mattocks as they dug, their steady pace across the hillside, the bits of words and songs in Mam, Quiché or Cachiquél that floated down into the valley. I'd swung a mattock enough myself to feel such work in my bones, and the Indians made an elegant job of it. After hearing their songs and smelling the turned earth, I was more convinced than ever that I wasn't finished with working the soil myself.

But the travel wore on Janir. He was demanding, he got bored, he cried, he was hungry, he had to pee, he slowed me down at everything I wanted to do. If I didn't pay him enough attention he broke into *Yo quiero a mi mamá* and drowned me in tears. One day I carried him on my shoulders a mile out into the countryside, then asked him to walk back to the truck. He wouldn't do it. He insisted that I carry him. When I refused he threw a fit. He tumbled to the ground, writhed around on the dirt and covered himself with dust. Why the hell had I brought him? He was too young for such a trip, and I wasn't made for this round-the-clock child care. What if I had to do this every damn day?

The next morning I took him for a swim. He hung from my neck as we paddled across the river, and there, sitting on the grassy bank, he started laughing. At nothing. Maybe it was the swirling water, or a bird that flashed by. The mirth poured out of him. I crouched beside him and looked into his wild eyes. He stuck his face in front of mine, hardly an inch away, arched his eyebrows and let his head quiver. He knew he could make me laugh, and did. It was delightful. It was just like falling in love.

● ● ●

Near the town of Cobán I found a gentle pleasing landscape, and from the sleepy local post office sent a letter to Peter Dutton, my friend from Chile. He was living in Mexico City with his girlfriend Rhonda, and I asked them if they'd like to start a farm. Then I drove back to El Salvador with Janir.

Though I had steeled myself to see him abandon me and run back to his mother, that didn't happen. After ten days apart his desperate attachment to her seemed broken. Instead he wore a guarded look, even when she picked him up and kissed him.

"What's the matter?" she asked him that night. "Don't you love me anymore?"

He watched her cautiously. "Yes," he said.

"Don't forget, *I* gave birth to you."

"No," he said.

"Who do you think? Him? Without me you wouldn't even be here."

"No," he screamed.

"Oh yes."

Another night she pinched him, the way she had pinched Doña Tencha's baby in Chile. Janir came running and told me, and when I scolded Clarisa she only laughed. "He deserved it," she said. "He's just like you, too full of himself."

A couple of days later her mother drew me aside.

"You should take him," she said. "He belongs with you."

Paquita had already decided something I was only beginning to imagine.

● ● ●

The rumor spread one weekend about a party at the beach. Enrique Suarez, a charismatic guru and ex-revolutionary from Guatemala, was said to be going, and I offered a ride to two different friends, Mano Echeverria and Antonia Brooke. At the last minute Clarisa told me she too was going, with Enrique and some others, and she was taking Janir. By now our marriage had come to that: we went to the same party, but almost by accident.

I picked up Mano and Antonia in the city, and we headed down toward the ocean in my truck. Mano was a street poet and musician, barely twenty, and Antonia a young half-English, half-Salvadoran woman with a light complexion and chestnut-colored hair. I'd met her some weeks ago while teaching, and we liked each other, but I was married. We had already talked that over.

Halfway to the beach, in the port town of La Libertad, I discovered I'd lost the key to my gas cap and couldn't fill the tank. Instead of driving on, I parked the truck behind the station and we waited for Enrique to come along with his pickup. La Libertad is one of the hottest places in El Salvador, and at three in the afternoon the sun still smacked us like a boxer. Antonia sat down under an almond tree, and Mano went across the street for some sodas, returning with three icy Orange Crushes. Antonia rubbed a bottle across her cheeks and neck. She was incredibly attractive—but I was not going to get involved. The three of us sat under the almond tree and watched the vendors pass by in the blazing light: boys with Chiclets, women selling *quesadillas* and a guy with a cart full of peeled coconuts.

Forty minutes later Enrique's old pickup rolled into view, and we waved him down. I climbed in up front with Enrique and a young couple from Guatemala, and Mano and Antonia piled into the back with Clarisa, Janir and four others, all stretched out on a mattress under the aluminum cap. Janir stayed close to his mom. In spite of our ten days in Guatemala, it was again his mother whose attentions he craved.

Enrique lounged behind the wheel, short and barrel-chested, his thick gray hair falling over his shoulders. On Haight Street he might have gone unnoticed, but here in El Salvador he stood out like neon. Mano had told me he was reputed to have done two hundred hits of LSD, and his whole truck smelled like marijuana. A couple of joints circulated most of the way to El Palmarcito, a little half-moon beach ten miles down the coast.

We parked, then started down the long sandy path to the ocean, walking under some giant frangipanis. Clarisa carried Janir and I carried our bags. We had hardly spoken, and I was completely absorbed in the roar of the waves when Clarisa stopped, spun toward me and said, "I know you want to fuck her."

I began to deny it, but didn't. Surely I would be honorable and never sleep with Antonia—but what difference did that make? I had thought about it and Clarisa knew. She stared me down, fearless and severe.

"Do what you want," she said. "I don't care. Here, take him, he's too heavy."

Janir slipped easily out of her arms into mine. All he wanted now was to get to the water, so I left the others behind and carried him down to the far protected end of the beach. There we played in the shallow water. He jumped into a little wave, got knocked off his feet, stood up and leapt into the next one and the next, a hundred waves without ever tiring of the game. His laughter rang out over the bay.

Clarisa reclaimed him an hour later as the sun dropped into the ocean. She looked strange, I thought, perhaps still angry—but I let Janir be the judge, and he went to her willingly. She carried him up the beach, someone lit a fire, and as the cove grew dark I fell into a long talk with Enrique. We lay on the glossy sand as the waves rustled up, soaked us and retreated. I asked him about the Guatemalan revolution of the early sixties, and he recounted tales of midnight killings, arrests and escapes. I might have doubted some of his stories but for his chest, which was covered with small welts: the smooth knurls of scar tissue that remain after cigarette burns. Such burns, everyone knew, were a common torture of the Guatemalan military. I had seen some before, but never in such profusion.

The two of us were still lying beside the sea when Antonia appeared out of the dark. She crouched beside me. "I think you should come," she said. "It's Clarisa."

Halfway up the beach I heard Janir crying. Clarisa stood to one side of the fire, illuminated by the flames and facing the others as if in some kind of standoff. She held Janir in her arms, but loosely, like a sack of wheat about to be spilled. His cries sounded desperate, and I was ashamed to have ignored him so long. Clarisa's hair was tangled, she wore a loose pair of pants and an open blouse with her breasts half-exposed. She squinted at me, then lowered her contorted face toward Janir.

"He wants *meeelk*," she said in English. Her words were so warped that at first I didn't understand them. "There's no *meeelk* and he wants some. He *neeeds* some."

She stared at Janir as if some alien creature had landed in her arms. Was this the result of the dope we'd smoked? She looked tormented, and Janir frantic. I tried to take him from her but she wouldn't give him up, nor did he want to leave her. In vain I offered him some sweet bread, then coconut juice. He ignored me, jerked up and down and wailed bitterly as he clung to her. He wanted her but couldn't have her.

Their long battle of need and rejection had finally come to a head. I felt confused, almost paralyzed—until Antonia stepped between us and fixed me with a look. "This isn't right," she said in English. "Either she has to love him, or she has to give him up."

Suddenly it all came clear to me. Clarisa was in trouble, but she would not let go of Janir. Maybe she thought he could save her—and maybe so far he had. But now his affliction echoed my own. I had imagined my marriage to Clarisa as a battle for her affection, a battle I'd been losing since his birth. But we were past that now. I had to protect my son from his own mother.

"I'm taking him," I said.

Clarisa stepped back and glared at me. *"Ni pensar, jueputa."* Forget it, you son of a bitch.

I hesitated.

Antonia said, "Do it, John."

I jammed my arm between Janir and his mother and pried him away from her. She yanked him back and all three of us went down on the sand. Then I had him and scrambled to my feet. I walked away with him without looking back, trusting the others to look after Clarisa.

All the way down the beach he raged in my arms. I knelt with him at the edge of the water, but he no longer cared about the ocean. He shrieked and sobbed. When I loosened my grip on him he tried to run back toward Clarisa, stumbling and crawling. I picked him up and pressed him to me. I felt monstrous. I'd torn him away from his mother against both their wills, and now I held him captive. He fought against me as I lay down with him in the shallow water and let the waves come up out of the dark and slap us: anything to distract him and stop this desolation, this frenzy of grief.

After twenty minutes he could take no more, and his cries choked to a stop. I carried him up onto the dry beach and lay down with him. The water, the air and the sand were all the same temperature. I held him in my arms as he clutched at me, then relaxed, then shuddered into sleep. I gave him ten minutes to drop off completely, then carried him back to the group and lay him on a blanket. Clarisa was calmer. Antonia sat next to her, holding her hand. I asked Antonia to keep an eye on Janir, took Clarisa by the arm and walked her back down the beach.

As usual after an outburst she looked subdued. I sat down in front of her on the sand, our knees touching. The moon had risen over the rocks to the east. I tried to make her look at me.

"Clarisa," I said. "You don't have to do this. Whatever it is, we can talk about it."

She didn't say anything.

"I don't want you to go crazy," I told her. "Is that what you're doing?"

There was something she was afraid of, I was sure. Since I'd always been afraid myself—of confrontations, of dangerous truths—I imagined it was the same with her. It had to be something so bad, I thought, that madness was more appealing than sanity. And in that moment I was certain I could save her. Only I knew her, so only I could rescue her. We had both been hurt, but together we'd get over it.

"Don't go," I implored her. "Come back to us. You can't leave Janir, he needs you. I need you."

She looked placid, unresponsive. She stared at her feet and didn't speak, but I went on pleading. I said it over and over. I was convinced she had a choice. "Please, Clarisa. You can fight this."

Finally she raised her face and stared at me. She said, "You don't know anything about it."

• • •

A week later I made a quick trip back to Cobán to rendezvous with Peter and Rhonda. We drove everywhere, found a twenty-acre farm for sale near the village of San Juan Chamelco and signed a purchase agreement with the woman who owned it.

When I got back to San Salvador on Sunday afternoon I asked Clarisa to come out with me to pick up some *pupusas* for the family supper. She came but she was wary: she knew something was up. We ordered the thick cheesy tortillas, wrapped them in a cloth and started home.

"I have something to tell you," I said.

"You're buying another farm."

"Yes. But first Peter and Rhonda want to go back to the U.S. and get married. So I'm going up for a few months myself. And I'm taking Janir."

"No you're not."

"I want him to meet Nana and my father and Alan."

"You can't have him."

"I'm buying the tickets tomorrow. I'm going to sell the truck and you can have the money. You can buy a car if you want."

She gave me a rancorous look, and I slowed down: if she was going to explode I wanted her to do it here, not back at the house. Silently, calmly, she picked up the cloth full of steaming *pupusas* and dumped them into the street.

At the house, before I was fully parked, she stormed out of the pickup and ran inside. I followed her in, then up onto the roof where I could hear her yelling. Janir, who'd been playing there with one of the maids, now cowered in front of Clarisa as she screamed at him.

"I'm your mother. You can't go with him. You'd hate it there, they're all racists. They don't like people with brown skin. You have to stay here with me."

"Clarisa," I said, "I haven't told him yet. He doesn't know anything about it."

She didn't listen. She kept repeating that he had to stay in El Salvador. I waited for Janir to break into tears. It was close, but he didn't. Instead he turned to me and lifted up his arms.

That was all I needed. "I'm taking him," I said and scooped him up, letting Clarisa rave on. Paquita and Eva Luz had come up onto the roof behind me, and I knew they were on my side. But it wasn't their support I needed, it was Janir's, and now he had chosen me.

•   •   •

Five days later we flew to Miami, then on to New York. I was unhappy on the plane, sitting with Janir on my lap. Clarisa had come to the airport with the rest of her family, but when it came time to board the plane she wasn't there, she had wandered off somewhere and we never said good-bye. I was angry at first, convinced she had done it on purpose. Then I was sad, then contrite. I was leaving her in the grip of neurosis, perhaps madness, and taking our son with me. It didn't help to remind myself that this was best for him.

Janir seemed happy to be off on an adventure. He charmed the stewardesses on both planes, the passengers next to us and anyone else he turned his attention to. My father picked us up at JFK and drove us out to suburban Connecticut over the smooth crowded highways. For me, coming back was always a shock: the million cars, the manicured lawns, the slabs of beef for dinner. But this new world didn't faze Janir. In May we went to Huehuetenango, in June to Westport, Connecticut. No culture shock for him. He was charming and ebullient and chattered to my dad in Spanish. I translated back and forth, and there was no talk at all of *Yo quiero a mi mamá*.

My father, though always great with kids, didn't quite know what to do with a two-and-a-half-year-old who spoke not a word of English. Even Nana, when we went to stay with her in Manhattan a few days later, seemed a bit unsure. We sat outside her project on the upper West Side, letting Janir explore the playground as we talked about my mother and Nana's niece Em. Janir kept interrupting us. He wanted me to push him on the swings and draped himself over my knees. When Nana spoke to him in English he watched her with suspicion.

After my mother's death Nana had become the nexus of my family. I got all the news and gossip from her, and spent more time with her than with Alan or my father. Her real name was Imogene Graves. She started taking care of me when I was less than a year old, and when my family moved from Manhattan to Connecticut she came to live with us—even though she was married and her husband worked in the city.

She was a black woman, light enough to "pass." In one of those slivers of memory from early childhood—I might have been five or six—I remember her telling me she was a Negro. I didn't believe her. "No," I said, "you're not."

"Oh yes, I am."

"You're *not*," I said. She couldn't be—though her husband clearly was.

"I am a Negro," Nana said.

She lived with us in Westport but spent every other weekend with her husband, Graves, in their apartment facing Harlem's Morningside Park. They never had children of their own, but when I was little Nana used to take me home on the bus to spend the night with her. Graves—his full name was George Graves, but everyone who knew him addressed him by his last name—was the manager of Sugar Ray Robinson's barbershop in Harlem. On my visits there

Graves would lift me up, set me down on one of the high red chairs and spin me around past the spotless mirrors through an air redolent of scented oils.

On alternate weekends Graves took the train to Westport and stayed at our house, and on sweltering Saturday afternoons he gave both me and Alan meticulous, hour-long haircuts that made me want to jump down from the chair, rip off the sheet pinned around my neck and fling myself into Long Island Sound.

Graves liked to tell us stories of the famous boxers and musicians whose hair he cut, and once gave me a colorful explanation of Harlem's numbers game and its runners. Nana had a favorite number, and he played it for her every week. She bet on boxing matches as well, and on Friday nights at least two little white boys in Westport, Connecticut were glued to the television for the Ballantine fights, rooting with Nana for the Negro boxer of her choice.

It seems a cliché now, or worse: we were white, she was black and she was devoted to us. But I was a greedy child who knew nothing of clichés or social justice. I loved Nana and she was mine. I had a mother, a father, a brother and Nana. When I got sick at night she was the one I called for. She was part of my family, and in many ways I am her son. What she knew about looking after children she imparted to me by example, and when Janir was born, though I'd never heard of meconium, colic or the fontanelle, I had it in my bones to be a father.

•   •   •

After Alan and I grew up, and Graves died, Nana stayed on for several years in Harlem. She liked her old apartment, but the neighborhood was falling apart. There were two overdoses in her building, then a murder. Finally my father found her a new apartment in a project on the Upper West Side. Though neither as handsome nor cozy as her old building, it was safer.

After dinner I let Janir lie on her bed and watch television. It was a corny show and all in English, but he was entranced. Nana and I sat at her kitchen table eating Fannie Mae chocolates and playing gin rummy. Over the ritual of cards there was time to let the stories out, especially about Clarisa.

"Doesn't sound like she can look after a child," Nana said. "You know Eva started out like that."

That scared me, for her sister Eva had wound up in the state hospital in Orangeburg, New York, a frightful institution I had driven Nana to several times after I got my driver's license. There was always a row of women inside Eva's building, looking out and clasping the barred windows. Some howled and some just stared at us as we got out of the car. Once inside we had to thread our way past other demented women. One rocked and moaned, wearing a sack dress and close-cropped hair. Another pulled her skirts up and scratched her exposed genitals. Another tore sheets of newspaper into smaller and smaller pieces, carefully guarding her handiwork. These were the days before Thorazine kept patients sedated. Eva was more lucid than most of the other women, yet she never got out of the locked ward. She died there.

No, I thought, Clarisa wasn't in that league. Not even close.

At nine-thirty Janir was still awake on Nana's bed. "Isn't it time that child went to sleep?" she said. "Turn the sheets down for him and we'll open the Castro later."

I had to explain to her that Janir could not go to sleep by himself, I had to lie down beside him.

"Don't be a fool," Nana said. "Turn the lights off and leave the door cracked. He knows we're here."

"He can't do it, Nana. He never has."

"What you talkin' about?"

"He's never gone to sleep by himself. Somebody always lies down with him. Clarisa or Paquita or me or somebody."

Nana was scandalized. "Is this some 'spanic thing?"

"I don't know. Clarisa started it in Chile."

Janir, who'd been listening to the conversation, came out of the bedroom and held on to my leg. Always alert to an argument or a dispute, he looked at Nana with distrust. He already had her pegged as the enemy.

Nana, in fact, had been the disciplinarian in my family. Though my parents didn't believe in spanking, they let Nana switch me and Alan on the back of our legs when we misbehaved. She would make us go outside, pick a shoot off the hedge, strip the leaves off and take it to her to receive our punishment. Now, with Janir, she thought it was time to be firm.

"Put that child to bed," she said, "and talk to him so he understands. Tell him we're not going anywhere."

I gave it a try. I brushed his teeth, I had him pee, I lifted him onto the bed and hugged him and kissed him and told him all he had to do was lie down and be quiet, and soon he'd be asleep. He didn't pay attention to any of it until I walked out of the room. Then he burst into tears, his cries reverberating through the apartment.

"You let him cry," Nana said firmly. "He'll get over it."

"Did you let me cry like that?"

"I sure did."

We sat at the table trying to play cards, but Janir's sobs did not let up. I knew their tenor: he wasn't lonely or afraid, he was offended. He wanted to get his way.

After fifteen minutes Nana had had enough. "Lord," she said, "go in and lie down with that poor boy."

I did, and only moments after I stretched out beside him he dropped off to sleep, his tired face streaked with tears. When I emerged from her room I found Nana still hunched over our card game, her hands clasped under her chin.

"I'm sorry, John. I can't do this again. I'm too old."

"You can't do what?"

"I always thought I'd take care of your children when you had them. Either yours or Alan's. But I don't have the patience."

I pulled my chair close and put my arm around her shoulder. I didn't want her to look after Janir. How could she, with the life I led? And *I* wanted to do it. "He's my son," I told her, "and my job."

"I'm seventy-three years old. It's all I can do to look after you and Alan. You're still my boys."

"We still are," I said.

"That's a beautiful child you got there, but he's a handful. Once you get settled you better make some time for yourself."

• • •

My mother, years before, had bought a rundown eight-thousand-dollar house in Sag Harbor, on the South Fork of Long Island. Now my brother owned it, but it was empty and needed some work. I still had friends in Sag Harbor—Patty Coughlan and her family, who had first invited us there in the early fifties—and I thought Mom's house on Garden Street would be a good place to spend the summer. I bought an old Ford Falcon from a widow in Bethpage, bargaining Salvadoran style until I got her down to $150, then drove out to Sag with Janir.

In the early seventies, even in the summer, Sag Harbor was still a peaceful village. The beach at Sagaponack, where we'd thrown my mother's ashes into the ocean, was only seven miles across the island, and I took Janir to swim there almost every day. It was late June, the potato fields behind the dunes were in flower, and except on weekends the long white beach was empty.

I cleaned the house, shopped, washed and cooked. No problem with any of that, for I'd done it all before, both on my own and with Clarisa. Domestic chores have always seemed to me the least part of child-raising. Far more trying was Janir's constant demand for attention.

Following Nana's advice, I went looking for some child care. I found a couple of women in Sag who looked after children at home, but neither wanted to take on a boy not yet three who spoke only Spanish. Finally I heard about a morning playgroup over in Springs, and drove Janir over to take a look. Judy Hubbard, who ran the group, didn't hesitate. "Of course I'll take him," she said. "He's lovely."

Janir was slower to decide. He looked the group over cautiously —but he could not resist the sight of ten other kids at play. He turned to me and nodded gravely, and five minutes later he was hanging from the jungle gym beside another boy. In the next few weeks at the playgroup he learned his first words in English: cat, dog, truck, hey. And his first full sentences: Take it easy, and Let me tie your shoe. I kept a list.

I loved having the mornings to myself, and immediately went to work on the house, which my brother was planning to sell. I re-roofed part of it, painted most of the rooms and sent all the doors out to be stripped.

I was lucky, once again, to have money in the bank, and used it now to spend time with Janir. My frugal nature was well established: I dressed and ate simply, drove an old car and kept the usual tight hand on my wallet. Over the years not everyone has considered this economy my most endearing trait. But having Janir only made me more thrifty. No sense in spending wildly now, I thought, when later we might need the money.

After playgroup we drove to Sagaponack to swim, make sand castles and kick around a soccer ball. Later a nap at home, then a snack, then a hose fight in the yard, and in the late afternoon we took a walk through the quiet streets of town. I'd bought a tricycle and pushed Janir on it from behind, using an old push broom. He loved a walk most when *he* could choose where to go, what streets to turn down, when to explore and when to head home.

One evening at dinner I made him a rash promise: if he would eat all his carrots, I would take him to the playground and push him on the swings as long as he wanted. He perked right up at that. Within minutes he had wolfed down the carrots and climbed onto his tricycle, ready to go. At the playground I helped him onto his favorite swing, one with a canvas seat that wrapped around him.

"Push," he commanded, and I began.

"Harder," he said, and I pushed harder. Every three seconds the swing rose back up into my hands and I thrust it down again. It was a repetitive task I'd often found soothing, for it was a chance to let my mind roam. I kept it up now for twenty minutes as Janir gripped the linked metal rods supporting his seat. Thirty minutes, forty, and he never said a word. Dusk came and I was still pushing. I was tired but determined not to complain. I would carry out my promise.

After an hour I was exhausted. "Is that about enough?" I suggested hopefully.

Janir shook his head. "Push," he said.

An hour and a quarter and I was still at it. Did he *have* a limit? Dusk was at an end, the sky was black. "Janir," I said, "let's go home."

"Me prometiste," he said firmly. I had promised him.

"We'll come back tomorrow," I pleaded. That wasn't much of a bargain, because we came all the time. "I'm falling asleep," I told him. "Haven't you had enough?"

"No."

"Janir, have some pity on your dad."

For the first time he glanced behind him. He paused, then said, "All right."

I stopped pushing and let the swing wind down to a stop. When it was almost still he jumped down with a smile. He had won. He went directly to his tricycle, looked back jauntily over his shoulder and said, *"A la casa."*

•   •   •

If I was now part of some social upheaval, I didn't feel it. I had never known a single father, either in Latin America or the United States, and didn't meet one all that summer. There was no movement to identify with: I was just a guy living with his son on a quiet street in the old, not-very-hip Sag Harbor. I had Janir, who wanted more attention than I could give him, and I was preoccupied with what had happened to Clarisa and our marriage.

One night I called San Salvador and talked to her mother. Clarisa wasn't there. She was out driving around in her car.

"She bought one?" I asked.

"Right away," Paquita said.

"And got her license?"

"She says so. I haven't seen it. She bought a Volvo. She drives it everywhere."

Paquita wasn't happy about it, but from this distance I was almost glad for Clarisa. Now she had what she wanted most, her freedom.

* * *

Nana's disapproval of Janir's bedtimes convinced me to make a change. Because we were in a new house in a new town, I didn't rush the plan, but prepared for it gradually. His bedroom was up-stairs next to mine under the sloping eaves, a lath-and-plaster room with plank floors, prop-open windows and a creaky old bed on casters. Though Janir could slide off the mattress by himself, it was too high for him to climb back on. At bedtime I lifted him up, then lay down next to him and read to him in English from the local library's simplest children's books.

He didn't understand much English yet, but he loved being read to. When I washed dishes or shopped or even pushed him around on his tricycle I was often on automatic pilot, thinking of something else. But I couldn't do that yet when reading him a story—and later, when I learned how, he would counter by demanding "a story from your mouth," meaning a story I made up on the spot. My mind, he knew, couldn't wander then.

Usually, after a couple of books in English, I told him a story in Spanish. Then "This little piggy," then a song, then a kiss, then I lay beside him until he went to sleep. The whole procedure took forty-five minutes, sometimes an hour.

We went on like that for a couple of weeks before I told him that the next night was going to be different. I would read to him, of course, and tell him a story and hug him and kiss him—but he was old enough now to go to sleep by himself. He heard me but hardly listened. Several times the next day I repeated the warning, and again that night as I got onto the bed with him. We went through the whole routine. But then, instead of lying there beside him, I stood up from the bed. He looked at me with alarm.

"I'll be right downstairs," I told him. "You go to sleep and I'll see you in the morning."

Before I got to the door he was off the bed and padding over the floor behind me. I picked him up. "If you don't stay in bed," I told him, "I'm going to close the door. You don't want that, do you?"

He looked at me wide-eyed.

"All right, then. I'm going to put you back in bed and leave the door open, and I'll be right downstairs."

"Papi, no."

Now he was looking panicked. I lifted him back onto the bed and draped the sheet over him—but the minute I headed for the door he followed me.

"I'm sorry," I said, and closed the door before he got there.

He gasped, he wailed, he threw himself against the bottom of the door and pounded on it. He was outraged. I sat above the stairs hunched into a ball while just inside the room, only three feet away, Janir gagged and choked, staggered and fell. He banged his head against the floor. He strangled on his own tears and did a close imitation of dying. I had to clutch my arms to my chest to stop myself from opening the door.

After twenty harrowing minutes his sobs let up. My heart felt like it was wrapped in barbed wire. He banged on the door again, broke into another spate of tears, then trailed off into silence. I waited ten more minutes, then raised the latch and eased the door open until it bumped against his head. He was asleep on the floor in his T-shirt and underwear, his hair tangled and his face still flushed. I squeezed into the room, gently lifted him up, lay him on the bed and covered him with a sheet. Finally I went downstairs and sat in a chair with a book. I tried to read but couldn't make it through a single paragraph.

The next day neither one of us said anything about it. But in bed, after his story, I told him that tonight, too, he had to go to sleep by himself. A terrible look came over his face. He was ready to slide off the bed again and try to stop me. I held him. "You don't want me to close the door again, do you?"

"No, Daddy. *Not the door."*

"Then you have to stay in bed. You just stay here and go to sleep, and I'll be reading. I'll never leave you."

He cried but stayed. I went downstairs and sat miserably in my chair and waited—and this time it only lasted five minutes. I gave him another five, then crept up the stairs and peered into his room. He was asleep but his body had not yet relaxed. His fists still gripped the sheet, and his breaths were so shallow I was afraid I might wake him up just by staring at him. I knelt beside the bed and listened to him breathe.

·   ·   ·

Sometimes I felt like I was having a great adventure with Janir. Other times I despaired of being such a loner, an outsider in a small town. In ways I lived a conformist life: I rose early, dressed my kid, fed him breakfast, took him to his playgroup, went to work. Yet we were hardly a normal family. Janir had no mother, and I had no woman to share my thoughts and feelings, or my bed.

As ever, Janir was an affectionate and physical child. I had grown up in a New England family in which no one draped himself over anyone else—but Janir was immune to those conventions. When we went to visit my old friend Patty Coughlan he crawled over me, flung himself against me, played with my ears and hair. I was a little self-conscious about it, but underneath I loved it. There was nothing I wanted or needed more.

Sag Harbor, I soon discovered, was full of women. Some evenings, after pushing Janir downtown for an ice cream, I stepped into the Harpoon Bar or the newly refurbished American Hotel to get a glimpse of the scene. There were always women there, drinking, smoking and chatting. But I never talked to anyone. With Janir on the sidewalk behind me making animal and engine noises on his tricycle, I could only stay a minute or two. I wasn't going to take him into a bar, and it never occurred to me that a woman might actually be attracted to a man with a small child.

I did meet an appealing woman one afternoon while visiting with Patty. Tall, slender and divorced, Sheila had—incredibly—two grown sons. Even harder to believe, she was seventeen years older than I was. She sat across from me in Patty's living room, wearing a little tennis skirt with white socks and sneakers, sipping a lemonade as we talked about divorce. She'd been through a rough one and was glad it was over.

She was affluent, sophisticated and far more sexually experienced than I. Or so I guessed. I didn't have the nerve to ask for her phone number. I'd have been mortified if she had refused to give it to me, and I was afraid of scandalizing Patty. So after a couple of hours I took my leave. I pushed Janir home on his tricycle, made him dinner and put him to bed. Then I sat in the darkened living room and thought about Sheila's smooth neck and long legs. If only I'd had a shred of self-confidence with women. It wouldn't have been a romance, I suppose, just an affair. Just what I wanted.

•   •   •

On the Fourth of July I drove over to Long Beach with Janir to watch the fireworks. On the way I tried to explain what they were, but "firecrackers in the sky" didn't mean much to him. We staked out a spot on the beach and sat on a blanket eating buttered spaghetti and fried bananas. As long as I could get some food down him I cooked whatever he liked. He wasn't skinny, but some days it seemed I could measure his intake in grams.

After dinner on the beach I read him one of the Babar books I'd loved as a child. He pointed to the string of elephants joined trunk-to-tail on the inside cover and announced, *"Elefante-camellos!"* We nestled down on our blanket as other people arrived and filled in the empty spots on the beach. There was a family on our left with three young kids, a basket full of food, a dog, a cooler and chairs for both big-assed parents: Zorba's whole catastrophe. On our other side a young couple wandered by and plopped down with only a six-pack and a sleeping bag.

Janir sat on my chest and played with my ears, completely unselfconscious. We were a pair of outsiders here: a brown child and a bearded father speaking Spanish in the midst of an American celebration. I felt I had little in common with the stolid parents on my left, and was far more interested in the young couple sitting face-to-face on their sleeping bag, holding hands and talking as if alone on the beach.

It grew darker. A covey of teenage girls strolled by, their hands tucked into their back pockets. Though clearly on the prowl, when three boys passed the other way both groups grew silent and ignored each other.

I had my son but no woman. Otilia, the one I'd given a ride to in Guatemala, had been wrong, for now I *was* lonely. As the light faded over Noyack Bay the young couple started kissing. Before long they had wrapped themselves up in their sleeping bag like a fat cocoon, wriggling and occasionally laughing.

Horns honked, and from behind us someone yelled, "Set 'em off!" A chorus of approval followed, but it was another twenty minutes before the first rocket whistled up into the sky and exploded with a thunderous clap.

Janir leapt to his feet. His eyes locked on the blaze of blue light —until a second rocket shot up and flowered brilliantly. Then another and another, heaving out of their tubes with a great *whump,* some exploding violently, some whistling and twisting across the top of the sky. Janir looked as solemn as a churchgoer. He backed up against my knees but didn't say a word. I could feel the concussive force of the salvos through his body, and bathing in his wonder, I was happy.

•　　•　　•

I called El Salvador a few nights later, and again Clarisa was out. Paquita told me she had taken a rock to the windshield of her car and smashed a hole in it so she could feel the wind in her face as she drove. She'd been hanging out on the coast with some American surfers. They were a bad influence, Paquita said: a decadent life and no ambition.

•　　•　　•

A few weeks later, a call from Paquita. Clarisa had gotten into an accident with two surfers, her car was totaled and she was in the hospital. One of her cheekbones had been crushed and the doctors were trying to reconstruct it.

My heart went out to her, an instantaneous and automatic response. Yet that same night, as I lay beside Janir after our nightly story, I could not stop imagining, in terrifying detail, an accident in which he was in the car with her. I saw him thrown into the shattered windshield, bounced around inside the Volvo, his face slashed and his bones broken.

I stood up, wresting myself out of this nightmare. Janir, already asleep, lay safe in his room. He would be fine, for I would look after him. But Clarisa was in trouble, and three days later we left for El Salvador.

I PACKED THE FALCON, PREPARED A LITTLE NEST FOR Janir in the backseat and left Sag Harbor at four in the morning to beat the traffic through New York. We didn't make it. By dawn the Long Island Expressway had filled with commuters, and by six o'clock it was stop-and-go. Heat shimmered up from the cars, and the sun glowed red over miles of tract houses. Janir woke up and climbed into the front seat.

"Daddy," he said, "I have to go."

We were locked in a grid four lanes wide. I crept ahead a few yards, stopped, crept again. All the drivers looked grim, staring ahead at the traffic.

"Daddy," Janir said.

I stripped off his underpants, rolled down the window and held him in the air. Everyone pretended not to notice. Janir completed a long and complacent urination, I pulled him back inside and we resumed our crawl toward the city.

Through New York, New Jersey and on into Pennsylvania. I'd bought a car seat but Janir would not stay in it. He played with his toys, he drew, he got bored, he put up with long hours on the road. We stayed with a couple of friends, and at motels where he could leap from bed to bed, treating the box springs like trampolines. He opened every bar of soap and packet of lotion, he used up all the towels and tore the wax paper off the glasses that had been sanitized for our protection.

After a full week on the road we arrived at Paquita's house. Clarisa's face was still discolored from the accident, and the doctors, in order to pull her bones into place, had anchored three wires to her cheek and temple. The stainless-steel wires emerged through her skin and formed a quivering triangle that stuck out five inches to the right side of her face. She looked disconsolate, and to protect the apparatus she moved with an unnatural stiffness. Janir allowed her to hug him, but it was an awkward embrace.

Though our own embrace was equally strained, Clarisa was candid about the accident. She told me how she had eaten a couple of Quaaludes with a pair of American surfers, who then persuaded her to give them a lift to the city. Quaaludes are a hypnotic drug and hell on motor control. Clarisa's driving was erratic, and one of the surfers insisted on taking the wheel. It was he who flipped the car, and she who got hurt. Then, though her face was lacerated, they waited until the next morning—when they could get a bus instead of a taxi—to take her to the hospital. They dropped her at the emergency room and split.

I wanted to kill them.

Clarisa tossed it all off as fate. She seemed to have no resentment at all. When I asked for details about the accident she recounted them as if it had all happened to someone else. I couldn't connect with her. Maybe it was the wires, but I had the eerie feeling I was talking to someone else, someone who just looked like Clarisa.

That night she took Janir to sleep in her room, and I sat on the front stoop of the house feeling isolated from everyone. Some neighbors I knew walked past on the street, and we exchanged the usual greetings: *Buenas noches, buenas noches.* But this was not my world, and suddenly it all seemed foreign: the dusty street, the paunchy and overworked women, kids playing soccer on the pavement with a ball that had lost its air.

On the long drive down there had been moments, even hours, when I had let myself imagine that everything would work out smoothly with Clarisa. Perhaps, I thought—so powerful is the engine of marriage—she might change her mind about living in the country, and the three of us could move to Guatemala. Now that seemed unlikely.

Some months ago I had witnessed an ardent reunion at the San Salvador airport. Like me, the man was American—or so I guessed from his buzz haircut and khaki pants. And the woman, like Clarisa, was Salvadoran. After emerging from customs he dropped his bags, took his woman by the waist and hungrily kissed her mouth and neck. She melted into his chest and answered with fervent kisses of her own. They paused to murmur a few words, and then, completely oblivious to everyone else, started kissing again. It embarrassed me to watch them. I felt as if I'd stumbled across a couple making love in a bedroom. Yet I couldn't take my eyes off them. I spied on them from across the room, even followed them out to the taxi stand and watched them get into a cab.

They weren't young, probably older than I by ten or fifteen years. I suspected the man of being a U.S. military advisor—and nothing, in the early seventies, could have been more contemptible to me than that. And the woman was no beauty: her waist was thick and her face flat. Yet their response to each other sent a chill down my back. Had I *ever* felt that way about Clarisa? By now I could hardly remember.

I was still sitting on the stoop when Janir came shuffling into the parlor. He wanted a story from me—and then to sleep in my bed. Clarisa watched us as I carried him past her room. Her face was set in a sad mask, accentuated by the wires that trembled to one side of her cheek. I glanced at her and looked away.

On our second night I took everyone out to dinner. The whole family doted on Janir and marveled at his English. Clarisa had relaxed, and her son with her. He no longer stared at the alien wires, and the two of them even laughed a little, sharing some joke. I felt torn. I wanted them to get along—but abruptly, fiercely, I did not want to give him up. Not for a day, not even an hour. I did not want to be the subordinate parent.

That Saturday night, as the rest of us watched television on Paquita's new set, Clarisa called her doctor's office. There was no one there. She paced around the room, one hand on her hip and the other at her chin. She was fed up with the onerous wires. She called the hospital, but they advised her to consult her doctor on Monday morning. It was not, after all, an emergency. But Clarisa wanted the wires out now. She stared at them in a hand mirror, looking angry and disturbed.

Paquita and I both argued with her. The wires were critical, we'd been told: only they could draw the bones of her face into their original alignment.

"They're not doing shit," Clarisa said. "They just get in my way."

I didn't understand myself how they were supposed to work. They were just three wires joined at the ends, with only the slightest bow to them. Clarisa brushed them with the back of her hand, and I winced.

"I can't sleep with them," she said. "Every time I turn around I bump them. I hate them."

"Wait until Monday," I urged her. "I'll go with you and we'll talk to the doctor."

She looked at me as if I were one of the enemy. Janir watched television, his hair dark and sleek after a shower. He focused intently on the show, ignoring all our heated talk. Clarisa went into the bathroom and locked the door. When she came out she had the wires in her hand. She looked flushed and triumphant. She had unscrewed them, simply turned them through her flesh. There wasn't even any blood.

In that stunning moment I recognized the woman I'd fallen in love with. But now she scared me. Her impulsive ways, which had first drawn me to her, now seemed dangerous and deluded.

●　　●　　●

A couple of days later I drove up to Cobán in Guatemala to meet up with Peter and Rhonda—and immediately the deal on the farm fell through. The owner didn't want to sell after all, and there was no way to force the sale. It was just as well, I thought. If I'd been lonely in Sag Harbor, what was I going to do with a three-year-old boy on an isolated farm in the Guatemalan highlands?

Though we looked around for other pieces of land, my enthusiasm for the project had disappeared. At the end of the week I returned to San Salvador, leaving Peter and Rhonda to explore on their own. Eventually they moved on to southern Belize, bought some land and started farming.

●　　●　　●

Paquita, upon my return, had made up her mind. She stood in her parlor in a slip, ironing a blouse, about to go back to work after her siesta. "She is too irresponsible," she said. "She can't take care of Janir. One of us will have to do it."

"Why?" I asked. "What has she done?"

"You've seen."

"You mean the wires?"

"She has no self-control. A child needs someone he can depend on."

"But she's his mother," I said.

It was a familiar dynamic: whenever Paquita attacked Clarisa I sprang to her defense. And in those moments I convinced myself that Clarisa wasn't crazy, just strange. Nana's sister had been crazy.

Paquita put on her blouse. "You know her father was in the hospital too," she said. "Before he killed himself."

"No, I didn't." All I really knew about her father was that Clarisa had worshiped him.

"He was a good man, but he had some of these same problems. And there are others in his family."

I'd heard some stories, but knowing nothing in those days about how dementia ran in families, I'd paid them little heed. There was an eccentric uncle in San Salvador and a batty aunt in California, both from the Rubio side of the family, and Paquita now mentioned what she called *la debilidad,* the weakness that surfaced among her husband's relatives.

We had never talked about schizophrenia, and my concept of the disease was foggy. From the sound of the word I thought it was a split into two personalities. Today I know schizophrenia is a psychotic disorder characterized by delusions, magical thought and other emotional disturbances—but in the early seventies I would never have weighed anyone's behavior so clinically. I had heard R. D. Laing's claim that madness was an appropriate response to an insane world, and that the demented were closer to the truth than the rest of us. That romantic notion held sway over me, and probably delayed my perception of Clarisa as someone with a medical problem.

One day on the street I ran into the handsome and engaging Ricardo Aguilar, a friend from my Peace Corps days and Clarisa's painting teacher. I watched him with some suspicion as we talked: had he been sleeping with Clarisa? There was no hint of it in his demeanor.

He suggested to me that Clarisa had lost her soul. "Someone has stolen it," he said with conviction. "You should take her to see Maria in Oaxaca."

"The *curandera,*" I said.

"She could perform a ceremony to get it back."

"How would I find her?"

"Just go to Oaxaca and ask. Everyone knows her."

"I don't think Clarisa would do it."

"Make her," Ricardo said. "Don't ask, just take her there."

For a few days I actually considered such a trip. But when I mentioned it to Clarisa she stared at me and said, "Don't be an idiot. Why should I talk to a medicine woman?"

"It might be like talking to a psychiatrist."

She waved me off with the back of her hand. "What good did that do your mother?"

·   ·   ·

Through our stay in Sag Harbor, Janir had been mostly a cheerful kid. Now he moped, he cried, he woke up with nightmares and couldn't get back to sleep. Every other night he wet his bed, and he argued with Clarisa almost constantly.

Sometimes she doted on him, and sometimes she badgered him. I found her in the kitchen one afternoon goading him to eat some *nances*, a tart yellow fruit the size of a grape. She was laughing, but she held him behind the neck as she pressed the fruit between his lips. Janir squirmed and yelled, *"No!"*

"What the hell are you doing?" I said.

Janir slid off his chair and ran out of the room. Clarisa only laughed. "I loved *nances* when I was his age," she said. "Something's wrong with him. You had him up north too long."

Her old acceptance of his concerns and curiosity—I remembered how she had let him crawl to the edge of a hayloft and look down at a ten-foot drop—had now completely vanished. She was insistent with him. She wanted him to eat what she chose, look at the books she chose, wear the clothes she chose. Actually, around the house, she didn't want him to wear any clothes at all. She thought it was healthier for him to run around naked. She didn't ask him how he felt about it, she just stripped off his shirt, pants and underpants and told him that was the natural way. Sometimes Janir was just as glad, for it was warm in the house and he was often happy to go without his clothes. But when he didn't like it she hid them and wouldn't give them back. That brought on a wailing protest from Janir, and either Paquita or I would have to step in and calm things down.

I came home early one evening, didn't see Janir, went to Clarisa's room and knocked on the door. She was there but Janir wasn't. "He's on the roof," she said.

"With someone?"

"I don't know."

I tore up the stairs. There he was, naked, playing in a pile of sand a mason was using to repair some tiles. He was fine—but there was only an eight-inch parapet around the flat roof, and he could easily have fallen to the street. He was barely three.

I wanted Janir to have a mother, but not like this. I carried him downstairs, asked the maid to give him a bath and left the house. I walked around the block—but I had already made up my mind. I entered the house, knocked on Clarisa's door, went in and stood beside her. She lay on the bed in her underwear and a T-shirt, reading the newspaper comics. Finally she looked up.

"I'm going back to the States," I said. "With Janir."

Her dark eyes narrowed. She glared at me but didn't move. I had expected rage, flying *pupusas,* a pitched battle. Instead she stared at me coldly, then turned away and drew her legs up toward her chest. She lay without moving in a fetal position. I wanted to touch her shoulder, to comfort her somehow, but I didn't dare.

"I'll take good care of him," I said.

"You better. Now get out."

•   •   •

The afternoon before we left, we split up all our possessions in ten minutes. Clarisa didn't care about the tools, so there was nothing to separate except a few books and albums, and we both knew who owned what. After five years of marriage we owned not a single object in common.

Since the day I told her we were going she had remained in a somber mood. Now she took Janir out to my car and sat with him on the front seat. I watched from inside the house. She put her arm around him and they seemed to be talking—but after five or ten minutes he climbed through the window, dropped onto the side-walk and came inside.

I was getting what I wanted, but it didn't make me happy. Clarisa looked sad, slumped in the car with her head on her chest. Her sorrow fed my own. I paced through the two front rooms of the house, pretending to pack and arrange things, but secretly keeping an eye on her. Everyone else in the house ignored her. Knowing how easily she could erupt, they kept their distance.

After thirty minutes I went outside, opened the door of the Falcon and sat down behind the wheel. For a long time neither of us said anything. We just sat beside each other, baking in the heat as we

watched the street in front of us. At some point she had acquiesced
to the fact that I was taking Janir away. Perhaps, I thought, she
sensed the trouble she was in. Finally she turned and stared at me,
her dark eyebrows gathered in a line.

"He's mine, too," she said. "Don't ever forget that."

•   •   •

The next morning the family gathered on the sidewalk for hugs
all around and benedictions for our trip. I had spent the last two
hours steeling myself against my own regrets, but Clarisa gave both
me and Janir a quick silent embrace, then stood back. The sun
blazed down on all of us: friends, family, servants and a cluster of
barefoot neighborhood kids. Paquita was crying freely. I would
write, I told her. I would send more money. We would all keep in
touch. But little was said about the future, and no one acknowledged that on one level this was the end for me and Clarisa. All our
hopes now rode with Janir.

We got in the car, Janir hugged everyone again through his open
window, and we drove away. Clarisa stood among her family, looking
small and hesitant and incapable of anything destructive. Janir
leaned against my shoulder. We left the pastel houses of the neighborhood, then the city itself. We drove past the coffee plantations
of Santa Tecla and down into the lowlands.

Janir tugged at my shirt.

"Are you thinking, Daddy?"

He meant, was I sad? "I guess I am," I said.

After seven years I was leaving Latin America for good. All
the way to the Guatemalan border I let a wave of nostalgia sweep
over me: for the times Clarisa and I had shopped in the central
market with its forty kinds of fruit, for the nights we had sprinted
to her mother's house through a wall of rain, for the secret
sweltering afternoons when passion had eclipsed every smaller
emotion.

Protecting Janir was my excuse to bail out of a marriage that had
overwhelmed me. Perhaps it was a reasonable excuse, but the truth
was I could love and look after my son, but not his mother, because
I needed someone to love me back. Clarisa couldn't do that, she was
struggling too hard with the chaos rising inside her. We were both
too fragile. She needed someone to trust and confide in, and I was
too afraid of her outlandish behavior to listen.

●   ●   ●

Janir took a long nap, then woke up fussing. I couldn't tell if it was leaving his mother and her family behind, or if he was simply fed up with being in the car. We'd just made this trip in the opposite direction, and now I was asking him to do it again. He complained and whined and cried, and only half a day into the trip I had second thoughts about the move.

Soon after dusk he fell asleep, and to spare him the tedium of the drive I stopped at a roadside rancho, filled my thermos with grainy black coffee and drove on through the night. Under the influence of a pint of caffeine the world seemed a friendlier place. I was going home at last. I'd find a farm somewhere, friends for me and Janir, then a woman. She would be as entrancing as Clarisa, but far more sensible.

How quickly I was forgetting how much Clarisa had meant to me, how much she had taught me, how deeply she was now embedded in my nature.

●   ●   ●

In the pale first light of dawn I pulled off beside a lake in the state of Vera Cruz. Janir turned under his blanket, his eyelids dark and still, his long lashes lying on his cheek. I stretched out on the front seat and immediately dropped off—only to be awakened an hour later. He was hungry.

We ate a pair of greasy omelettes at a restaurant overlooking the water, then drove around the edge of the lake. I hoped to find a place to swim, but there were no beaches or easy access. Finally I left the car by the side of the road and we walked down a brushy slope. I was still groggy, and getting into the water helped. Janir clung to my neck as I swam out twenty yards. Then I dropped him in the shallows, where he leapt about and thrashed his arms as if he could swim. He almost could. He was happy but I was fading fast. I put on my clothes and lay down in the delicious warm sunlight.

"Janir, I have to take a nap. If I go to sleep you can't go in the water, okay?"

"Okay."

"Not one step. Not even your toes."

"I won't, Papi."

"You promise?"

"I *won't*."

I rested my head on my arm. "Just a little nap," I said.

I drifted off delectably as he sat beside me, chattering in Spanish, *"Mira, Papi, mira al pájaro."*

Look at the bird, he said. I opened my eyes, then closed them. Oh, God, just to sleep.

"Mira a las hormigas," he said, look at the ants—but I was floating away.

"Mira, Papi. Mira. Mira a la culebra."

I jumped straight into the air. Not ten feet away a snake as thick as my wrist was gliding over a log. I could only see a foot of it at a time as it emerged from and slid back into the grass, but it must have been ten feet long. I grabbed Janir and backed up the slope, the adrenaline prickling the ends of my fingers and toes. I set him down on the hood of the car and gave him a belated warning about snakes.

We headed north toward Veracruz. I was fully awake, but kept seeing the snake slide over the log. It made me wonder how I was going to pull this off. Having left the protective fold of Clarisa's Salvadoran family, I had no idea where we were going. We had no destination at all. My brother was selling the house in Sag Harbor, and Long Island was too crowded anyway. It was November and winter was coming. I felt like hibernating—yet only five minutes into my first nap I'd been jolted awake by an enormous serpent.

At one in the morning we crossed the Pánuco River by ferry. Janir was asleep but I woke him so he could watch the crossing. He didn't say anything, but took it all in with an air of reverence: the dark sweep of water, the smell of wet soil and branches, the big ferry working at a slant against the current until it nosed into the dock with a crunch. We disembarked among semis and buses, passed through Tampico and pushed on toward Brownsville, Texas. My sleep pattern was shot. The old Falcon purred as we cruised across the plains of Tamaulipas under a sky full of stars, the passing trucks lit up like ships and Wolf Man Jack growling on the radio.

Two days later, in Beaumont, Texas, I traded in the Falcon on a Chevy half-ton pickup. The truck was stable and warm, and Janir did somersaults on the roomy bench seat as we rolled over the velvet interstate. I was eager now and a little afraid. This is it, I thought: I have my boy and I'm going to raise him.

On OUR WAY EAST WE STOPPED FOR A LOOK AT ATHENS, Ohio, a small town in the southeast corner of the state, and the home of Ohio University. A friend and fellow gardener had suggested it as a place to live. "Beautiful country," he had told me, "and good soil."

I asked around for the health-food restaurant, took Janir there for lunch, and within the hour we had met a dozen people. It was 1973, but still the heart of the sixties there, an easy time for a long-haired father and his three-year-old son to make friends.

Roger and Linda Jahnke had a son slightly older than Janir. They owned land in the woods, managed an herb-and-plant store and helped run the local alternative school. I loved how relaxed they were with Janir. Roger lifted him up and carried him over to their store as naturally as if he'd known him for years—and Janir let him.

We'd only been talking for thirty minutes when Roger said, "Why don't you live here? Land's cheap and our school is great." He smiled. "Besides, we could use another student."

The next day I followed a winding gravel road up to an old ridgetop farmhouse. Kay Woyar was the lone teacher at the White Oak School, and she opened the door as soon as we parked: "I heard you were coming!"

She was a woman of boundless energy. Her two-year-old daughter Joy ran ahead of us as Kay led us through the book room, the dress-up room, the music and science room. Most of the kids were a little older than Janir, and he watched them with a fascination that bordered on hunger.

After our tour Kay fixed me a cup of tea and explained the school's philosophy. "We're based on the British primary system," she said. "We don't track students by age or grade. They learn whatever they're ready for, and work with both older and younger kids. And I try to let them choose what they want to do, and to stay with a project as long as they like. There are no bells here."

When we finished our tea she said, "Why don't you leave him for a while?"

I glanced at Janir. He looked around for a moment, then nodded. "Come back for me later," he said.

"When? An hour?"

He thought about it. "Two hours."

That afternoon I drove nonstop over the back roads of Ames and Bern townships. The land, as promised, was beautiful. Stubbled cornfields filled the snug hollows, and hardwoods covered the hills. There were orchards, meadows, old farmhouses and fenced gardens. It felt like the right place to me.

In early December we went back to New England. My father and brother both lived there, and I looked at some land in both Vermont and Massachusetts. But property was expensive, and most people aloof. So after Christmas Janir and I returned to Ohio, I enrolled him at the White Oak School and we moved into a cabin on Roger and Linda's land. It was a tiny primitive dwelling with no water, electricity or telephone, but we had lived that way before, and it would do until we found a farm.

I knew I'd never make a lot of money running a truck farm in Appalachian Ohio. But I wanted a job at which I could set my own hours and spend lots of time with Janir. It took me four months, but I found the right place: half an old fruit farm, seventy acres altogether with ten in bottomland. The apple and peach trees had all been abandoned or cut, but there were two creeks, a small house, a shaky barn and a working natural gas well that provided free heat. The price was $23,000—almost exactly what I'd been left by my mother's estate. The only hitch was that we couldn't move in until the fall.

In June, when the White Oak School closed for summer vacation, I organized a playgroup with four other parents. Four days of the week I was free, and each Wednesday I took my turn with the kids. Janir and I were still living in the Jahnkes' tiny cabin, so we spent most of the day outdoors. The kids hunted minnows in the muddy creek, we built a castle out of bricks, old lumber and bits of cloth, and sometimes I drove them to Dow Lake to swim. Lord, I think now: five riotous kids on the single front seat of my pickup, and not a one buckled in.

Always after lunch I told them a story in a clearing under the oaks and hickories. One quiet day in July I carried out some blankets and three books from the library, planning to read them to sleep as I had before. We stretched out on the blankets, and I began with Beatrix Potter. The kids lay all around me, three and four and five years old. I finished with Peter Rabbit and began the next book. A couple of chipmunks scurried about. The light was muted and there wasn't the faintest breeze. My eyes grew heavy.

When I woke, the kids were gone. I scrambled to my feet and ran panicked through the woods, calling out for them. A couple were close by, happily poking through the underbrush. "Stay there," I told them, and ran off to find the others. Joshua Jahnke had gone back to the cabin, but Janir and Sara Dewees had wandered out to the drive and were climbing around on a pile of bricks, a great place for copperheads.

I got everyone back inside and tried to give them a lecture. "Next time wake me up," I said. "Okay?"

They didn't look concerned. What was my problem, anyway? "We won't get lost," Sara said.

"I'm five," Joshua announced.

"Yeah," said three-year-old Janir. "He's *five*."

*   *   *

Though we couldn't move onto the farm until September, I was free to work the land. I went there every day, planted a garden, cleaned up the fields and prepared for next year's crop. I bought a hardworking nine-hundred-dollar tractor, a 1942 flathead Ford with a power takeoff and weighted tires. I found a big rototiller that mounted on the tractor's three-point hitch, and a bush hog to keep the fields mowed. On Saturdays Janir and I drove around to farm auctions to buy shovels, rakes, chains, pry bars, pitchforks and sledgehammers.

Once a week, sometimes every other week, I'd work a child-care trade with another parent and get a night free. Usually I went to town, ate dinner and wandered over to Swanky's, a noisy Athens bar full of hippies, pot growers, architecture and dance students, junior faculty from the university and occasional bikers. There, without feeling self-conscious, I could dance alone on the crowded floor. I

met a few women but never asked one out. How could I date anyone? I had few nights off, and Janir and I were still living in our
cramped little cabin in the woods.

•   •   •

In town one evening we called his mom from a pay phone. She
had renewed her U.S. residence, moved back to San Francisco and
sent us her number. As a pair of fat moths flapped against the glass,
I lifted Janir onto the phone booth shelf and fed quarters into the
telephone. After ten rings someone answered and went to call Clarisa. I couldn't tell if it was some kind of commune or just a house
where she had a room. We had written, and I'd sent her money
every month, but we hadn't spoken in half a year.

"How's Janir?" she asked.

"He's fine. He's right here."

I passed him the phone and he said, "Hi." He listened, sitting
upright on his shelf. He nodded, he said, "Yeah," and "No." Sometimes he had trouble hearing because of the traffic. He looked so
cautious it made me want to cry. Finally he said, "Okay, 'bye," and
handed the phone to me.

"He sounds worried," Clarisa said.

I didn't tell her he hadn't been that way over dinner, or that
twenty minutes later he would probably be chattering and singing
songs. "He's made some friends," I said. "There's a great school
here, and he's in a playgroup for the summer."

"Are you going to stay there?"

"Yes, I'm buying a farm."

"So I can come and see him."

I hesitated only a second. "Sure."

For a moment she didn't say anything. Then, "Is everybody white
there?"

"Not everybody."

"What about his friends?"

"Most of them," I conceded. "Not Jesse."

"You better take care of him."

"Clarisa, I do."

There was a silence. Finally she said, much softer than before,
"He sounded so far away."

"He's doing fine," I assured her. I put my arm around Janir and
told him, "Your mom sends you a hug."

Already he looked more lively. "Tell her we went to the lake," he said.

"He should swim a lot," Clarisa said. "Swimmers get good muscles."

There was another long silence. "Where are you living?" I asked.

"People here are rude. I'm going to find somewhere else."

"Send me the new number," I said. "I'll have a phone in a month."

Two days later I talked to a lawyer. He advised me to get temporary custody—it would help if there was a battle later—and we started the process.

·   ·   ·

I met a young woman at an ice cream social, and after a night of square dancing and Virginia reels she invited me to her house for dinner the next Friday.

"Great," I said. "I'll bring my son."

"Your son?"

"He's three."

"Well, sure," Deborah said. "Bring him. I'd like to meet him."

I wasn't convinced she meant that, but she did get an envelope from her car and draw me a map on the back with crossroads, stop signs and mailboxes. In those days everyone lived on a farm.

Janir and I arrived at seven, which felt like late afternoon. Deborah's decrepit ridgetop house looked as if it might collapse in a puff of wind—but there was no wind, only the blue August air and a hazy orange sun that glowed above the hills to the west. Ripe peaches bowed the branches of a tree outside the door, and Deborah stepped out wearing only shorts and a sleeveless T-shirt. Her arms were smooth and her hair soft.

"Hello," she said brightly. "And what's your name?"

Janir wasn't used to adults who were nervous around children. "Janir," he said coolly.

Deborah said his name but didn't get it quite right.

"Ja-NEER," he repeated.

"Would you like some lemonade?"

"Sure. Do you have a television?"

"No, I'm sorry, I don't have . . . anything for kids."

He shrugged. He was used to boring places: the post office, the feed mill, the agricultural extension office, too many yard sales. Either there were kids or there weren't. If not, he put up with it.

I scanned Deborah's living room and found him some old *National Geographics*. After a while she relaxed, when she discovered she didn't have to entertain Janir to keep him happy.

Her meal impressed him. "This is a *good* dinner," he announced as she served a cheesy lasagna and a salad from her garden. Later he filled himself up with her homemade peach pie.

Deborah and I washed the dishes, then sat beside each other at the kitchen table, our legs almost touching. I took her hand and held it. A few big flies buzzed around the kitchen, then settled down with dusk. Outside, the trees were no more than silhouettes. Janir had dropped off to sleep on the living-room couch.

"He's very nice," she said.

"I can't believe he went to sleep without a story. Oh *shit*." I jumped up from the table. "Hold on."

I had forgotten to have him pee. I picked him up and carried him outside, his head as loose as a newborn's against my neck. He had already dropped into the depths of sleep. I stood him on the grass, unbuckled and lowered his Osh Kosh B'Goshes. If he didn't urinate now, it almost guaranteed he would wet the bed. "Janir, wake up. You've got to pee."

He stood on the moonlit grass, swaying slightly, holding himself upright but still fast asleep. Deborah stood to one side, watching.

"Janir, you have to do it."

Wrapped up with visions of kissing Deborah, I had ignored his bedtime rituals and let him slip away. He'd dropped off to sleep on me before, so I knew the stages. In the first ten minutes I could wake him easily, and even after a half hour it was possible to drag him back to consciousness. But soon after that he descended to an unreachable level.

It was now or never, while he was still on the edge. I shook him a little, but he threatened to collapse.

"Janir," I told him, "just pee. Go ahead." His penis stuck out in the moonlight, but nothing happened. "Do it," I urged him. "Just let it go. You can do it."

"*Okay,*" he said, annoyed. He could talk but he couldn't urinate. He was too far under.

I was not going to give in. Without any running water at the cabin, cleaning his sleeping bag was a major chore. I jiggled him and tousled his hair.

God damn it. This *one* time, with the first woman I'd gone out with since splitting up with Clarisa, I had forgotten him for thirty minutes. I considered setting him back on the couch and suffering the consequences later. But when I glanced at Deborah she took a step back. She looked wary, not at all like a woman who had kissing on her mind.

"Janir," I said, "wake up. You have to pee."

He wavered, then took a step forward. "I will," he said. But nothing happened. Deborah watched in silence as I pinched his fingers, his ears, even nudged the responsible organ. I kept talking to him, telling him to relax and let go. It went against all his training —but finally, after five long minutes, he let a great stream shoot over the grass, and his angry face relaxed. By the time he finished he was tumbling back into sleep. I tucked him into his overalls and lifted him up.

"I guess I better go," I said.

"That was amazing."

"Maybe . . ." I said, "maybe I could get him covered some night and we could go out to dinner in town. Go dancing at Swanky's."

She hesitated. "You know, I'm kind of like an egg these days." She put her fingers to her chest and tapped. "There's a shell around me, and I don't want anyone to crack it right now."

Yeah, sure. She didn't want *me* to crack it. But I just nodded and said I understood.

I carried Janir to the pickup and laid him out on the front seat. Deborah followed and said good-bye, but we didn't touch. I climbed into the truck, gave her a wave and drove off down the winding township road. I did understand. I was ten years older and I had a kid. I'd just forgotten, after living with Janir all this time, how scary the job could look to someone else.

•   •   •

On the first of September we moved into our new house. Now we had plumbing and electric lights and, more important, that vital device for a single parent, a telephone. Now I could call other parents on the spur of the moment, arrange overnights for Janir or invite his friends over.

I sent Clarisa the address and phone number, and one Saturday in October she called. But surprise: she wasn't in San Francisco, she was at the Columbus airport and could we pick her up?

Janir ran ahead of me into the gate area, stopped in front of her and let her pick him up. She held him with her eyes closed, swaying slightly. Janir hugged her back. Not tightly, but he seemed glad to be in her arms. It made me wonder if I'd done the right thing. She was his mother, and maybe I should have fought to keep them closer. Seeing them together, their dark heads side by side, for a moment I felt I'd made a terrible mistake.

Clarisa had a tiny suitcase and a tattered Raggedy Ann doll as big as Janir. He thought it was for him, but she said, "No, she's mine." When she lowered him to the floor he inspected the doll. One eye was missing and some stuffing protruded from its waist.

"It's broken," Janir said.

"You can carry her if you want."

We started for the truck with Janir carrying the doll sideways. Its feet dragged on the ground.

"Why do you have a doll?" he asked.

"Don't you have dolls?"

"I've got animals."

"What kind of animals?"

"Paddington Bear."

We sat in a row across the truck's front seat: me, Janir, Raggedy Ann and Clarisa. "Won't your father let you have a doll?" she asked.

"He can have whatever he likes," I said.

"I have a doll," she told him, "because I don't have you any-more."

"You have me," he said. He was indignant.

"Okay, why don't you come back to San Francisco with me?"

Janir folded his arms. "I can't. Daddy and I have a house now."

"Don't be so snooty about it."

"I'm not snooty, *you* are."

I turned off the city street into a fast-food restaurant, before they could launch into a battle. Not much had changed from the old days.

•   •   •

Sunday, the following afternoon, the three of us went to a harvest festival at the Athens Fairgrounds. We ate, saw some exhibits, took Janir on a couple of miniature rides and played volleyball. Or I did, taking advantage of Clarisa's visit. There were no other kids around, and she sat at the edge of the court with Janir, who jumped up a couple of times to chase the ball. He was slow to give it back: he wanted to play, of course. It flew past him again and he ran to get it, but one of the players, a woman, beat him to it. She snatched the ball up and said with a laugh, "Oh no you don't, you're much too slow."

Clarisa charged the woman, screaming. "*Leave him alone!* Don't touch him!" She grabbed Janir and held him in her arms as if the woman had gone after him with a knife. "What do you know about kids? Do you have a kid? You're selfish and sick. You don't know anything."

Janir looked terrified and Clarisa deranged. Her long skirt dragged on the ground and her tangled hair fell around Janir as she hunched over him. I was embarrassed and confused. I took Janir from her and we headed away from the court, across the grass toward the parking lot. When I glanced back the two teams still stood without moving on either side of the net, everyone watching us.

I kept Janir out of school for the next four days. We had a fairly peaceful time, but Clarisa and Janir argued a lot, and she was a cranky visitor. She was critical of the farm, which was too far from town. She didn't like how I dressed Janir or what I fed him. She didn't like a friend who stopped by to borrow a towing chain.

I had hoped to get some work done, but instead spent most of my time refereeing between the two of them. I was glad, at the end of the week, when she said she was ready to go home. I bought her a ticket, we drove her to Columbus and she got on the plane to San Francisco. She had left her Raggedy Ann for Janir.

I was relieved to see her go, for everything was simpler with just the two of us. On the way home I said, "I told her she could come back whenever she wants to. Is that okay with you?"

"Yeah."

"For sure?"

"It's okay," he said—but that was all I could get out of him.

•   •   •

I led such an odd life compared with what I had imagined for myself when younger. I'd certainly never thought of being a farmer. I remember driving across New Hampshire one cold winter dusk, my final year in college, staring through the frosted windows of my Volkswagen at a broad snow-covered field and a white farmhouse with smoke rising from the chimney straight up into the sky. A severe and beautiful scene, I think now. But at the time I could not imagine living in such a godforsaken place. I wanted an urban and intellectual life, not the desolation of a small farm.

I remember, too, reading George Eliot's novel *Silas Marner,* in which an old weaver adopts a young girl and devotes the rest of his life to her. How depressing that seemed in high school. The very last thing I wanted to do in life was raise a child on my own without having a woman. Yet here I was at thirty-two, looking after a young boy who meant more to me than anyone on earth—and living on a small farm besides, fully convinced that taking care of my soil was the most vital work I could be doing.

*   *   *

On Halloween the parents from the White Oak School put on a party for the kids at Maren's hillside farm. Maren was a Ph.D. candidate in chemistry with a son Janir's age and a redneck boyfriend—a guy who would one day drop his pistol on the floor and shoot himself in the stomach, but survive. The night before the party I had made Janir an inadequate costume: an orange sweatshirt with a black mouth, nose and eyes sewn on to look like a pumpkin. Janir wore it to school, but not with any enthusiasm. He wanted to be a cheetah. He had loved cheetahs ever since hearing they were the fastest animal on four legs. "I'm *fast,*" he'd say, a half dozen times a day. But a cheetah costume was beyond my seamster skills, so he'd had to settle for the pumpkin.

A friend drove me to the party at four in the afternoon, and Janir caught sight of us as we approached. He came tearing down the hill, all flash-haired and wild, wearing a spotted cape and a stiff piece of rope frayed out at the end for a tail. Kay, his teacher, had fixed him up. He crashed full-steam into a ditch beside the road, but scrambled to his feet without complaint to announce triumphantly, "I decided to be a cheetah!"

He had entered the age of fabulous imagination. When we played monster at night he brought the beast right into our living room: "Did he sting you, Daddy? Did he put fire on you? I'm gonna put fire on *him*! Look out! Here he comes, he's right here!"

Now he squirmed into my arms and told me about the spooky

house in Maren's living room: "It's black *black* inside, it's *real* scary."
He hunched his back, rolled his eyes and curled his fingers in an
ecstasy of fear. I lifted him up and carried him toward the house,
but halfway there he scrambled down and ran ahead of me, eager
to get back to the other kids.

Ellie McGlynn was there, standing by herself on the front porch.
Her son Teague was one of Janir's friends at school, but I had only
spoken to her a few times, and had always found her reticent. She
still looked reserved, standing alone outside the party—but also
graceful, with her luxuriant blond hair falling onto the black shoulders of a long-sleeved woolen dress. She wore black tights, and
maroon socks that stuck up above her boots.

We shook hands, we were still that formal. And as we did a charge
shot up my arm. I stared at her, trying to cover my confusion. "Is
Teague here?" I asked.

"He's inside with the kids. I just stepped out. I can't seem to get
enough daylight these days."

"And daylight savings ends next week."

"I hate that, don't you?"

She didn't seem reticent at all. Maybe it was because we were
alone, whereas at school there were always people around. She slid
her hands into the square front pockets of her dress. "It makes me
want to go south," she said.

"Didn't you just get back from a trip?" I'd heard that from Kay
at school.

"We went to England."

We, I assumed, was Ellie and Teague and his father Michael. "Did
you have a good time?"

"It was lovely. Though not much fun for Teague. We went to
Blake's house to see his manuscripts. That was wonderful."

"You went to England to see Blake's manuscripts?"

She hesitated. "I guess we did."

She looked away, which gave me a chance to watch her smooth
throat. I tried to be polite about it. I was just noticing, just absorbing
her presence. Though we stood only a few feet apart, the gap between us was enormous. She was married.

After a while I went inside and said hello to the other parents.
Michael wasn't there. I ate a little, then did a turn in the spooky
house, a cardboard room within a room. I wrapped myself in a
blanket and scuffled around in the dark, grunting and bellowing

and terrorizing the kids who dared to come in. They entered in packs or bravely on their own. I gripped the closest by their ankles and dragged them back into my lair, gargling like a fiend as they howled in alarm. Then I let them squirm away, back to the door and the safety of their friends.

After my stint I wandered through the downstairs rooms of the house. No Ellie, so I stepped back outside. She was still on the porch, sitting in a rocker with a plate at her feet. Her legs were drawn up and her fingers tucked into the tops of her boots. The sun had set and the light was draining out of the flat fields. Her face seemed to glow in the dusk.

I sat on another chair. "Michael didn't come?" I asked.

"He's not very sociable."

I almost laughed. "Neither are you."

"I'm not so good with gangs of kids."

"And Teague?"

"He loves a gang."

"Same with Janir," I said.

"He's never had that many friends, but he talks about Janir. I think the two of them get along."

"I had him by the foot in there. He's so blond I knew it was him."

Ellie tucked her own hair behind one ear. "Kay told me you're raising Janir on your own."

I nodded. "I've had him for almost a year now."

"Is it hard?"

"Sometimes I can't believe this is all there is to life."

"Oh, God, I know."

We looked away. I'd complained about the job to other parents, but not usually to someone I'd just met.

"It must get easier as they get older," I said. "Can you get Teague to help? Like clean up his room or anything?"

"Are you kidding?"

I laughed. I liked everything she said. "Janir just wants to play," I said.

"Teague too. And we want them to."

"Yes, but . . . I like to read. I went to college, I used to have ideas about things."

She smiled. "You might have to give those up." I wasn't sure if she was joking. She stood and slipped her arms into a wool jacket. "We give up everything else," she said, "don't we?"

"Just about."

It was almost dark. Ellie cinched her jacket around her waist, then skipped down the porch steps onto the stone walk, where light from the windows spilled out onto the lawn. "It's getting colder," she said. "I can't stand to think of winter, can you? Cold cars and cold houses." She stomped on one of the stones, making the bottom of her skirt shake. "Do you need a ride home?"

We both lived on McDougal Road, our houses barely a mile apart. After rounding up our sons and their Halloween treats we maneuvered the kids into the backseat of Ellie's Volkswagen. Within minutes they fell asleep as she drove the back road home, winding through fields and dark woods on a route so untraveled that blankets of tan oak leaves lay across the road. Slowly she plowed through them. She dropped into second gear and stayed there, doing no more than twenty miles an hour. She asked me about Janir's mother.

I might have tossed off my usual quick explanation. Instead I thought: I'll get closer to her, I'll tell her what actually happened. First I reached around and put my hand on Janir's chest to make sure he was asleep. We talked often about his mother, but I knew it would sound different when explained to someone else. He had dropped into sleep, his arms flung out like an infant's.

Ellie listened in silence as I described our life in Chile and the slow breakup of the marriage. For a while I thought she wasn't going to say anything. Maybe these intimate stories, coming from someone she hardly knew, had overwhelmed her. She kept driving, even more slowly now. Finally she glanced into the backseat.

"Janir is beautiful," she said. "Does he look like his mother?"

"A lot."

"She must be very pretty."

"She is."

"And how does he feel about living without her?"

"I think he misses her sometimes. But she's difficult, and things are more stable with me."

Ellie watched the road. She was quiet. By now we were close to my farm, coasting down off the ridge, the headlights turning the gravel road white. She kept her foot on the brake. She went slower and slower. Finally she looked over at me and asked, "But how did you know when the marriage was over?"

• • •

Janir and I shared his first Thanksgiving. I made a couple of apple pies and we joined a potluck at Helpless Far, a local commune. At home the following morning, with school still on vacation, I got a call from Ellie.

"Teague is driving me crazy," she said. "He needs someone to play with. Any chance you could lend me Janir for the day?"

"Hey, I'll walk him right up."

Even at Janir's vagrant pace it took us less than thirty minutes, and when we arrived the McGlynns were still eating breakfast. Michael stood up and I said hello. We had met by now, because Ellie and I were sharing the drives to school: I took the kids in the morning, and she brought them home in the afternoon. But I'd never been inside their two-story log cabin. It was clean and cozy, with a tidy kitchen, a gleaming coal stove, and handsome finish work on the wooden cabinets. At home, in my own plain house, the carpeted living room was little more than a playground for Janir.

Here all the furniture had been chosen with care. There was a tall dresser, a church pew and a delicate writing table. A death mask of William Blake hung on one wall beside some of Ellie's paintings.

"Sit down," she said, "don't look at those. I'm just a beginner."

"No, they're good."

I didn't know if they were good or not, but I found them arresting: dark forests, chimerical beasts and women floating through the air.

"Have some breakfast," Michael said. "There's plenty."

I couldn't tell whether he was gruff by nature, or whether Janir and I made him feel awkward. But breakfast looked good and I sat down. Not Janir. He and Teague ran up the stairs to play in Teague's room.

"You going to farm that place?" Michael asked.

"Just a truck farm, a couple of acres to start. The farmers' market looks pretty good here."

"Ellie tells me you lived in South America."

"We had a beautiful farm there. My wife and I."

"Where's she?"

"She lives in San Francisco now."

Ellie moved gingerly between the table and the kitchen counter, buttering toast and pouring cups of tea. For a while she stood next to the coal stove and warmed her hands on the backs of her legs. Michael ate fast and gulped his tea. He was blond, Ellie was blond and their child was blond. I was dark and my boy darker.

I'd barely finished when Michael pushed back his chair, stood up and said, "I've got some brush to clear. In weather like this we're pretty much outdoor people."

The hint was clear, so I thanked Ellie, called Janir to give him a hug and followed Michael outside. He showed me their garden, and the tiny studio where he wrote poems. Then I walked home.

At dusk I returned and was invited in again, this time for a tea with pound cake. The table was set with matching cups and saucers, bright silverware, old plates and a small pitcher of milk. Michael added chunks of wood to the stove and swept up around the wood-bin. He only sat down after Ellie served the tea. Twice she passed behind his chair and lay what seemed to me a soothing hand upon his shoulder.

Though there were undercurrents here, I was absorbed by the sense of family, the polished details of hearth and home. How appealing all that seemed.

I ate four slices of cake, told stories about Peru and Chile, and finally made ready to go. I bundled up Janir, took him outside and lifted him onto my shoulders. The nighttime cold had a new bite. Ellie followed me outside with a flashlight she wanted to lend me for the walk home.

Both my hands were clasped around Janir's ankles. I lifted them and smiled. "No way to hold it," I said.

"The drive's pretty steep."

"I'll make it. And thanks for looking after Janir."

"I was glad to have him."

"Bring Teague down when you need a hand. Any day."

"I will, but don't worry about it. Janir, you were a delight. Take care of your dad, okay?"

"Okay. But he takes care of *me*."

As she reached up to pat his leg, the side of her hand brushed mine where I held him. I stood still, but my whole arm tingled. Ellie said good night and went back inside.

I wanted to stop and spy on them, peer into the house to see how she and Michael responded to each other in private. Though they seemed to have refined the outward form of marriage, I suspected that underneath not everything ran smoothly. Of course, it rarely does.

The drive was gravelly, and I had to focus on my steps so as not to stumble and spill Janir. Then, once we got to McDougal Road, he was perky and wanted to talk. He held his palms against my forehead, and I strode along with no chance to think of Ellie, too busy answering Janir's string of questions about stars and cars and what he'd done as a baby.

*   *   *

Years later, when I ran across Ellie at a potluck, she told me this story:

That first fall, when we still hardly knew each other, she had gone to lunch with a pair of friends. They were all married, and that day all three of them agreed that they had mated for life. Ellie was as confident as the others. She and Michael had been through some hard times, but she was certain they would remain a couple. In all her life she would have only one man.

She and I had met by then, but we'd hardly spoken. That fall I was volunteering at the school a half day a week, making maps with the kids: big simple maps of the school and nearby roads and houses. Ellie drove up to get Teague one afternoon, and as he gathered up his things to go home Janir ran into the schoolhouse, crying. He had cut his hand on some broken glass. I found the first-aid kit, cleaned and bandaged the wound, then sat with him on the porch. I held him and let him cry.

"That was all there was to it," Ellie told me. "But that afternoon I went home and took a look at my marriage, and I understood what wasn't there."

*   *   *

Ellie gave us a ride to the schoolhouse for the Christmas party. Michael didn't come, and I didn't ask why. Every other parent was there, and we walked with the kids a quarter mile down the road to carol a group of neighbors, braving an icy wind that knifed over the top of the ridge. After three or four carolings we retreated to the toasty schoolhouse for hot chocolate and Christmas cookies.

At first we kept our distance. I held Ellie in my peripheral vision, watching her long neck and the swell of her chest from across the room. I talked to every parent but her, and every word was a feint to conceal my obsession.

Finally I gave in. I made my way toward her through the crowd, we exchanged a few words and slowly drifted into the music and science room. There we talked about the Christmases of our youth: snowstorms in Pennsylvania and ice on Long Island Sound. Ellie leaned back against the school piano, her gray skirt revealing the camber of her thighs. We talked about our parents and our sons.

Her restive fingers toyed with the battered keys. If I stood any closer, I thought, they might land on me. The score to *South Pacific* lay on top of the piano. We had both seen the musical when young, and soon were singing songs from it: "I'm Gonna Wash That Man Right Outa My Hair," and *"Dîtes-moi, pourquoi, la vie est belle."* I'm not a singer, but I sang. We had just started "Some Enchanted Evening" when Roger and Linda Jahnke peered into the room, studied us for a moment and withdrew. We stopped singing and took a step apart. The last notes hung in the air. I was nervous. Surely anyone could see what was going on. If it *was* going on.

When the party broke up we dressed the kids in coats and mittens and shuffled them out to Ellie's car. Janir was exhausted and fell asleep under a blanket in back. Teague crawled into the front seat and sat on my lap. He didn't say anything, but occasionally twisted his head to look up at me. The car warmed slowly as Ellie drove over the icy gravel roads, and for the first few miles our breaths were vaporous. The lights from the instrument panel fell across her skirt. On her right wrist, just above her glove, a white oval of skin was exposed to the air. Teague nodded, twitched once, twice, then relaxed his head against my chest and slept.

We drove all the way home in silence. We were turning onto McDougal Road, only a quarter mile from my house, when Ellie finally said, "There's a place I go in town, a friend's house. She works during the day, and sometimes I paint there. Would you like to come for lunch?"

My fingers went numb, my toes, my lips. I managed to say, "Yes, I'd like that."

ONCE A WEEK THAT WINTER, SOMETIMES TWICE, WE MET in secret at an apartment Ellie rented after Christmas, the bottom half of a house on Hanlin Avenue. Michael didn't know about it. Ellie, who had the only key, arrived first and turned up the gas heater in the large bright bedroom. There was no furniture, but light streamed onto the scarred wooden floor as we unfolded a pair of quilts in front of the heater. There we knelt, still a bit shy, our hands and faces cool, exchanging the first delicate wafer of a kiss. Our clothes came off slowly, or sometimes in a flurry: my checked shirt and corduroy pants, her dark blue dress and white knee socks.

Later we ate lunch in front of the trembling gas flame. Ellie brought yogurt and fruit, I brought date-and-peanut-butter sandwiches. She put on my shirt. She wanted to hear about every woman I'd ever kissed. "Tell me everything," she said.

So I did. When I finished she looked unhappy.

"There weren't that many," I said.

"More than me." She stared at the heater. "I've never done anything."

"You've done this. And you've been married."

"I *am* married."

"Are you going to tell him?"

"Please, don't hurry me. I've been married for seven years. I just want to know what this is like. If Michael finds out, it's going to be bad. I love this, I don't want him to come in and knock it apart."

She turned and leaned back into my lap, her shirt falling open. I knelt above her. I massaged her face, then her neck and breasts. She had a narrow waist and a rich small belly. Her ribs rose and fell. She closed her eyes and let me go on for twenty minutes.

Later, when we had to go, she was slow to put her clothes back on.

She lingered over each button—and then, once she had finished, I stood before her and unbuttoned them all again, so she could repeat the job. How reluctant we were to part.

•   •   •

On a soggy winter afternoon I stood eighteen inches down in the adhesive clay of my farm, digging a footer for my new greenhouse. I'd worked up a steady sweat. My boots were six inches wide with mud, and though I'd paraffined my shovel the clay still clung to it after every thrust.

I didn't want a clandestine affair. Ellie had told me, two weeks after renting her apartment, that soon she would move out of the cabin. Yet her marriage wasn't over. Not even close. She still lived with Michael, still slept with him every night. When I asked if they still had sex, she looked away and wouldn't answer.

I pried the clay off my boots. Finally I made a decision: I would tell her it was over. I wanted a woman of my own, not someone who was married and lived a mile up the road. This was a dead end for me. I'd had too much heartache already, and I didn't want to get hurt again.

An hour later Ellie rolled down the drive, bringing the kids back from school. They ran inside, and we stood out of sight under an apple tree. Her wintry complexion was flushed from the cold.

"Janir is such a sweetheart," she said. "Sometimes when I'm driving he stands on the seat behind me and plays with my ears."

"He loves ears."

"And he's great with Teague. He's so full of life and imagination. He makes us play games. We have to count red cars or play Pooch. Did you teach him that?"

"I played it with my brother when we were kids."

"One point for a horse, two for a dog . . ."

"Three for a rabbit," I said, "and four for a sheep."

"But fifty for an elephant?"

"He likes elephants."

"I love your son," she said. She opened her coat, took my cold hand and slid it under the belt of her jeans onto her bare skin. "But all day, all I can think about is seeing you."

We started kissing. I kissed her eyes, her lips, her teeth. I never said a word about my decision to break up with her. I didn't remember making it. I wanted to run off with her and raise our boys together. Our family would be ready-made. Janir could have a sibling, and Ellie was the perfect woman. She was sane and brave and beautiful, and she loved my son.

•   •   •

Janir came down with a fever, and by midnight his temperature stood at 104.8. I knew little about kids and illness, for in his four and a half years Janir had never once been sick: never a cold, never a flu, not even an earache. The only time he'd seen a doctor was when I took him to get his vaccinations when we first came to the States. I knew no doctors in Athens, and the emergency room, in my experience, was a place to get bones set and cuts sutured.

But I did know high fevers could be dangerous. Ignoring his shrieks of outrage, I wrapped him in wet towels until his temperature dropped to 102. Aspirin kept the fever at bay after that, but he slept fitfully all night. I woke often myself, whenever he stirred. I bathed his forehead with a damp cloth and took his temperature as he slept.

The next day I left the house only once, for a short walk to the pond. Coming back I was exhausted, dragging my heels through a four-inch snow. By the end of dinner I could hardly move. I crawled into my sleeping bag, covered it with blankets and spent the next five hours shivering ecstatically. Around two A.M. the chills broke, and I soared into a fever. I got up, soaked myself in a cool bath, took four aspirins and went back to bed. But again I slept erratically. I kept hallucinating that Janir had woken up and gone out into the snow without his boots: that his teeth had all fallen out: that he was trying to cook us a ravioli dinner in the living room on a camp stove.

We spent the next day together in my bed, half delirious. Janir made ramps with the sheet and ran his cars down them. He drew in his coloring books, and at one point rolled over onto his crayons and broke most of them in two. He cried miserably. "I don't feel good," he said.

"I'm sorry, Janir, I can't help. Do what you want. Find something to play with."

He slid onto the floor and came back with his marbles and a box full of Legos. The bed was chaos, it looked like the earth's last hour. Periodically one of us dropped into a fevered sleep.

That afternoon, on her way home from school, Ellie stopped by to see how we were doing. Though I kept her and Teague out of the contagious bedroom, after dinner she returned alone with a pot of chicken soup. I couldn't get any down, but Janir was hungry. She fed him in bed, tipping the soup into his mouth with a spoon. I sat back against the wall and watched as she looked after him. For once I watched her impartially, untouched by desire. I wanted to marry her.

Two days later Janir and I were still as weak as young mice. We couldn't seem to pull out of it. Ellie called her doctor and drove us into town to see him. He shot us up with penicillin—no more fooling around with herbal teas and orange juice—and the following day we were on the mend.

·   ·   ·

Michael went to Pittsburgh for the weekend, Ellie and I found friends to look after our boys for twenty-four hours, and we spent a day and a night together in her apartment in town. We bought a mattress and lay on fresh sheets with the sunlight pouring in above the curtains. She undressed me playfully, tugging off my clothes with her teeth as she hummed, *"Dîtes-moi . . ."*

Just at six we stepped outside into the last purpling light of dusk. The cool unhurried peals of the bells of St. Paul's were still floating down over our end of town. We walked to the Chinese restaurant on Union Street, cased the place, found no one we knew, and ate together for the first time in public. The thrill of this was undeniable.

That night we lay face to face on her new mattress, her hands curled inside my T-shirt.

"We've never been so bold," I said.

"I don't know what got into me." She smiled, already half asleep.

"You're not worried?" I asked.

"I'm never going to let you go."

A few minutes later she pulled back her hands and tucked them between her legs. She dropped slowly into sleep, like a stone wobbling down through the water.

"Ellie," I said. I watched her in the dim glow from the street-lights. "Are you awake?"

She wasn't, she was far below the surface.

"Ellie, I love you."

Any minute, I thought, she would open her eyes and break into a smile.

"Ellie McGlynn, I'm in love with you."

I was practicing for the daylight. I was slipping those words—the most dangerous and vital in the language—into her unconscious, because when I told her for real I didn't want her to jump.

In EARLY MARCH, BEFORE THE START OF THE GROWING
season, Janir and I flew east to see my father. In the past few weeks
I'd been obsessed with Ellie and hadn't given Janir enough attention. Now he hung from my neck in the airport, held on to me as
we boarded the plane, asked me endless questions. Once in the air
he stood up on his seat and peered out the window.

"Is that a river, Daddy? Is that snow down there? Can we eat on
the plane? When are we going to get there? Is the plane going to
land? Is Nana going to be mean? Is she going to switch me? Can we
get a dog? Did you have a dog when you were a kid? Where's the
bathroom? Can I go by myself?"

He had entered his question-asking prime. For five straight days
he asked me hundreds of questions a day, and I did my best to
answer them. But we'd only been on the plane for an hour when I
broke down the first time.

"Janir, quit bugging me. Let me read or something."

"*No,*" he said, "you have to tell me. Did you ever crash on a
plane? Did you ever see one crash? Did I go in a plane before? How
old was I? Is my birthday soon? What am I going to get? How come
you gave away my blue coat? I liked that coat. What do you call those
things where you go up the stairs? Yeah, escalator. When do I get to
ride the escalator? I want to do that when we get there. I want to do
it right away!"

"Janir, shut up."

In our house that was the one forbidden phrase, far worse than
any swear word. He sat down in an instant sulk, close to tears.

"I'm sorry," I said. "But sometimes you just drive me crazy."

"Sometimes you just drive *me* crazy."

He stared out the blurry window for a few minutes, then slowly

recovered. He looked around, pointedly inquisitive and auto-
nomous as he explored the pocket in front of him with its magazines and airsickness bag. He studied the plastic-coated ditch
instructions, running his finger under the words as if he could read
them.

"Then you put this on," he said softly, following from one illus-
tration to the next. "Then you open the door. Then you jump out
here."

I could have kissed his darling face. But I didn't, because I didn't
want to interrupt him while he was acting so self-reliant. When the
stewardess came by he stood up again on his seat and asked her—
bypassing me entirely—"Can I have some more Coke, please?"

"Certainly, young man."

When she brought the soda, a whole can, Janir looked directly at
her and said, "Thank you very much."

Wow! Where did such language come from? At home he could
go a month without using the words *please* or *thank you,* for I never
insisted on them. I figured he'd pick them up the way kids picked
up everything else, by example. Of course I liked it when he was
attentive, polite and articulate—but I wanted all that to spring from
his own disposition, not from a set of rules. I didn't believe in
rehearsing my kid so he could make adults happy.

I heard parents do it all the time: "Can you say please, Jennifer?"
and "Thank the nice man, Freddie."

I could never stomach that indoctrination: Say hello, say good-
bye, say you're sorry, tell them what a nice time you had. Clarisa, I
was sure, would never have trained Janir that way.

She was with me always as I raised our son. Sometimes I could
almost see her flowing through his veins. A couple of days ago I'd
introduced Janir to someone in the hardware store. Joe was a
friendly guy, a carpenter who was going to help with my greenhouse
—but to Janir he was just another in a long series of adults parading
through his life.

"Hi there," Joe said brightly.

Janir looked him up and down. His eyes narrowed slightly, he
bared his small teeth and growled like a dog: *"Grrgghh."* It was his
way of saying, "I see you but don't get too close. I don't know you
yet and I'm not sure I want to."

Joe, to his credit, found it amusing: he simply smiled and growled
back. And I thought Janir was completely reasonable. Why should a

four-year-old child be subjected to the adult protocol of shaking hands and exchanging small talk about things that bored him?

Yet I have to admit I was delighted on the plane by how polite he was when the stewardess brought his Coke. After all, it vindicated my theories that when the time came he would learn all this on his own. I was so charmed by his manners that I didn't remember until after he'd finished his second soda that his limit was one a day.

Sometimes he growled, sometimes he was a beguiling child. After we landed in New York he charmed the bus driver who drove us in from La Guardia, then three elderly women from Queens in a donut shop near Grand Central, then a dour-looking black woman on the subway. Janir skipped ahead of me into the car, stood directly in front of her and announced brightly, "Me and my daddy are gonna sit here."

"Oh you are?"

"Yeah!"

She squeezed over and made room for us, and Janir sat down beside her.

"Where are you going?" she asked him.

"To see my grandfather and ride the escalator. What's in there?" He poked a gift-wrapped package in a shopping bag held upright between her legs.

"That's for my godson. He's about your age."

"What's a godson?"

"You know . . . a godson. I had him baptized. I take him to church."

"What's baptized?"

The woman shot me a look. "A boy like you should be baptized."

Janir held his hands in the air, disclaiming all responsibility. And he was right, of course, it was all my fault, I was a long-haired hippie agnostic. He pinched the woman's package. "What did you get him?"

"A garage with cars and trucks. You think he'll like that?"

"Are they Hot Wheels?"

A moment's pause. "I'm not sure."

"Those are the best."

The train roared past a local stop, then on through the dark tunnel. Janir and the woman talked until the train slowed down and I stood up. He slid off the seat and took my hand. I gave the woman a nod, and when the doors opened Janir and I stepped out onto the concrete platform. He didn't look back or say good-bye—and my first impulse was to remind him. But I didn't. He had started the conversation, and I let him end it as he chose.

•   •   •

At my dad's office Janir picked out his grandfather the moment he entered the reception area. "My *grand*father!" he shouted, and ran into his arms.

"My grandson," Dad said, and picked him up. He carried him around and introduced us to people, and showed us his own office, where the layouts for the next *Horizon* magazine were pinned to a corkboard on the wall. What interested Janir was the view from the plate-glass windows, and the sounds of the city floating up from the street. Dad set him on a table where he could stand in front of the window and push his palms and nose against the cold glass. I put an arm around him and tucked his shirt into his pants. Here on Sixth Avenue his corduroys and sneakers looked a bit shabby.

Dad took us to lunch at a typical New York restaurant: crowded, noisy, small tables, no room for a child to play or even fidget. Janir ate half his meal, then looked through a book, then sat in my lap. Finally I let him stretch out on the carpeted floor beside my feet as Dad and I talked. I gave him the contents of my pockets—keys, change, pen, wallet—and let him play with them on the floor. Finally the waiter could stand it no longer.

"No, no," he said, as he approached the table and drew himself up. "This is impossible."

Go fuck yourself, I wanted to say. In those days I was quickly incensed about the demands placed on children. But I picked Janir up and sat him on his seat—and spent the next ten minutes imagining what Clarisa would have done. She would not have just taken it the way I did. She would have stood up to the guy, told him off, made such a ruckus he'd have been desperate to calm her down. And which one of us was more imprudent, I thought: she or I?

•   •   •

After lunch I took Janir to Bloomingdale's to ride the escalators. I didn't tell him he could ride them as long as he liked, but I resolved to try. It's rare for kids to get enough of what they want:

enough attention, enough hugs, enough stories, enough rides on the rocketship. So periodically I tried to let Janir set his own limits and do something for as long as he liked.

Bloomingdale's busy first floor was filled with mirrors, makeup counters, stylish women, chiming bells and the smell of perfume. We rose past glassware and ladies' shoes, past patio furniture and leather suitcases, all the way to the top floor and down again. And up again, and down again. The metal stairs rose and fell, disappearing at the end of their run in a maneuver Janir found endlessly fascinating, just as I had when I was a child.

I interrupted him only once, to buy him a shirt, some pants and a pair of brown-and-beige two-tone leather shoes he immediately christened his "city slickers." He wore them back to the escalators for our next round of trips.

He wanted to ride up a floor and return by himself, and I let him. I could see him almost the whole way. But then testing, always testing, he wanted to do two floors. I let him do that, too, and was relieved when he came gliding back into view, looking as if he'd been to the top of a Himalayan peak. He was only four and a half. Though enjoined not to, he leapt from his stair before it flattened out, hit the floor in front of me, did a shoulder roll and came up smiling.

We stayed with my father, with Nana, and with my brother in Maine. Altogether we were away for ten days. I thought about Ellie constantly, but only told Nana about her. I was embarrassed to be having an affair with a married woman and doubted I could explain to Alan or my father the overwhelming impact of it: the rapture that justified the transgression.

I swore Nana to secrecy, then told her the whole story. "Lord," she said a couple of times, but otherwise she heard me out. We sat at her kitchen table playing cards and eating Fannie Mae chocolates, the same as ever.

"Is she going to leave her husband?" Nana asked.

"I don't know."

"Is she as much in love with you as you are with her?"

"I think so."

"Would she make a good mother for Janir?"

"She's a great mother. But sometimes it's confusing. He already has a mother."

"He can have two mothers," Nana said.

"Yeah, I guess he can. I did."

She took my hands in hers. She looked older, her eyes were worn and soft. "Do what you have to, John. But be careful. You don't need any more trouble than what you got already."

●   ●   ●

Back in Ohio I found a postcard in the mailbox with a quote penned in Ellie's small hand:

> *"Through the sureness of fire and times burnt clear—hear it in the lineaments' song. Breathing sigh. Two virginities meet, commingling showry head to braided feet."*

Blake, I thought. In "showry head" I saw our long hair tangled up on the pillow, and in "braided feet" our toes intertwined as we lay on our backs after love. Below the quote she had added:

> And John, when can I see you? I've moved into town.
>
>   E.

I sat on the couch, nothing unpacked, as Janir ran around looking at his bed, his toys, the lawn outside, everything new to him after ten days away. I'd come home doubting the whole affair, but now Ellie had moved out of her cabin. She and Michael were finished, I was sure. They had argued too much. The marriage was in its last days.

Hoping to spend a whole night with her, I left Janir with Will Dewees and his son Jesse, drove to town, parked three blocks away from her house and made my way furtively along the cold streets. In the middle of March, spring was still only a promise: the stiff buds of elms and sweet gums stood tightly furled above the bony lilacs. I kept my eyes out for Michael's truck, took a short cut through a backyard and emerged on Hanlin Avenue.

Teague had gone to sleep in his living-room bed. Ellie and I talked in the kitchen, whispering, both a bit timid. We had been ten days apart and might have changed our minds. But no. Before long she was in my arms. Her kisses fell on my neck like slices of melon as I traced, under her sweater, the fine stretched skin that covered her ribs.

"Thank God you came back," she said.

"Of course I came back."

"It scared me how much I wanted you."

"Don't be scared. I'm in love with you."

"Are you?"

"I told you before I left. While you were sleeping."

She pulled her skirt up onto her thighs. "I think I heard you."

But first I had to talk about Michael. "Have you told him?"

"I don't want to hurt him. I have to go slowly."

"How slowly?"

"John, don't make me think about that now. Not when you've just come back."

Suddenly, at the door: *tap tap tap . . . tap tap tap.*

"I won't answer it," she whispered. "It's probably the boys up-stairs."

"Go ahead," I said. "Open it. I'm ready."

"No, let's wait and see."

Tap tap tap . . . tap tap tap.

Finally whoever it was stepped off the porch, got into a vehicle and drove off. It sounded like a truck to me: what Michael drove.

An hour later we lay naked in bed, her hair in my face, her breath in my mouth. The telephone rang. Ellie jumped up, threw a quilt over her shoulders and ran into the kitchen to pick up the phone. From her hushed and protective tone I knew immediately it was Michael. And as I listened she fed him lies, one after the other, he could take his pick: she'd been out, she'd come back late, she wasn't feeling well, she hadn't heard him knock.

By the time she got off the phone I was dressed and tying my shoes. I couldn't live with this. She tiptoed into the bedroom, her shoulders slumped. "What's wrong?" she asked.

"What are you going to do, lie to him forever?"

"He's hurt. I think he knows. I just want to protect him."

"No you don't. You want to protect yourself."

I was angry and jealous and there was nothing more to say. I grabbed my coat and left. I ran down the streets to my truck and drove out to Will's to pick up Janir. I wanted him back. I lifted him out of bed, warm and loose, and carried him to the pickup. He never woke, but clung to me in the depths of sleep. How secure we are, I thought: as long as we are man and boy we're going to stay together. Can any couple say that now, and know it to be true?

•   •   •

Ellie came out to the farm and stayed for three days. At night we lay in bed and read the love poems of Ovid from a book she had found in the library. In the morning I took the kids to school and came back to seed long rows of lettuce with her, then spinach, peas and beets. I was aiming for the June opening of the farmers' market. We worked hard, stopped for lunch, then lay on the grass with Ellie's head on my stomach and the sun lighting up the downy hairs on her arms. Sometimes we had nothing to say, love had given us such a clout.

•   •   •

On the third day Clarisa called as we were finishing lunch. She needed some money: five hundred dollars and right away. She sounded worried.

"What for?" I asked her.

"I need it."

"What for, Clarisa?"

"Just send it, will you?"

She wanted it wired that afternoon. And though Ellie and I had planned a walk at Dow Lake, I dropped everything, left her to fend for herself and drove to town before the bank closed.

When Clarisa called I still jumped. It had nothing to do with being married or separated. It was because of Janir. And knowing that, I wondered how much Ellie would ever cut loose of Michael.

CLARISA AND I GOT DIVORCED. I TOOK THE MORNING off, put on the same blue suit I'd been married in and drove to the county courthouse. She'd been served notice in San Francisco about the divorce and custody hearing, and though she hadn't responded, I worried I might find her in the courtroom at the last minute, determined to fight for Janir.

There was no sign of her.

"The mother understands that custody is to be decided today?" the judge asked my lawyer.

"Yes, your honor."

The judge arched his eyebrows. "She doesn't seem very interested in the child."

"No, your honor."

The Jahnkes and Will Dewees spoke for my parenting skills and general responsibility, and in fifteen minutes it was all decided. I got full custody, Clarisa was granted "reasonable" visitation rights, and the judge set her child support at a token ten dollars a month.

When she called a few weeks later I told her about the divorce, the custody and the ten dollars.

"I pay *you* ten dollars?" she said. "You've got the money, why should I pay you?"

"It does seem unlikely," I admitted.

She wasn't interested in anything the state had decided, and instead of challenging my legal custody she ignored it. "I want to see Janir," she told me.

"When?"

What a foolish question with Clarisa. "Now," she said.

I put her off for a month, but at heart I agreed with how she saw things. The state had nothing to do with the question of visitation.

My true authority came from Janir, and he was the one I asked about it. Did he want to visit his mom?

He thought it over briefly. "Okay," he said.

But I balked at letting Clarisa have him in California. He was not yet five, and her life seemed too unstable there. Eventually I agreed to take him to El Salvador, where Paquita was eager to see him and would guarantee his well-being. I'd have to fly him down myself, but then I'd have two months free to work on the farm.

•   •   •

After a couple of nights at Paquita's we all drove out for a stay at her childhood home in Atiquizaya, a town that reminded me of García Márquez's Macondo. There, in the family's ancestral house, Clarisa's spinster aunt Blanca had been born and would live her entire life, rarely venturing as far as San Salvador, a two-hour trip by bus.

Like many homes in Latin America it was a self-contained and secretive dwelling, a residence that divulged little to passersby. From the street its pocked adobe walls and eternally shuttered windows looked neglected, but inside, the high-ceilinged parlor was lined with ancient photos of the Betancourt family in all their stiff splendor. There were several cool and shuttered bedrooms, a covered porch and a huge patio with ten-foot walls. Inside this rustic courtyard Blanca raised chickens, pigs and vegetables, and harvested fruit from a dozen trees: avocados, mangos, pomegranates, oranges, limes, plantains and a pair of hundred-year-old tamarinds.

It was the rainy season, El Salvador's winter. Each afternoon the skies darkened and a violent cleansing rainstorm swept the town. The adults waited it out on the porch, but Janir and his cousin Frankie stripped off their clothes and played in the gushing downspout. I had come with some doubts, but now felt comfortable about leaving Janir with his mother. Both here and back in the capital city he would be surrounded by family and people who loved him. Clarisa seemed calm, submissive to her mother and reasonably attentive to both Janir and his cousin. Sometimes she brooded—but the old house in Atiquizaya seemed a good place to brood, a somnolent enclave that had always induced in me long naps and desultory conversation.

At dusk Blanca started her tortillas on the clay *comal,* feeding the fire beneath it with sticks she had bought from an old man with a donkey. Evening settled in almost unnoticed. The chickens roosted in their darkened coop, and when it was too dark to see across the courtyard Blanca grudgingly turned on a pair of forty-watt bulbs. We lay beneath them in coarse sisal hammocks worn smooth by decades of use. Time may not have stood still there, but it was close.

I said nothing to Clarisa about Ellie. If she found out by grilling Janir, so be it. After supper one night we went for a walk around the plaza. We passed the town hall, an open pharmacy, a movie theater in which, when we were first dating, we had made out through an entire Mexican western.

Near the edge of town she surprised me by taking my hand and leading me to the gates of the cemetery. They were locked, but we climbed over the fence and made our way past the stones and small mausoleums to her father's grave. He'd been buried here in his wife's family plot. For ten minutes we stood in front of his gravestone, holding hands in silence, joined by the fact that we had both lost a parent.

Back in the family's timeworn house Janir and his cousin were asleep. Blanca and Paquita, the two sisters, swung in their hammocks, exchanging a sentence every now and then, listening to the mangos and avocados drop with a thud onto the soft earth. Occasionally one clanged against the bathroom's zinc roof, making everyone jump.

Bedtime came early for us all. Paquita had staked out her territory when we arrived, and Janir now slept with her, not with his mother. I unfolded a wide canvas cot in the parlor where I'd been sleeping, and made it up with a pair of sheets. I read for a while under a single dim bulb, then turned out the light and drifted off to sleep amid the faint sounds from the street: someone passing on horseback, a pair of young men talking, an occasional car or truck.

Sometime in the middle of the night I woke with a start, as Clarisa climbed onto the cot. She slid between the sheets and put her arms around me. Her hair smelled of tortillas and smoke. As I held her familiar spare body she began to cry. Our long sad history was at my throat again, and I was almost crying myself. But then she began to rub my back and neck, and to kiss me. I hesitated, I tried to hold back—but in spite of lawyers and judges and even Ellie McGlynn, I was both aroused and tempted.

Finally I shook myself out of my trance and rolled over on the cot, facing away from her. She went on massaging me until I pushed down the sheet and got off. I stood on the cool tile floor. "That's over," I said in a whisper. "I don't want to do that anymore."

"Don't be so proud," she said. She reached out quickly and touched me. "See?"

I stepped back. "We're divorced now. Things have changed. I have a girlfriend."

At that she went still. She watched me coldly, then got off the cot without a word and went back to her bedroom. I lay down and stared at the dark tiles of the roof, unable to sleep, sorry to have used Ellie like a club.

•   •   •

Back on the farm, without Janir, I was free to work twelve- and fourteen-hour days. Occasionally, after watering until ten at night, I went back to work at dawn, spreading manure or seeding soybeans in a field I was preparing for next year's crops. A wet season delayed the beans, but eventually I got them in, broadcasting them with a hand seeder and tilling them under with the tractor-mounted roto-tiller. Behind the blades the earth churned up dark and friable, and six days later the seedlings sprang out of the soil like little cadets.

Nana died of a heart attack. I flew to New York and took the subway up to Harlem to view her at the funeral home. She would have been uncomfortable, I thought, with the hushed tones and formidable bronze casket. "When I die," she had told me more than once, "just put me in a box and put the box in the ground."

The next day Dad and Alan and I went to her funeral service in a Harlem church, then to her burial on Long Island. There a rapacious young funeral-home rep in black tails and a glistening conk presided over the service, holding a lone yellow rose to his heart. I could almost hear Nana telling him to get his fool self back to the limousine.

Once again I was slow to grieve. I was too busy trying to do the right thing. I'd worn my blue suit and tied back my hair, but I was the lone white pallbearer and acutely conscious of the fact. Instead of thinking about Nana I thought about race. Race had rarely been an issue between us, but out in the world, skin color seemed to overwhelm all else—especially, for me, when *I* was surrounded by black people.

•   •   •

Ellie had been fighting steadily with Michael, and now decided to put some distance between them. She settled on Yellow Springs, a small town near Dayton and the home of Antioch College. One Saturday after the farmers' market I swept my truck clean, filled it with Ellie's furniture and followed her and Teague across the back roads of central Ohio. After eight years in Athens she was leaving her home, her husband and all her friends.

Without Janir as a buffer, Teague was more reserved with me. He was six now and understood that I had played a role in his parents' separation. In Yellow Springs he refused to help as we unloaded the truck, and when I put my arm around Ellie on the way to dinner he said, "Don't, Mom."

I took the seat across from them in the booth. Ellie kissed and held him, but when his hamburger came he refused to eat it. "I'm not hungry," he said. "I just want the milk shake."

It had been a long day. "Eat what you like," Ellie said gently—and halfway through the shake he started in on his burger.

As we drove back to their new apartment he fell asleep across her lap. He was getting too heavy for her, so it was I who lifted him out, lugged him inside and lay him down on his mattress. I didn't stay the night, partly because of Teague. But the next Saturday I returned, and the weekend after that.

*   *   *

In the drugged heat of summer, with the temperature locked at eighty-five and the western sky still light at nine-thirty, Ellie and I lay naked on the sheets of her bed. Beside us the lace curtains bellied in with a faint breeze, then hung inert. Ellie reclined against a pillow, her breasts slack against her chest, her neck damp beneath her hair. I'd always been drawn to dark women before, but that was irrelevant now, for I was in love with *this* woman, blue-eyed and flagrantly blond. I kissed her slowly, almost at random, from her toes to the top of her forehead.

In the morning I woke to find her staring at me, her hand beneath her chin. We watched each other in the cool green light. Then she lay a finger on my lips and slid out of bed like a dancer, one leg extended. Even if Teague knew we slept in the same bed, she didn't want him to see us there together.

*   *   *

Three weeks after leaving El Salvador I put in a call to Paquita's house. The maid answered and sent out to the street for Janir. He ran in out of breath, picked up the phone and said, *"Sí?"*

"Janir, do you know who this is?"

"Yeah! It's my dad!"

"How you doin', buddy?"

"I want to go to your house *right now!*"

How gorgeous to hear his voice, it made me laugh and talk and want to hold him. But he wasn't having a good time in San Salvador. I listened to his complaints about his mother, then got the details from Paquita: the two of them had been quarreling, and Clarisa was doing worse each day.

After hanging up I sat on the porch behind my house as dusk fell into the hollow and the whippoorwills began their insistent calls. I hadn't missed Janir that much. I knew single mothers who couldn't go two days without their children, but I wasn't like that. I loved having time to myself and almost always wanted more. But now a wave of longing broke over me. I imagined how he had looked as he held the old black phone to his ear in Paquita's living room, hopping up and down at first, then growing sad and standing quietly, his eyes fixed on the floor.

I called again a week later, and the first thing he said was, "I want to go home." He almost cried but didn't, and stuck to his plea throughout the call.

I talked to his grandmother about it. Victor, who now worked for Ford in Kentucky, would be flying up to the States in ten days, and I made Janir wait to go with him.

I met them at the Louisville airport. Janir saw me from a distance, dropped his uncle's hand and came running toward me. I crouched in the middle of the busy corridor and let him knock me over backwards, head over heels onto the floor. It was an old game between us. He scrambled onto my chest and rubbed his face against mine. God, how I loved him.

Other passengers streamed around us. Finally I stood up, and the three of us headed for the baggage carousels. Janir didn't walk, he cavorted in his city slickers. He tore past the carousels, raced around columns and flew back into my arms.

Victor and I had a cup of coffee, then I carried Janir to our truck and found the highway out of town. He stood on the seat beside me, playing with my ears, then lay his head on my lap and asked for a story. I was ready with a long one I'd made up on the way to the airport, a fairy tale about a farmer and a boy who could talk to animals. Janir began to drift off, but each time I paused he said, "Keep on telling it, Daddy."

I felt him unwind beside me, his arms and legs twitching as his muscles relaxed. Finally he slept, as limp as a young rabbit. Though I'd gotten along fine without him, it was lovely to have him back. His hair was shiny, his arms tanned, his eyelashes thick and long. I lay a hand on his chest and felt him breathe, mile after mile through the Kentucky night.

•   •   •

The pleasure of having him was immediately tempered by the extra work. The next morning I couldn't just roll out of bed and start pruning tomatoes, I had to unpack his bags, fix his breakfast, clean up the kitchen—and then he wanted someone to play with.

I called Suzanne Sweeney, drove into town and brought back her son Matt. The next day another friend, and the next day another. I owed some child care to almost everyone on my list, so it was a good time to make that up—but it all meant lots of work. I couldn't stay in the garden, I had to go back to the house repeatedly to check up on the kids. I fed them lunch, read them a story, set up a water slide on the lawn, knocked off work altogether and took them swimming at the pond. After three days I was exhausted. But there was no retreat. Like a marathon runner upping his miles, I bent my will to the unending round of meals, games, clothes and cleanups. The house was a mess. There was never enough food. Janir ran through every friend. There was nothing to do.

"Why don't we have a TV?" he said.

I shrugged. "No reception. Not down in this hollow."

"You just don't want one."

"Well, that's also true."

"You could get it for me," he said. "Lennie has one. And a puppy, too. Why can't I have a puppy?"

"Because puppies grow into dogs, and dogs are work and I've got plenty of work already. *You* are plenty of work."

"I am not."

In two minutes he was close to tears. In San Salvador he had lived in a house full of family where there was always someone to pay attention to him. Here we argued, we fought, slowly we strapped ourselves into the yoke of our common life. It would have been easier if we had a television. It would have been easier if my family lived nearby. It would have been easiest of all if I were married to Ellie, for then Teague would have been an instant sibling. But Ellie wasn't ready for that. She was still clawing her way out of her first marriage, not thinking about the next, as I was.

•   •   •

Some nights, too worn out to cook, I drove Janir into town for dinner. We liked the old Towne House restaurant where we could always get a booth. We took Paddington Bear with us and sat him in a corner as we ate.

No health food at the Towne House, just big juicy burgers, chicken-fried steaks, and chocolate sundaes served in scarred metal cups. After the meal Janir slipped around to my side of the table and I read him a story as if we were at home on the couch. One of the waitresses, Marie, a tiny Irishwoman with stockings rolled down below her knees, was especially fond of Janir. Sometimes she brought a sliver of pie "for Paddington" on a separate plate, then sat in the booth behind us when I started to read. She would tap out a cigarette and pretend to smoke it, as if on break. She didn't actually light it, because she knew I hated the smell. She just liked to hear the story.

One night, after I'd finished reading and Marie had left to fill the ketchup bottles, Janir sat up and asked, "What's Mom doing now?"

"She must be back in San Francisco by now."

"Where's that?"

"In California. That's where your mom and I got married. Before you were even a dot in eternity."

He was not in the mood for jokes. He gripped my shirt and pulled on it, frowning. "She's not at Paquita's?" he asked.

"I don't think so. Do you miss her?"

He didn't say anything.

"How come you were so ready to come back?" I asked—but still he didn't answer. "Was your mom good to you down there?"

"She laughs at Tia Blanca," he said. "Because she eats tortillas funny."

"Blanca doesn't have any teeth."

"And sometimes she gets angry."

"At you?"

"Yeah. And I get angry at her. When she gives me bad food."

I wanted to know how things had gone in El Salvador during his visit, but peering through the screen of his five-year-old consciousness was little more than a guessing game. I waited to see if any more bits of information were forthcoming—but he had said all he cared to.

On the way home he sat beside me in the truck. It was simple this way, to be the single parent of an only child. No one helped, but no one got in the way. Though Janir hardly had a mother, and I only half had a woman, day after day we had each other. There were times that was all I wanted.

•   •   •

The next weekend we drove up to Yellow Springs, and from the moment I stepped into Ellie's house I could feel her uneasiness. It was the aftermath of Michael's visit the previous weekend. She kissed me on the cheek, then picked up Janir and asked him a dozen questions about his trip. Then she went back to fixing dinner.

I let her be nervous. Finally, when we got into bed that night, I asked her what was wrong.

"I don't know," she said.

"Yes you do."

She wrapped the sheet around her legs. "It's the same old story."

"You mean Michael."

"He's so insistent."

"About what?"

"You know. He wants his family back."

"And you?" I asked.

She sat rocking slightly, binding the sheet to her calves. "I don't know what I want."

I knew what I wanted: for Ellie to leave Michael. Yet I understood her dilemma. Just as she was now separating Teague from his father, I had separated Janir from his mother. And two years later I still worried about that.

All that weekend I was ruled by doubt. I remembered Ovid's maxim from one of his poems in *The Art of Love:* She who follows, I fly from, she who flies from me, I follow. Ovid wrote some delightful poems—but he also claimed that what keeps love alive is insecurity. I hated that idea, it didn't sound like real love at all. Yet the truth was that when I feared Ellie would leave me, I ached for her all the more.

I watched her struggle with the juggernaut of her marriage. I had done the same myself and emerged single—but she might not. And if she didn't, how much time would I have wasted? Janir was getting older, he was already five and I wanted him to have a sibling. What if I had to get started with some other woman?

But I didn't want some other woman. I wanted Ellie.

•   •   •

A couple of Sundays later, after reading the kids to sleep, I sat at the foot of Ellie's bed. She closed her book on her finger. "It's too bad, John. You should have a woman who likes kids."

"Hey, I know you like kids. Our kids, at least."

"They're driving me crazy."

It was true her patience had been eroding. Recently I'd tried to take up the slack and do more than my share of child care, as she had done at the start. But this hadn't solved the problem of finding time alone for the two of us. Some weekends we didn't have a single moment apart from our boys until they went to sleep at night.

We spent all our days with them. We took them to the movies, to caves, to Clifton Gorge, to the duck pond, to a festival in Dayton, to the state fair in Columbus, to the library, to the college green, to the playground, to the reservoir, to the mill. The boys got along well together, but often it was our attention they wanted.

At home in Ellie's small apartment we tried to be discreet when sharing our affections. But Teague was six, he knew what was going on, and it was impossible to disguise the fact that I had taken his father's place in his mother's bed. I worried about that, but I slept there every weekend.

When Janir was away in El Salvador I gave Teague lots of attention. I read to him, played catch in the alley and taught him how to ride his new bike. On one level we got along fine—but he also threw some wild tantrums that month. One night when Ellie had gone to the store he ran screaming into his room, tore the covers off his bed, kicked his toys and flung them against the walls. When an airplane banged against a window I lost my temper. I picked him up and pinned him against the wall, holding him there until he broke down and cried. Though I didn't actually hit him, I manhandled and overpowered him.

Immediately overcome by remorse, I lowered him to the floor and tried to apologize. He wouldn't listen. He ran to his bed and buried himself under a sheet. I knelt beside him to explain, but he cried out over and over through his tears, "I don't want to hear it, I don't want to hear it."

Of course not. Who wants to talk things over after being physically subdued and humiliated? I had reacted hotly, angrily, and done something I hated.

When I confessed to Ellie she said she understood. But for the rest of the weekend I felt a slight cool distance between us, the scrim of her restraint.

•   •   •

Janir never flew into tantrums the way Teague did. Instead he whined and complained—which over the long run drove me almost as crazy. What set him off was often a mystery, and I could never predict when he would lapse into a three-year-old's nagging tone of voice. Sometimes he whined when I didn't give him enough attention, and sometimes after I'd spent all day with him.

It was clearly not beyond his control, for he never whined to other parents or kids—only to me. One afternoon as I sat on Ellie's couch reading, I heard him ask her in the kitchen, "Can I have a soda?"

"I don't think so, Janir. We'll have dinner soon."

"I'll eat my dinner." He sounded agreeable, even perky: his best shot with Ellie. "All of it, I promise."

"Well, you can ask your dad."

He stuck his head around the corner, his mouth turning down, his face already pinched. "Can I have a soda?" he complained.

I shook my head.

"Why not?" he said, drawing out the words in a dismal mix of lamentation and defeat.

The intensity of his complaint was seldom keyed to the magnitude of his grievance. At home he put as much work into "I don't *want* peas for dinner," as he did into "I don't *want* to go to the dentist."

I wondered if he whined instead of crying, if the misery in his voice was an expression of some primal loss, an ache I could not assuage. Though he rarely talked about his mother, perhaps this was the mark of how much he missed her. On his visit to El Salvador the two of them had fought constantly, and he'd been adamant about coming home early. Still, he must have mourned her absence.

He had seen his mother drift away, and now he saw how much in love I was with Ellie. Knowing he might fear I too could leave him, I assured him often that I never would. I told him I would always love and take care of him—but perhaps he feared it anyway.

Most days Janir was a robust and sunny child. Then, for no apparent reason, the whimpers would overtake him.

"When are we going to *eat?*" he moaned, even as I cooked dinner. He made it sound as if I'd threatened to cut off his food.

"I don't *know* where my shoes are," he lamented.

"I don't *have* any friends."

"Why don't we ever do what *I* want?"

Occasionally, when relaxed, I could stand back and admire his delivery, the artful way he bent his notes. He might have been a bluesman playing a mournful sax. Other times, when he whined about the heat or the rain or some small impediment to his desires, and when he kept it up too long, a rage would boil up inside me. I'd want to spray him down with the garden hose or lock him in his room. I'd want to take off in my truck and let the little bastard fend for himself for a couple of hours.

Over two or three years I waged several campaigns against his whining. I tried punishing him for it, but that only made it worse. I tried to ignore it, but couldn't. In the end all I could do was weigh his comments and act on them as neutrally as possible—because if he whined for dinner I was going to feed him anyway, and if he whined for a candy bar at the checkout counter I wasn't going to give it to him.

I was always careful about promises and threats. If he acted up in the car, I didn't tell him I was going to put him out beside the road and make him walk home, because obviously I wasn't going to do that. And unless I was prepared to stand on it, I didn't tell him he could only have ice cream if he finished his potatoes, or that he couldn't go to the circus until he cleaned up his room. I certainly didn't threaten him with that if I'd already bought the tickets.

I also tried not to lie to him, ever. All around me I saw parents lying freely to their children. They told them the doctor's shot wouldn't hurt, that there were no cookies left, that they didn't have enough money with them to buy that toy. All lies, and the kids usually knew it.

I tried not to lie—but there were times I wasn't completely candid. "Daddy," Janir said one night as we were eating dinner, "I want to spend the night at Joshua's."

"Okay, sometime you can."

"No, I want to go tonight."

"Well . . . we'll have to see about that."

That was a lie. We weren't going to see about it, because I already knew I wasn't going to drive halfway across the county and back at seven-thirty at night. But I also knew that if I admitted to that in so many words, Janir would start fussing. With the natural perspicacity of a five-year-old, he understood that although I resisted it, whining sometimes worked.

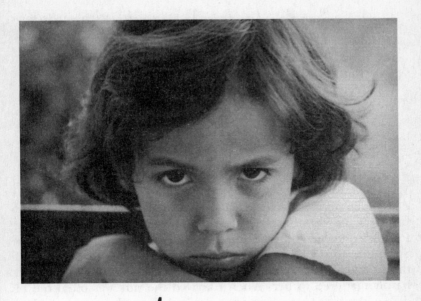

Janis at 5

T H I R T E E N

ALMOST EVERY SATURDAY THAT SUMMER I CAME HOME from the farmers' market, cleaned out the truck, packed a bag for Janir and me and made the two-and-a-half-hour drive to Yellow Springs. And week by week I watched Ellie change. By the end of the summer her domestic life, so important when we'd first met, hardly mattered to her. When I arrived the sink was often full of dishes, the floors were dusty and the beds unmade. Teague looked after his own room, and it was trashed.

"I've been keeping house my whole life," Ellie said. "I'm sick of it."

Though our sex was still compelling, she was no longer interested in anything that smacked of taking care of me. At night we had often brushed each other's hair—my own was almost as long as hers —but not anymore. There had been a time when she'd served me cozy dinners with artichoke hearts and a glass of Beaujolais, and brownies for dessert—but now either I did the cooking or it was pizza by phone.

I got by. I didn't need anyone to wash or cook for me. But I missed our old easy touch, and for a month I tried to set up a trade: if she would cut my fingernails, I'd shave her legs in the tub.

That was kind of a joke and kind of not. My mother, as I'd told Ellie, had trimmed my nails until I was well into my twenties. When I came home for vacation from boarding school or college we often sat and talked as she clipped, then smoothed them with an emery board. It was a ritual we'd held on to: a last excuse to hold hands after physical contact became awkward for us.

"Think how pleasant it would be," I joked with Ellie. "And think of the symbolism. You could trim my claws back to nothing."

"Think of how your mother did it, and now you want me to do it. There's your symbolism."

We laughed, but she ignored my nails and I no longer got invited into the tub with her.

In August she took a weekend job tending bar. At ten before seven on Saturday nights, only a few hours after Janir and I arrived, she pinned up her hair and left for work. She had never been gregarious, and bartending wasn't easy for her, but that was partly why she took the job. She wanted to work, to make money and get out in the world. When she returned after midnight she smelled of beer and cigarette smoke.

Everyone at the bar must have wanted her, I was sure. Men were watching her—and women too, for there were many lesbians in Yellow Springs. Late one night as we lay on her bed after making love she said, "I wish someone would tell me what casual sex was all about, so I wouldn't have to do it to find out."

"It's nothing, El. It's nothing at all."

"Maybe not, but I want to know anyway."

I lay beside her, both frightened and stung by her honesty: the candor I had always asked of her.

•   •   •

At the end of September Michael drove up to Yellow Springs for a second visit. All weekend he tried to talk Ellie into coming home —and she was half persuaded.

"Why couldn't I love you both?" she asked me the next time I saw her.

"I'm sure you do."

"Who says it has to be either him or you? Who says it has to be one life or the other? You still love Clarisa, don't you? That's what you told me."

"But I'm not going back to her."

"Well, I still love Michael."

All day the topic came at us like waves against a beach. Ellie, who sometimes smoked a cigarette after dinner, but never around the kids, now lit one after lunch and smoked it at the kitchen table with nervous fingers. She sat down, stood up again, stubbed out the cigarette, crossed her arms under her breasts. There was her wedding ring on her left hand, the same as ever.

I reached out and tapped it. "Is that how you feel? That you're still married?"

"I *am* still married. And I feel all kinds of things. Don't box me in here."

It rained all day. The apartment was in shambles and the kids in a frenzy. I felt like I might explode myself, and at dusk took Teague and Janir over to the Antioch gym so we could work out on the tumbling mats and trampoline. Afterward we sprinted home through the dark as a chill rain pelted the ground and gusty winds shook loose storms of sodden leaves. It was too cold for early October.

By the time we got back, Ellie had left for work. I cleaned up the house and fixed dinner for the kids, gave them a bath and read to them from Roald Dahl. By nine they were both asleep. Taking care of them, somehow, was easier with Ellie out of the house. But once alone I could not just sit and read. At ten I put my coat on and took a solitary walk through the storm, trying to settle my heart. I made one loop and then another, returning to check up on the kids. I peered in at them through the window. In the dim glow of a night light they lay curled on their mattresses on the floor, one dark boy and one blond, each embracing an animal.

I wanted Ellie and no other woman. I wanted to marry her, or at least live with her and our boys. If she didn't want that, I didn't know how much longer I could wait, or how much sorrow I could live with.

•   •   •

Halloween came round again, a year since Janir ran up to me in his spotted cape and tail and announced, "I decided to be a cheetah!" This year the older kids from his school had discovered trick-or-treating and didn't want to settle for a party in the sticks. So Will Dewees, a couple of other parents and I drove them into Athens and turned them loose in one of the town's wealthier neighborhoods. There our ragamuffin crew of ghosts, pirates and astronauts moved hard for the plunder, hustling straight across the manicured lawns from one big house to the next. The city only gave them ninety minutes. At first Janir looked fierce and exotic, wearing a papier-mâché mask I had worked on for hours the night before. But the mask was too large and heavy and kept slipping down his face. After the first couple of houses he ran up and handed it to me without a word. It was defective. It didn't work.

He had asked for a simple store-bought costume, but instead of buying what he wanted I'd tried to live up to some image I had of my own childhood Halloweens, when my mother had gotten up elaborate costumes for me and my brother. And so the exotic mask: unique but useless.

After handing it to me Janir turned and sprinted after the other kids, his black cape trailing behind him. The cape was my college graduation gown pinned up so he could walk, and now the pins were coming loose. He stumbled on it, almost fell, then picked up the front of it and hustled after his friends. He wanted to keep up with the bigger kids and fill his bag with treats—but now, without the protection of a mask, he had to face one stranger after another and answer their inevitable questions about his disintegrating costume. Once he passed by close to tears, one hand clutching his cape and the other his paper bag. I stepped aside from the other parents in case he wanted some help, but he barely gave me a glance.

On his own turf Janir was often self-assured, even forward. If I picked up a hitchhiker on our way back from Yellow Springs he would check the guy out, start a conversation from the backseat, sometimes climb into his lap and play with his ears.

Other times, like tonight, the world threatened to overwhelm him. All the way home in Will's old Dodge I held him close. He didn't say anything but nestled against me, his candy forgotten in its bag on the floor. Will dropped us off, and I carried Janir into the house. I felt so tender I never let go of him as I set his treats on his dresser, took off his clothes and put on his pajamas, brushed his teeth, pulled back the covers, lay down beside him and read him a story. After that a song about a lady and a crocodile, then a hug, then the world's shortest story: "Once upon a time there was a fly on the wall, and that's all." I tucked him in with his animals, turned off the light and lay beside him until he slept.

•   •   •

Over Thanksgiving I tried to plan something with Ellie for Christmas. "We could visit my brother," I told her. "Or just go to North Carolina and rent a place on the Outer Banks. It's peaceful there."

She stared out the window. "It sounds cold and lonely."

"Perfect for you," I said, and left the house.

She didn't follow me, we never talked it out, that night we had hard brilliant sex. In the morning we were polite with each other, distant and guarded.

•   •   •

My friends Peter and Rhonda were farming in Belize, and I had a long-standing invitation to visit them. I didn't want to sit around over Christmas being miserable about Ellie, so I sent them a letter to say Janir and I were coming, and bought two round-trip tickets to Belize City.

Janir dozed off on the late-night flight out of Columbus. I carried him off in New Orleans, laid him on a bench and sat beside him the rest of the night, immersed in Lael Wertenbaker's luminous book about her husband's cancer, *Death of a Man*. Death, loss, endings: that was all I wanted to read about.

In the morning Janir and I washed up, ate breakfast and confirmed our seats on TACA for the flight to Belize City—a flight booked mainly by wealthy Salvadorans who were continuing on to El Salvador. The lobby was jammed with men in dark suits, and stylish women in calf-length skirts and platform shoes. It was 1975. The little girls wore flouncy skirts, and the boys wore nylon shirts printed with soaring seagulls. Janir shared the color and physiognomy of most of the kids in the lobby, but there the resemblance ended, for they were all restrained Latin bourgeois, and Janir was a fanatical cowboy-and-Indian. The night before, he'd chosen his own clothes for the trip: sneakers, a worn but favorite pair of pants and his Big Foot T-shirt, on which a monster pickup crushed a row of other vehicles.

A boy about Janir's age was playing with a small Hot Wheels car. Janir had several of those at home, and I was immediately sorry I hadn't brought one along, for the glazed lobby floor made a perfect track. Janir, though often outgoing with other kids, didn't mosey over and ask the boy if they could shoot the car back and forth. I understood why. First, the boy spoke Spanish—which Janir, in spite of all my efforts, had almost entirely forgotten. And second, the boy was fastidious with his toy. He knelt down, watched to make sure no one was walking by, then sent it on a judicious ride and ran immediately to pick it up. He never allowed his hands, his striped short pants or anything other than his polished shoes to touch the floor.

I kept thinking Janir would sidle up to me, hang on my knees and ask me in a whisper, "Daddy, will you buy me a car like that?" Instead he took out a Canadian quarter, given to him by a man at the ticket counter, and held it between his fingers. When a space opened up in the lobby he shot the coin underhand so that it slid across the floor directly in front of the boy with the striped pants and leather shoes. Then he sprinted across the lobby and hit the polished floor at full tilt, sliding up to his quarter like Phil Rizzuto into third base. He picked up the quarter, rose to his knees, turned to the other boy and delivered him a long even stare. Janir had taken his measure. The kid may have had new pants and a nifty toy, but he couldn't dive and slide and clean up the floor with his clothes.

For a long time the two of them played side by side, the boy with his car and Janir with his quarter. They watched each other but didn't speak. Janir was not very careful. He slid all over the floor, ran among people's legs and sometimes poked among bags and suitcases for his coin. But I didn't stop him. I sat there once again, thinking about Clarisa. So much of how I raised Janir still came from her. It would not have been her way to make a little adult out of him at five. She would have let him test and explore at will, I was sure.

●　　●　　●

Both Janir and I found Belize City intimidating, with its raucous street life and strong smells, and the baffling English dialect most of the black population spoke. We spent the night in a flimsy wooden hotel where coughs and sighs filtered in from the other rooms, and at seven in the morning caught a bus for "PG," Punta Gorda.

An hour into the ride Janir's culture shock disappeared. He climbed over the seats, made friends with everyone on the old U.S. school bus, sat down next to portly black women and their children and got them to join his chant, "One-two-three . . . *PG*!"

Instead of one-two-three it was a twelve-hour trip, and by the time we got off the bus in the rural Toledo district it was already dark. A teenage boy offered to show us the way to the Duttons' farm, and after a mile on the white gravel road Janir grew tired. I lifted him onto the top of my knapsack, where he clutched my head, nodding and falling asleep. The road curved on through open pastures and the encroaching jungle, until the boy stopped at a grassy pathway lined with banana and orange trees, all carefully mulched.

"Down there," he said, and promptly went on his way.

Janir woke up and said he would walk. After three hundred yards we came to a clearing with a dark house. We stood watching it for a moment, listening to the sounds of the night. Then I yelled, "Wake up, *compadres!*"

"Yeah, you guys," Janir chimed in, "wake up!"

Peter and Rhonda appeared at the upstairs window, at first mystified. They hadn't gotten my letter.

Rhonda was the first one down. "And what," she said, "is this peanut doing way out here in the bush?" She lifted Janir up and spun him around.

"I'm not a peanut," he said. But he was pleased.

Rhonda was a California girl, handsome as an actress. She'd grown up in the suburbs, married Peter, and now she was chopping bush with a machete, raising vegetables and selling them at the farmers' market in PG.

"You just looked like a peanut in the dark," she said. "Aren't you sleepy?"

"I had a nap and my daddy carried me. Now I can stay up all night."

Peter and Rhonda had built their house out of posts, planks and palm fronds. There was a dirt-floored kitchen downstairs and an airy bedroom on the second floor. There we sat on mats and talked. It was a simple life here in Belize: they worked the soil with mattocks and machetes, while I tilled the ground in Ohio with my old Ford tractor. But we were all glad to be farming, and it was a joy to see their smiling faces again, to forget briefly about Ellie, to talk about composting and the tilth of our soils. Peter and I found we could both still quote from memory the advice of an Indian chieftain we had once found inscribed in Spanish on a wall in Mexico City's Museum of Anthropology:

> *Take care of the things of the earth.*
> *Do something. Cut firewood, work the ground.*
> *Plant prickly pears, plant maguey.*
> *You will have to drink, to eat, to dress.*
> *With that you will be upright. You will be truthful.*
> *With that you will be spoken of and praised.*
> *With that you will make yourself known.*

This advice from a simpler world had reached across centuries and gripped us both. *Haz algo:* Do something. *Ten cuidado de las cosas de la tierra:* Take care of the things of the earth.

• • •

When I rose at five Peter had already finished cooking both breakfast and lunch. All morning we seeded beans and corn, threshed sesame seeds and transplanted young peppers. Then a midday meal of tortillas, beans, tomatoes and squash, then a swim in Cacao Creek, then more work in the garden and finally, at dusk, a bowl of rice grown on the farm.

Shortly after sunset each night Janir volunteered for bed. Down he went with only a brief story, and by eight Peter and Rhonda were asleep as well. Alone in the downstairs kitchen I hung the Coleman lantern from a nail next to the open shutters, stretched out in a hammock and read *The Rainbow,* escaping into the tumultuous English farm world of Lawrence's novel.

After an hour, though still wide awake, I crimped the page and turned off the light. The lantern's hiss grew soft, then died away. Let it be, I thought, still trying to calm myself down. If Ellie had to leave me she would, and there was nothing I could do about it here in Belize. Yet I could not relax. I knew how easily she could find a new man—if she didn't have one already.

• • •

Christmas morning I woke with the first blue light. Peter and Rhonda had already built a fire, made coffee and laid out the presents we had wrapped the night before in banana and dasheen leaves. The three of us knelt beside Janir and nudged him.

"Wake up, little peanut," Rhonda said. "I think Santa came."

He struggled to his feet, crashed back onto his mat, then looked around and saw the presents in the glow of the candlelight. He leapt up, his eyes shining.

"Look at that! He was here!" He examined the remains of the offerings we had set out the night before. "He ate part of a cookie."

"It might have been just an elf," Peter suggested. "It's a long way down here from the North Pole."

"*No.* It was Santa Claus." Janir stared at the plate with reverence, as if Santa's hand had just touched it. "He ate all the papaya, there's just some slime left. And he didn't drink the milk. I *knew* he wouldn't like that goat milk. Hey, this present's mine! It's got my name on it!''

We opened the presents—I'd smuggled down a slingshot and a rubber-band airplane in my knapsack—and ate the cookies and sweet bread we had baked the day before. We drank the traditional campesino beverage, *maiz tostado,* a bitter black coffee made from toasted corn.

Rhonda and Peter were great with Janir, recounting Christmas stories from their own childhood and local legends from Belize. I tried to be part of it but could hardly listen. My heart would not calm down. I couldn't evade the dream I'd woken up to, in which Ellie and her sister floated past me through the trees, both silvery and naked.

"Have you heard?" her sister asked me.

"No, what?" I asked.

"Oh, I must tell you."

But she didn't. Instead I woke up in a panic and immediately guessed the news: that Ellie was leaving me.

•   •   •

That night I lay again in the kitchen hammock with the lights out and everyone else asleep. The bush whirred and shifted outside the window. There were tarantulas in the woodpile—Peter had smashed one our first day there—and scorpions that sometimes dropped onto the bedroom floor from the rafters. Creatures moved through the nearby bush, and all I could think about was Ellie.

She was going to leave me. I'd been the one to spring her from her marriage, but now I held her back. She had to wander and be free.

I lay in the swaying hammock. I tried to make it come to a complete dead stop, but couldn't. Perhaps it was the rosewood posts it hung from, oscillating faintly under the bulk of the house and a breeze too light to feel. Perhaps it was my breath that made the hammock move, or the beat of my heart, but it would not hang motionless.

By now I'd long accepted the limits on my freedom that came with being a father. Years ago I'd moved to the far end of South America to study the "true necessaries" of peasant life— only to discover in Ohio the change that dwarfs most others: the elemental servitude of raising a child. In the last few years Janir had quartered my involvement in sports, music and writing. He had drawn me down into the unceremonious backwaters in which educated men and women spent their time packing lunchboxes, washing muddy sneakers and playing ludicrous board games. Yet it never occurred to me that I had learned less about life because of him.

Ellie had married at nineteen, had a child, lived for seven years in the conjugal box. Now she'd had enough of it. I was in love with her at the wrong time. She wanted to flirt and dance and find out how attractive she was to other men. She had not the least interest in a conventional life.

The coals were extinguished in the earthen stove, and the darkness absolute. Only forty feet away the jungle was full of noise. It was so warm at night the vegetation never stopped growing. I listened, trying to distinguish one sound from another. Finally I got up and walked out of the house toward the bush. I was afraid of snakes but went anyway. I stood next to the curtain of moist vines and creepers, my bowels churning and my heart slamming against the walls of my chest.

Ellie McGlynn had been a dream. I had thought I could fly off with her and our two boys, make an instant family and forget all about my history with Clarisa. But that wasn't going to happen. I was not going to wind up in some cozy house with Ellie. I was going to wind up with my son and the specter of his mother, a disturbed and unruly woman bound to us by blood forever.

I stepped inside the curtain. I thought of the story a neighbor had told us two days before: he'd been chopping weeds with his machete, heard a muffled sound from inside the bush and stepped in to see what it was. He went farther, his eyes adjusting to the dim light, until he saw what was making the noise: a small deer struggling in the coils of a giant snake. Snakes sometimes caught their prey here by dropping from above.

I felt like that deer, squeezed by the coils of my own life. What I had started with Clarisa would never end. I groped a few more feet into the bush. Leaves brushed my face, a vine touched my arm and made me jump. There were noises. I stopped and listened.

Something stabbed my ankle. A fer-de-lance, I thought, a coral snake. But there was another bite, and another. They were fire ants. I burst back into the clearing, scraped them off, removed one sandal and then the other as I stumbled into the house. I stood in the kitchen breathing hard, then felt my way to the ladder. I climbed it in the dark, found Janir and crouched on the mat beside him. He was stretched out on his back, his sheet tossed off, completely naked and heedless. Just waiting, I thought, for a scorpion to land on him. But none had so far, and none would in the days that remained before we headed back to Ohio.

SHE LEFT ME.

I raged across my farm, crashing through the underbrush, flailing my machete at crabapples and wild grapevines. I took Janir to school in the mornings, came home, lay on the living-room rug and wept. I shaved my beard. I worked too much and gave my son too little attention. I joined a men's group. Each morning I jerked awake at four or five after dreaming of Ellie. I gathered all her letters and photos and burned every one. Nothing helped.

And that was the year every woman seemed to want me. Was I marked somehow? Was it the heartache that drew them? In the next twelve months I went out with five spunky and attractive women. I told them all exactly where I stood, for having suffered so with Ellie I didn't want to hurt anyone else. But they got hurt anyway, and my reputation spread through town as a guy with a careless heart. It was unfair, I thought, after I'd been so honest. But the truth was I should have stayed home. I wasn't ready to be kissing anyone.

I heard about Ellie through her friends: she got divorced from Michael, and after a few brief flings she found another man. I prayed she would fall in love with this new guy and he would leave her, so she would know how much it hurt. Or else he would die in a car crash. I imagined all the details: the telephone call late at night, her agony as she identified him at the morgue, her long nights of weeping.

Then he did have a car crash. The trouble was that Ellie and Teague were with him. That woke me up. I loved her, I didn't want her to suffer. Teague was okay, but Ellie fractured her neck and was in the hospital for weeks. Her recovery was slow but full.

• • •

Clarisa didn't come to Athens that year. I heard from her family she was pregnant, but no one knew anything about the father. I was thankful then for my restraint the previous summer: at least I knew *I* was not the father.

A month after her second son was born she called to tell us the news. Janir talked to her first. He turned to me and said, "I've got a baby brother!"

This was not the sibling I'd had in mind for him, but I was happy to see him so excited about it. When I got on the phone Clarisa told me her new son's name: John Leslie Thorndike.

At first I thought she was kidding. She wasn't. "Where's the Leslie from?" I asked.

"Nowhere. I just liked it."

Though at the time it annoyed me that she had commandeered my name, I later came to view it with some humor. The original John Thorndike had come to Boston in 1632, and he'd had several American namesakes since—but probably none quite like this boy, who had no Thorndike blood at all. What were the matrons who kept track of our genealogy going to make of that?

"How's your girlfriend?" Clarisa asked me on the phone.

"We're not going out anymore," I said.

"She dump you?"

How did she know that? I was too surprised, and still too hurt, to pretend it wasn't true. "Yeah," I admitted, "she did."

"Serves you right."

"For what?"

"Fucking her."

Clarisa could still put an arrow through me, any time.

•　　•　　•

One of my salvations that year was a men's group I joined with five or six friends. Those were early days for men's groups: we didn't read Bly or Jung or go on quests, we just met at Don Harse's every Monday night, ate pineapple upside-down cake and talked about our emotional lives. Sometimes we cried about our broken families or unhappy love affairs. Four of us were single parents, so our kids were often a topic.

In our eyes, more and more men were raising their children. In 1976 the counterculture still had a solid beachhead in Athens, Ohio. Outside the county, mainstream culture might have been dragging its feet, but here on our farms and communes we were in the thick of a continuing revolution. For single fathers—or anyone outside the norm—it made life easier. While child care could still weigh us down, it always helped to feel like a pioneer.

Will Dewees, the most evangelical of our group, drove up to New York State one weekend to deliver an unsolicited speech at a meeting of La Leche League. Will was a Ph.D. with a ponytail and a teaching job at Ohio University. He was also a single father, and he had a message for the members of the league, who had gathered to encourage the practice of breastfeeding. It's hard on fathers, he told them. It separates men from their children. It makes it difficult for a man to bond with his daughter. He pleaded for at least the occasional use of a bottle, starting in the earliest days of an infant's life.

They gave his speech a cool reception, but we laughed and shouted when he returned with his report.

●   ●   ●

That fall, at the age of thirty-four, I got serious about a new sport. I joined Ohio University's club volleyball team, submitted my will to an exigent coach and traveled to tournaments all over the state. My teammates were undergraduates in their teens and early twenties.

I took Janir to dozens of practices at OU's Grover Gym. While I ran drills with the team he wandered through the building exploring the locker rooms, the weight rooms, the racquetball courts and tumbling mats. Occasionally we practiced across the street at the giant Convocation Center on a glossy maple floor under a ninety-foot roof. There Janir shagged balls for the coach or chased the pigeons that clapped back and forth under the dome.

"Hey, Daddy!"

I looked up from the middle of a spiking drill, scanned the building and found him standing on a chair on the topmost row of seats. It was steep up there. I'd already told him ten times to be careful.

"What are you doing?" I yelled.

"I'm chasing the bird!" Some two dozen pigeons lived inside the building. No one could catch them, and Janir had taken a fancy to a white one that stood out from the others. "The bicentennial bird!" he cried.

He was six, and the country two hundred.

I often took him to tournaments at Ohio Wesleyan, Oberlin and

Kent State. He liked to go with a friend—Matt or Joy or Jesse—and I let them roam the gyms at will. If there were mats to crash on, they found them. If there was a pool with open hours and a lifeguard, they swam. Inevitably they ran up against managers and custodians, but Janir could usually charm them. He was always a scammer. He's still that way. He loves to get ahead in line, sneak into a movie, get something for nothing.

We couldn't find a friend for him one Saturday for a tournament at Miami of Ohio, so he had to look after himself. He got bored but waited it out, and his reward was a shower and a long game of slip-the-soap after our last match. He ran ahead of me into the shower room, lifted his arms and cried, "Let the wild rumpus begin!"

I tossed a bar of soap on the floor and he stomped on it, driving it across the tiles. Then he careened after it, diving past other players. His feet were slippery and the floor hard, but I let him take the risk, because he loved this game above all others. He pushed past everyone in his way, chased the soap between their legs, showed not a hint of modesty about his naked buns.

No wonder I got along so well with the college kids on my team. They didn't care if Janir jumped around and banged into them. They thought it was fun. The rowdier he got, the more they liked it. And they loved him for his reckless comments. When one of the Miami players—an exceptionally hairy young man—stepped into the room and started to take a shower, Janir paused to inspect him.

"You look like a goat!" he cried.

Somebody dropped a towel over the room's central drain, and soon there were three inches of water on the floor. That was heaven for Janir. He pushed off from one wall, ran two steps, did a belly-flop and sloshed across the floor. For twenty minutes he kept it up as the players finished and left the room to the two of us. I turned on all the shower heads and let them run, wasting hundreds of gallons of water to make my boy happy.

•   •   •

Sometime that year he stopped whining. Maybe it was because I'd split up with Ellie. Maybe he just grew out of it.

In the spring Clarisa asked if I'd let him fly across the country to meet his half brother. They would all stay with Clarisa's Aunt Teresa in San Francisco, so I agreed. He would be safe there.

Janir, at five and a half, was eager to take his first flight alone. I kissed him good-bye at the Columbus airport, and a stewardess walked him over the concrete apron to the plane. She tried to hold his hand but he wouldn't let her. He marched along beside her, then scampered up the aluminum stairs. At the top he finally looked back, found me and waved.

When I called him that night he was full of details about the trip. "I ate steak," he said. "Mom was at the airport. Teresa has a *good* house."

He sounded fine, so at the last minute I joined my volleyball team for a road trip to Daytona Beach and a week-long tournament on the sand. I caught a ride with my teammate Bill Renz, his girlfriend and another couple, and we spent five days swimming, eating, playing volleyball all day and dancing half the night. It didn't matter that I was fifteen years older than everyone else. I'd missed spring break and everything like it when I was in college, so I soaked it up now. I slept on the beach and lived out of my knapsack. I hadn't been so irresponsible in years.

At dusk of the fifth day I stood under the bonnet of a public phone and dialed Teresa's number. The night was warm, the sky full of pastel clouds, the beach crowded with cars. Teresa picked up the phone.

"Hi, Teresa," I said cheerfully. "Is Janir there?"

"Oh, John. I better let him talk to you."

I knew there was trouble. He said, "I want to go home," and there was a catch in his voice. "I want to go now."

"Janir, I'm at a tournament in Florida."

"You're not at my *house?*" He was outraged. "Where are you?"

I explained, but he didn't want to hear it. I was supposed to be at home waiting for him, sitting by the telephone, eating dinners alone. Forget my own life.

"I hate Mom," he said. "She's mean. She doesn't let me play with anyone. And she pinched me."

Clarisa grabbed the receiver and started in with her own complaints. "He won't listen to me," she said. "He won't do what I tell him."

I could hear Janir screaming and trying to get the phone back. Finally Teresa waded in and took over. "It's like this every day," she said.

I talked to Janir again and tried to calm him down. "I'll go home tomorrow," I said. "As soon as I get there you can fly back, okay?"

"Okay," he said—but when we hung up he was still close to tears.

Goddamn it, I couldn't get one miserable week free. And Janir had flown off to see her with such confidence, with such hope and trust. For once, like every other kid he knew, he was going to have a mother. Even I had let myself be persuaded of this dream. It was why I hadn't called him for five days. Now the truth had hammered us once again.

•   •   •

I caught a ride as far as Columbus, then hitched to Athens. I got Janir's return flight changed and met him two days later at the airport. He seemed resilient. He'd had a sorry visit but now he was home.

That night there was a kicker. As we nestled over a bedtime story he scratched his head. He did it again, and again. I sat him up so I could take a look at his scalp under the light. He'd never had dandruff before, but tiny white specks now dotted his hair. They were nits. He had lice. The eggs clung fiercely to individual hairs, and the only way to remove them, I discovered, was to pinch them and slide them out to the end of the hair. I searched around for a live insect but didn't find any.

"What is it, Daddy? What's there?"

I lifted him off the bed. "Time for a shampoo," I said.

"I just had a bath."

"I have to wash your hair. I think you've got some bugs."

"*Bugs?* I don't have any bugs."

"If there are any," I said, "we'll wash 'em out."

I doubted that would have much effect, but gave him a double shampoo and put him to bed. In the morning I sent him to school. His alternative school had closed, and he was now at Amesville Elementary. The nurse there would have a fit if she stumbled on this, but I didn't think the little buggers could jump from one head to another. Anyway, I'd take care of them that night.

As soon as he got on the bus I drove to town and bought some Rid-Ex. I read the directions on the enclosed sheet, went back to the farm, took all Janir's bedding, my own sheets and blankets, all the clothes he'd taken to California and everything those clothes had come in contact with, including the covers from the couch, piled everything into the bed of the pickup and did a humongous wash at the laundromat in town. It took hours. I set the dryers on high and baked every load. God *damn* Clarisa.

After school I soaked my head and Janir's in a hefty dose of the Rid-Ex. It smelled strong enough to eradicate anything smaller than a dog, and was supposed to kill both lice and eggs. Included in the package was a fine-toothed comb designed to extract the nits—but the comb didn't work on Janir's fine hair. No matter how many times I ran it through it failed to capture more than one egg in twenty. I did comb out a single dead louse, and we inspected it on a sheet of white paper. Janir poked at it, then we burned it just in case.

The next morning I sent him off to school again, reasonably confident that the problem was solved. Yet only a few days later I saw him scratching his head over dinner. In the bald white light of my desk lamp I took another look—and there were more eggs now than before. I parted the forest of his hair and peered down into it, exploring tiny sections of his scalp. I looked everywhere, and finally saw a single brown louse scurrying out of sight, losing itself in the hairs.

One day of treatment followed the next. Rid-Ex, Nix, A-200, finally a prescription for Kwell. I searched the town for finer combs, washed all our clothes again and shampooed both of us morning and night. Nothing helped. Outside, the organic fields of my farm went free of all chemicals, while daily I poured these toxins from bottles labeled Danger! onto my child's scalp. And none of them worked. Every medication promised to kill eggs as well as lice, and none did. I could tell, because when still alive, the eggs would pop between two fingernails. I spent an arduous thirty minutes removing individual nits from Janir's hair—but by then there were thousands of them. It was like trimming a lawn with nail clippers.

I knew the one sure remedy: I could cut off his hair. But Janir had lustrous beautiful hair, and I didn't want to send him off to school with a ferocious buzz cut that would make him look like . . . well, like a kid with lice. Slowly I faced the truth. Chemicals and combs were not going to solve the problem. The only sure way was to pick out all the eggs by hand, every last one of them.

We did it in the spring sunshine, on the lawn behind the house where I could throw the eggs to the ground. We spent two hours a day at it, and it drove Janir nearly mad. I used a pair of needle-nosed tweezers that sometimes caught and pulled at his hair.

"Go ahead," he screamed, *"Just cut it all off."*

I came close, but didn't. After devoting a full week to his scalp and hair, I pronounced them clean.

•   •   •

One night in the car, on our way to dinner in town, Janir and his friend Clayton got the giggle fits in the backseat. I don't know what set them off: what is it, ever, but the mad joy of youth? I drove without a word, letting myself float on the wave of their hilarity. They were doubled over, poking at each other, making cryptic comments and bursting again into laughter.

They calmed down enough to get through the serving line of the new family steak house in town, but once in our booth they started laughing again, clowning and making faces. I was aware of the other diners, of the polite teenage waiters coming and going. But to me the giggle fits were sacred, and these my saints: a couple of six-year-olds cackling at the wiggle of an eyebrow, falling into convulsions at a single word. They ignored their steaks. They laughed so hard they slid under the table.

I kept eating. Half the restaurant must have heard them. I felt the pressure but I was not going to yield to it. My kid could laugh where he wanted. At the next table a beefy father was staring at me openly. His own prim wife and kids ate like prisoners in the Gulag, their heads down, their eyes on their plates.

I ignored them. I thought about a summer night at Lake Winnipesaukee with my brother, the first year we were old enough to be entrusted with a trip alone to the hotel restaurant. We were eight and five. Once seated we had started laughing. We goaded each other with funny words and faces. We were practically in tears when our hamburgers came, and from then on it was a battle to stifle our outright laughter. Once the hostess appeared to ask if we were enjoying our meals, and I managed to give her a silent nod. But as she walked off I risked a glance at Alan. His mouth was in his napkin, but his eyes bulged with glee, and for a horrifying instant I coughed out a burst of laughter.

We finished half our burgers, skipped dessert and signed the chit for the meal. We had to get outside. As we scurried past the hostess she remarked coolly, "I trust you boys are feeling better now." We nodded, opened the door and ran outside under the pine trees, eager to wallow in our laughter.

It was gone. We tried to get it back as we walked down to the lake. We made faces. We repeated the phrases that had seemed so comic inside the restaurant—"dumb doodlebug" and "baldheaded bastard"—but our delirious euphoria had vanished.

Out of the corner of my eye I could see the father at the next table, still staring at me. Maybe he thought his own children might catch the virus of Clayton and Janir's muffled laughter. Finally, girded by my abiding sense of loss from that night at Lake Winnipesaukee, I turned and gave the guy a fierce look, unblinking, Patton against Rommel: Shut your face, asshole. And amazingly, he looked away. Eventually my kids got up off the floor and onto their bench, and calmed down enough to eat their rib eyes. I sat there surprised at myself, exhilarated.

●　　●　　●

One Saturday in town we ran into Michelle Ajamian, who had been Janir's teacher for a year at the White Oak School. We were headed for the playground, Janir's reward for accompanying me on a series of boring errands. After that we had to go shopping, then out to the farm to meet a guy coming over with a load of manure.

Janir hung from my hand, mildly trying to drag me away as Michelle and I talked. After a while he gave up and entertained himself by poking along the gutter, looking for pennies or bottle caps, anything of interest. Michelle and I had lots to talk about, for she and Bill Renz and I were planning a party together. Finally, after Janir had been so patient, I realized there wasn't enough time to go to the playground before getting our shopping done, and home in time to tell the guy with the manure where to dump it.

"We'll have to go another day," I told him.

"*No,*" he said. He was outraged. I had promised him.

"I'm sorry," I said. "We can't do it. We've got to go shopping and get home."

He crumpled onto the sidewalk and thrashed about in his overalls, smacking the concrete with his hands and feet.

"You *promised,*" he cried. "You *have* to take me." He wailed and gagged as people walked by. Their glances only drove him to greater histrionics. When I tried to pick him up he squirmed wildly, jerked away and threw himself to the ground again. By now I'd had enough of him.

"I'm sorry," I said coldly. "It's too late."

"It's not too late!" he howled.

Michelle took it all in stride, as if one might commonly find an ululating child on the town's main street. She leaned over and whispered to me, "I love Janir. He's so passionate."

Janir sulked in the car as I blazed through the supermarket, and we got home just in time: the big tri-axle full of turkey bedding had just turned down the drive. But after the truck left I stood beside the rank pile regretting that I'd made Janir a promise and failed him. I could have taken him to the playground and gone shopping the next day. I'd just been annoyed when he started flailing around on the sidewalk, and had taken it out on him by claiming it was impossible to do what he wanted.

It was like a marriage. I made mistakes every day, and often repeated them.

·   ·   ·

Attention was all: knowing when Janir needed it, and slowing down enough to give it to him.

One snowy night I took him and Joy to the Shop Hop, an annual party at a friend's woodworking shop. I unloaded a sled and a plastic disk I'd brought along for the kids to play with on the steep front lawn of the house, and watched for a while as they forged a track and trudged back up the hill. It looked safe enough, so I told them to come inside when they got cold.

When they did, forty minutes later, I was dancing with Michelle to the Pointer Sisters and didn't want to stop. Joy was no problem. She pulled off her snowsuit, threw it in the corner and went looking for food. But Janir wanted me. He stood between me and Michelle and raised his hands. He wanted me to pick him up.

"Janir, I'm dancing. Take your suit off. Go upstairs with Joy and get something to eat."

"No." He stood doggedly in front of me. "Don't dance, Daddy."

I dragged myself out of the music and crouched beside him on the floor. "Are you okay?"

He shook his head. He looked sad.

"What is it? Did you hurt yourself?"

He shook his head again.

I stripped off his snowsuit and boots, checked his limbs, looked him over. "What is it?" I asked again, but he couldn't say.

Ahh, I thought. How simple it was. How could I be so dense? "You need some attention, don't you?"

He nodded soberly. I fussed with him, combed his hair with my fingers, kissed him, hugged him, then picked him up and danced with him.

It only took five minutes. By then he'd had enough of me. "Okay," he said.

"Don't you want to dance?" I'd made the transition, by now I was having fun with him.

"I'm hungry," he said, and squiggled to the floor. "Where's the food?"

•   •   •

Two years had passed since Ellie McGlynn, and my crying days were over: no more nights facedown on the living room rug with Mick Jagger on the stereo reminding me that you can't always get what you want. I still missed Ellie, but it was closer to how I missed my mother or Nana: I wanted to talk to her but couldn't.

By the time I met Natalia Fisher I'd almost forgotten how thrilling a romance could be. She was funny, fresh and daring. We had a breathtaking start but then ran into some barriers. My own, I'm afraid. I was still wary. I had a cautious, not a careless, heart and sex made me think of Ellie.

Natalia was younger and had lots of free time. I had Janir. I couldn't go dancing on Thursday night, to a movie on Friday and a party on Saturday. I was lucky to get out twice a week, and often it was only once. And the truth was, as Natalia pointed out, I didn't want to get out any more than that. Most nights I wanted to stay home with my boy.

After six months she took me for a walk by the Hocking River. "This isn't enough for me," she said. "I want to spend more time with you."

"It's enough for me," I said.

I might have couched it in softer terms. I was an idiot not to. But ever since Ellie I'd been prickly about the truth. I had to speak baldly. There could be no secrets, no hidden agendas, nothing left unsaid.

"Why don't you get a baby-sitter?" Natalia suggested. "You've got the money."

"Well, let me think about that."

I thought about it but never got one. I'd shared a few baby-sitters with other parents but had never hired one myself, not once in all those years. I knew Janir didn't want to be dropped off at somebody's house where he had no one to play with, and finding someone to look after him at home was equally problematic. Our farm was eight miles from town, with no television and no neighbors within hailing distance. At night it was dark and lonely. If a fifteen-year-old girl were there alone I'd have thought about getting *her* a sitter.

In fact, not having a baby-sitter was rarely a sacrifice, for when I went out to a party I wanted to be free for the night, not tied to a midnight deadline. Instead of hiring child care I traded it with other parents: I had a list as long as my arm. And our trades worked coming and going, for whenever Janir's friends spent the night at our house he had someone to play with.

•   •   •

He turned seven, then eight. His limbs grew longer and thinner. He had a quick smile, smooth skin and a booming fascination with his own anatomy. About the time I started going out with Natalia he entered a boisterous sexual phase of his own.

Psychoanalysts define *latency* as that period from about five years old to puberty when children repress their sexual urges. I have my doubts about that. From what I saw, the repression all seemed to originate externally, from parents and the rest of adult society.

My goal with Janir, as always, was to let him make his own choices. I extended that ideal to his friends when they came to visit, and for two or three years Janir and Kerri and Clayton and Allis and Millie and a half-dozen others, in pairs or small groups, periodically dropped their pants and gallivanted around our living room, shrieking and laughing with their butts stuck out.

In Yellow Springs Janir and Teague had invented a game called "The Bitch and the Peewee." I never stuck my head into Teague's room to see what they were up to, but the game was marked by periodic silences, then squeals of laughter.

Now, on the farm, Clayton and Janir disappeared into his room for thirty minutes. Thumps and laughter and odd noises filtered out to the living room where I was working, and finally the two of them tumbled out with their pants and underpants around their ankles, laughing hysterically about "buttbones" and "teeny tiny teeny little boobs."

Six months later I sat at my desk typing a letter. Janir and Joy were in his room, so silent I'd forgotten about them as I tapped away on my old Olympic portable. Then behind me a sound. A flop, then another. It was a quilt, working its way across the floor like some amorphous animal. *Flop flop flop*, until it came to rest near my feet.

I joined their game. "I wonder what those kids are up to in Janir's room?" I asked out loud.

More rustling and bumping and muffled giggles from under the quilt.

"What good kids they are," I announced. "So well-behaved and quiet. So mild-mannered."

At that the quilt flew into the air and Joy and Janir erupted from it stark naked. They hopped up and down like jumping beans, poked each other and twirled around to make sure I saw everything there was to see, then ran shrieking back into Janir's room, dragging the quilt behind them.

Though I didn't know what the kids did when alone, I imagined it was everything possible. Perhaps that was only a projection on my part: an adult wish that *I* had tried everything when I was a child, which I had not. But I never tattled to other parents about their games. Janir took his clothes off with some friends and not with others, and I figured they could work it out among themselves. In those relaxed days I never worried that an adult might hear the kids talking and accuse me of something wicked. Today God knows.

In the last dozen years, since Janir has grown up, I've noticed a subtle change in the way I look at kids and sex. I can't tell if it's me, or the kids, or how society has turned up the volume about sex and children. But these days I notice sassy twelve-year-old girls in newspaper advertisements, ten-year-old boys on parade at the mall, even madcap six-year-olds at picnics—and I'm not sure what I'm seeing. What I used to read as pure animal spirits is now tinged with something sexual.

Thankfully, in those days when I was surrounded by Janir's child-hood friends, sex was not such a loaded topic. For years we all swam naked at the pond, and plenty of his friends, both boys and girls, joined us as we wrestled on the couch at home, or as Janir jumped me in bed in the morning.

Janir had his limits and let me know them. When Natalia spent the night he sometimes snuck upstairs in the morning while we were still asleep and snatched the sheet off our naked buns. But one morning, after she grabbed him in the act and tried to pull *his* pants down, he got angry.

"Hey," Natalia said with a laugh, "you did it to us."

"Yeah, but you liked it."

We did. We thought it was funny. It wasn't sex and it wasn't dangerous.

Today I'd be afraid to go swimming naked with someone else's young children. Today, whenever an adult touches a child, people watch and worry. Today a conservative white-haired New Englander tells me how he played horsey with his four- and six-year-old grand-daughters, how they climbed on his back and he shook them off. Though the girls loved the game, after a while he started worrying about what other people might think. He even worried about how he felt himself: was he taking some strange pleasure from the game, something perverse? Finally he stood up and cooled his grand-daughters down, ending the fun before they wanted to quit.

Certainly we have had to expose the scourge of incest and sexual abuse that has wounded so many children in our society. At the same time, the harsh light we now shine on all physical contact between adults and children has taken a toll on our natural show of affection.

I RARELY PRESSED JANIR TO HELP OUT WITH THE REPETI-
tive farm chores of planting or weeding. But on Saturday mornings
in the summer I needed his help selling at the farmers' market. I
gave him a roofer's nail apron like mine, and he concentrated on
making the right change, counting it back out loud and storing his
ones and fives in separate pockets.

I loved the commotion of the market, where I bagged and
weighed and bantered and made change for three different customers at once. I loved the first hour after the opening bell, when
customers gathered three deep and the money poured in.

Later, as the crowds abated, Janir got bored. As soon as I released
him he handed me his apron, then scrambled up onto the hood of
the truck, onto the cab and the wooden cap. He was a natural
athlete with a crackerjack body, a fearless climber who often jumped
from walls and ladders twice his height.

"Daddy, watch."

When I turned he dropped six feet through the air, hit the grass
and rolled, his knees slamming into his chest. He made the same
jump five times, ten times, and each time I had to look back and
watch him do it.

One Sunday afternoon at home I heard him call to me from
outside. I stepped out the door and looked around. It was early fall
and the big sycamore leaves, some of the first to go, were floating
down in lazy spirals and landing on the grass. They lay there like
little boats.

"Where are you?" I called.

He gave a chirp, so small and sharp I couldn't tell where it came
from. We often played hide-and-seek like that. I looked under the
house, inside the shed and behind the paper compost, but couldn't

find him. He gave another chirp, then another. I was stumped. Finally he laughed, directly above me. He stood on one of the top milky branches of a sycamore, a nonchalant forty feet off the ground. My toes lit up with adrenaline. They do again now as I write this, years later.

"You're up pretty far," I said.

"I'm way up." In his eight-year-old search for excitement, courting danger was a standard practice. "Come on up, Dad."

I stood under the tree with the hope that if he fell I could catch him. "I think I'll wait for you down here."

"Da-ad's sca-ared."

I was. My palms were sweating. I stared up into the tree, watching the white bottoms of his sneakers pivot on the branch he stood on. For two or three minutes we stayed like that, I on the lawn and Janir in his aerie, proudly surveying the hollow. Finally he started down.

"Keep a good grip," I told him.

He didn't bother to respond to that. How stupid did I think he was? He picked his way down, handhold and foothold, until I could reach up and take him by the knees. He squirmed onto the ground and pointed up to where he'd stood.

"Way up on that branch," he announced with satisfaction.

•   •   •

Clarisa called with no warning from the Columbus airport. We drove up to get her and found a surprise: she had brought along John Leslie, Janir's three-year-old half brother. She was not supposed to have him, for after a rocky stretch—including a month in the locked ward at Napa State Hospital—she had lost custody of him, and he was now living with her cousin Cecilia and her husband. Clarisa had been granted a six-hour visit, but instead of taking him to Russian River she'd bought a one-way ticket and flown to Ohio.

From Athens she called Cecilia and told her what she'd done. Cecilia called the boy's state guardian, the bureaucratic wheels turned and three days later we got a visit from a young man and woman from Athens Children Services. They interviewed us both, checked out my house and assured themselves John Leslie was not in danger. Though I had mixed feelings about what Clarisa had done, I saw that no one else was going to take her side, so I did. I told them the boy would be fine with me. I'd look after him myself and he could stay at my house until they sent him back to California.

"We'll see," they said.

The next day they came back and removed him to a temporary foster home. There he stayed for three weeks with a family he didn't know. I thought it was outrageous, and Clarisa was beside herself. The day they took him she followed them out to their car, berating them in Spanish.

A week into John Leslie's stay at the foster home we were allowed a visit with him at the Children Services office. He looked tense and anxious, and Clarisa seethed as she watched him play. Catherine, the same young woman who had come to the farm, supervised the visit in a fenced-in playground. There, while Janir pushed his brother on a tiny swing, Clarisa drew me aside and said, "I know she's sticking her thumb up his butt."

Wow. Where had that come from? Had I missed some question-able behavior on Catherine's part? I didn't think so.

On the way from the playground to the office Clarisa walked between her and John Leslie. "You can't take him away from me," she said. "He should be with me, not people he doesn't know."

"I'm sorry," Catherine said. "We can't allow that. You broke the rules in California, and now—"

Clarisa turned and slapped her face. The blow was so sharp, so shocking, I felt like I'd been hit myself. I grabbed Clarisa by the shoulders and pulled her back. "Are you out of your mind?" I said.

Catherine put both hands to her face and visibly restrained her-self. Finally she brushed past us toward the office, her cheek bright red. The slap had woken me like a gunshot. What had I been think-ing? There was no way Clarisa was going to get her son back now.

And she didn't. Two weeks later they flew him to California, and she lost what visitation rights she'd had before.

●　　●　　●

In 1977 I took a year off from farming and built a house farther up the hollow. It was two stories, all brick, weatherproof and fire-proof. I did most of the work with a friend, David Moran, a mason who taught me his trade as we went along.

Bricklaying is a slow deliberate job. Each day David and I mixed the mortar, built corners, strung a line, laid and laid the 28,000 bricks. The joists and rafters were rough-cut oak from a state mill. The windows and doors were salvaged from a building the university had torn down. The gas stove and heaters were yard-sale items, and the total cost of materials came to under $15,000.

The large, high-ceilinged living room was designed for dance parties and indoor sports. The rule I'd hated most from my own childhood was "No playing ball in the living room." With Janir I changed that to "Play ball in the living room!" We played indoor soccer and floor hockey. I bought a gym mat so he and his friends could wrestle. We laid out tape on the varnished pine floor and played violent games of foursquare. And volleyball: I spiked the ball to Janir, he bumped it back, I set it to him, he spiked it back to me. We went through two or three lightbulbs a week, but at a quarter a pop, who cared?

Had we lived with a woman—if we had lived with *anyone*—we certainly could not have been so boisterous. But we lived alone and took advantage of the fact. And I followed Janir's lead. More than a tidy house, he liked one he could play in.

I was never much of a homemaker. My style was to keep the kitchen and bathroom sanitary, sweep the floors, wash the dishes and let everything else slide for a couple of weeks. Then I'd throw myself into a cleaning frenzy. After Janir taught me the joys of a Walkman, I mopped the floors to Led Zeppelin and scrubbed the stove to Prince. As long as the tape ran I looked around for more work. I could clean the oven! I could scour the trash cans! Hell, I'd *iron* to Stevie Wonder.

It did help that in those years Janir cared nothing for household niceties. He had his own bedroom but rarely used it, preferring to throw one of his sleeping bags on the couch and have his bedtime in the living room. I read to him there, sang him a couple of songs, and then he went to sleep close by as I worked at my desk. After he drifted off I got up from my typewriter, knelt beside the couch and stared at his face. The refrigerator hummed and the water heater gurgled, but otherwise the house was still. The foundation went down three feet and the double-brick walls were ten inches thick. Nothing moved or swayed. Janir's face glowed in the dim light, and his eyelids fluttered. He was in the midst of some dream, a life of his own.

•   •   •

In the fourth century B.C., Plato wrote that every man—it was always a man for the Greeks—should do four things in life: plant a tree, father a son, build a house and write a book. Nineteen seventy-seven was a banner year for me, because I was doing all four at once.

A year earlier an editor at *Country Journal* magazine had asked me to write an article on Louis Bromfield's Malabar Farm. Bromfield was a prolific novelist who, in the 1940s, had used the profits from his books to rescue an Ohio hill farm from erosion and exhausted soil. Now the editor, an old friend of my father's, wanted to know what had become of it.

Though I'd written little since Janir was born, I drove up to the farm and talked to everyone in sight. I was nervous but determined, and came home to write and rewrite the article a dozen times. *Country Journal* published it, and before long I was writing three or four pieces a year, often about farming, for several different magazines.

The articles paid well, and financially I'd have done better to abandon vegetable growing and take up freelance work full time. But I was devoted to farming. In a decade when organic foods still had limited appeal in the marketplace, I was a passionate advocate of J. I. Rodale's organic methods. I built up my soil, added trace elements, made compost, never used herbicides or chemical insecticides. In those days there seemed no higher calling than the care of my own fields.

Like so many men in their thirties, I worked compulsively. I planted fruit trees, built a solar collector, bought and fixed up a house in town, planted more acres, built a shop and cut firewood. I worked most Saturdays and too many Sundays. I wrote in the evenings after Janir went to sleep—or if I had a night free I sat in a carrel on the sixth floor of the university library, working on the first rough chapters of a novel, *Anna Delaney's Child*, a story of a single mother whose nine-year-old son dies in a car crash.

Janir had never been in an accident. He was sensible and sturdy and the healthiest kid I knew. But I worried about him anyway. I worried he might die, and in my dreams I sometimes lost him. He would disappear into a crowd or a maze in the jungle, and I'd search for him in a panic until I woke. In one terrible nightmare I took him sailing, he shrank to the size of a chipmunk and was sucked out into the ocean through the boat's drainage hole. I woke wailing from that one.

Now I feared for Janir when he traveled with other parents. Everyone had to wear a seatbelt: I'd become a crusader. If he was late getting home from a trip I paced through the house, imagining that the car he was in had lost its brakes on Sharpsburg Hill, and now he lay mutilated and dying by the side of the road. Or else a runaway truck had plowed into a gas station where his soccer van was parked, igniting the pumps in a giant explosion.

Janir had his own strange fantasies, sometimes regarding my devotion to him. One snowy winter evening he looked up from a book and asked, "Would you go barefoot all night in the snow for my life?"

"Of course," I told him. "I might lose my toes, though. You'd have a dad with short feet."

Though I'd answered with a joke, his solemn expression told me he was serious. Not literally, perhaps—but he wanted to know how much I would go through for him, how much I would sacrifice.

And how much would I? Sometimes I created elaborate scenarios that tested my will to save him. In one I had to sit all night in the woods, completely still, while the bad guys circled nearby. Somehow, like the night in the snow, I could save his life that way. In another I was forced into a grim contest in which I had to outrace another father to the top of a mountain: the loser's child would be shot by terrorists.

Lord, where did such thoughts come from?

I envisioned what I would do if Janir died: where I would bury him. Not in a cemetery, but on our farm in a small clearing near the pond. I would dig the grave myself, six feet down into the dense clay soil. Then I'd wrap him in blankets or mats, as they did in Central America, and climb down into the grave with him, holding his body close as I inhaled the pungent smell of the soil. Finally I'd get out and shovel in the dirt on top of him: first the loose earth, then the clods and matted chunks of grass.

With that I had faced the worst I could imagine, the utmost desolation.

•   •   •

When Janir was nine one of his schoolmates died. David Richards was a feisty kid with a small nervous body and shoulder muscles as tight as wires. The first few times I grabbed and hugged him he went rigid in my arms, but eventually he relaxed enough to let me sling him across my back or toss him into a pile of leaves the way I did Janir.

David had a bad heart. His parents knew about it and made a choice I honor: instead of keeping him at home and restricting his activities, they let him play hard and take his chances. But one night, in an empty neighborhood lot, he collapsed in the snow. In spite of an elaborate search he wasn't found until almost dawn. Though he was still alive, it was too late to save him.

After school the next day Janir and some of his friends went to investigate the spot where David had been found. "It looked like this," Janir told me that night. He lay down on the rug to illustrate the exact configuration of David's limbs as they had melted down into the snow.

His death was a blow, one Janir struggled to understand. When I took him to the funeral parlor he stood by the edge of the casket and stared at the pale form inside. He held back from tears, but his shoulders jerked as he watched.

On our way home he delivered his own eulogy for his courageous friend. "He wasn't afraid of anything," Janir said. "He rode his bike down that rocky chute behind the school. He climbed a telephone pole. He walked across the Hocking on the ice. Last year he climbed out on the trestle and sprayed his name on it."

•   •   •

Janir could talk about David's death, or even his own, but the one taboo subject in our house was my death. That could never be mentioned, not even as a joke. Any reference to it brought a piercing look from Janir, sometimes a hint of panic.

One of the songs I sang to him at night was Leadbelly's "Good Night, Irene," in which there was one forbidden verse.

> *Sometimes I live in the country,*
> *And sometimes I live in town.*
> *Sometimes I have a great notion,*
> *To jump into the river and drown.*

If I started to sing that verse Janir would sit up in bed and press his hand across my mouth. There was no joking about that, ever. For while he boarded planes on his own and flew fearlessly across the continent to see his mother, while he casually spent the night or the weekend with a dozen different friends, and while there were always other adults in his life, I was his one true lifeline. If I had died, my brother Alan and his wife Ellen would have raised him. The three of us had discussed it more than once—but Janir didn't want to hear about anything like that.

Sometimes I thought that if one of us had to die, me or Janir, it should be him. This sounds scandalous now, even to me. But in those years the more terrible fate for either of us would have been to live through the death of the other.

CHILD CARE IS A MINEFIELD OF COERCION. SOON AFTER babies are born we start telling them how to behave: Stop crying, eat this, sit up straight, don't hit the dog. We even tell kids how they should feel: You should be happy you got that nice pair of mittens for a present. Or: Don't be sad you have to leave the party, you should be glad you got to come at all.

Of course we do know more about life than our children do, and can often make better decisions for them than they would make on their own. But it's coercion, and a hard habit to break.

One summer night Bill Renz and I sat on the front steps of my house talking about a woman we knew whose boyfriend sometimes pushed her around. Over the years even mild-mannered Bill and I had made some mistakes with women: not violent mistakes, but comments or embraces that proved too leading. Evangelistic sinners, we founded that night the initial chapter of the Men's Noncoercive League.

But Bill's clever mind never rests. "And now for our first bylaw," he announced.

"What's that?"

"Sometimes you have to be coercive."

There's the rub, because sometimes you do and you're never sure when. A friend, for example, might need to be urged into talking about some problem. A child might need to be prodded or compelled to keep a promise, or simply pressured to do a job well.

The question came up often for me when Janir played sports at school or in local leagues. I couldn't understand how a kid who was so bold and exuberant at home could hang back on the soccer field and consistently let other players take the lead. He had grown up kicking balls of all kinds, and with me or his friends he was a natural competitor, quick, agile and fearless. But on his city league team he had no drive, no hustle. He could control the ball but not take control.

I thought I could explain that to him. It was so clear to me that with a little ambition he could be a star, or at least play up to his level. I didn't want to be one of those overamped dads who pace up and down the sidelines goading and berating their children. Yet at halftime I couldn't restrain myself from taking Janir aside and saying, "*Go* for that ball. Take it away from them. You can do it."

Janir sucked on a slice of orange and wouldn't look at me. I was embarrassing him. He didn't want the advice and didn't profit from it in the second half. He couldn't, because his entire being—including a new public diffidence—was expressing itself on the field.

It was the same over at the baseball diamond, where I watched the game from a set of tiered aluminum benches, surrounded by other parents and siblings. Janir stood out in center field wearing his cleats, his uniform and the new glove we had bought and oiled. How he loved these accoutrements of the game. But baseball is such a slow affair: a foul tip, a pitch in the dirt, the repeated *thwock* of the catcher's mitt. I knew it was hard, idling out in center field, for Janir to stay focused, and from my seat on the bleachers I willed him to pay attention. Sooner or later the ball would come his way.

It did, and he wasn't ready. He took a step in, then it was over his head. He ran after it, grabbed it, threw it hard to the shortstop. He had a good arm, and they held the runner at third, but his throw was followed by a deflating silence. And then, only an inning later, his catcher threw hard to second base, trying to cut down a steal. The ball flew over the infielder's head, and Janir hadn't moved to back up the throw. Again the runner went to third.

Oh, what did it matter? It was just a game. The field was freshly mown, birds sang in the brush behind home plate, and clouds puffed by overhead trailing shadows the size of houses across the verdant outfield. And Janir's coach was great. Eager and energetic, he never chided the players for their mistakes. And yet . . . and yet. Baseball seems such a symbolic game. What if Janir were to sleep-walk through his whole life? And did his lack of focus reflect some other problem? Was I failing him somehow?

He went one for four at the plate, finally knocking a solid single over the outstretched glove of the shortstop. After the game he was still jubilant.

"You see that hit, Dad? I really tagged that one!"

That was his whole afternoon. He ignored the rest and focused on that one satisfying impact of bat against ball.

•   •   •

Next week's game was rained out by a downpour that started at two in the afternoon and continued all night. By dawn the creek was out of its banks and roaring over the concrete ford. Matt Sweeney had slept over, and the boys spent the morning tossing logs and branches into the water and racing after them as they bobbed along through the coffee-colored water. By early afternoon the creek had settled back within its banks but still flowed hard, and they wanted to run it in a pair of inner tubes.

"We can do it," Janir assured me. "No problem. Dad, we're nine."

I made them wear sneakers, strapped them tightly into a pair of life jackets and turned them loose. They leapt onto their tubes and bounced down the current, yelling and laughing, completely unafraid at the big curve where the creek slammed into the bank. I ran along beside them. No problem, just as they'd promised. In the water Janir was totally attentive. Here there was no hanging back, never a space-cadet moment as the ball flew past.

At his birthday party that September it was the same. I laid out a big rope circle for dodge ball, and Janir was the star. He ducked, he jumped, he danced, he threw hard and was gracious in both victory and defeat. This was the real Janir, I thought, the one without an ounce of shyness or indecision.

That fall his soccer team had no coach, and someone had to volunteer.

"Dad, *no,*" he said.

He could already smell the awkward situations. And he was right, it was probably unavoidable, for the one thing I wanted to elicit from the kids was the kind of hustle Janir had not been showing on the field.

I set up a drill, one on one. Two players dashed in, one from either side, as I bounced the ball between them. I urged them both on, one of them made off with the ball and I threw the next one. Janir sprinted forward, then hesitated. He waited for the ball to settle—and in that moment Justin took it away.

"*Go* for the ball," I yelled. "Don't wait for it, attack it."

Janir glared at me, a look of pure hatred. On the drive home he brooded in silence, drowning the car in his indignation. At the farm he jumped out the minute I parked, his anger undiminished. "*You* couldn't do any better," he said.

• • •

I was never big on discipline. The worst punishment in my house was for Janir to be sent to his room, away from the action. Even that was rare, because there wasn't much to punish him for. Child care is easier when you don't insist on proper behavior, proper respect, proper language.

Because I swore myself, I let Janir swear. There were no language rules in my house save for that peculiar taboo from my own childhood, *shut up*. Those two words—which still raise my hackles like no others—were forbidden, but otherwise Janir and his friends could say what they liked, and often did. Occasionally, back when they were seven or eight, they had run through the house from room to room, giggling madly and crying Shit! and Penis! and Asshole! This was not how I'd grown up myself, but I couldn't see any harm in letting the words out of the closet.

Now and then I heard more respectable parents refer coyly to "the *F* word," both among themselves and around their children. I thought they were dotty. How long did they imagine they could protect their kids from the language of the streets?

One night I took Janir and Matt to a hockey game between Ohio University and Miami of Ohio. The rivalry between the two teams was strong, and Bird Arena drew a rowdy, beer-drinking crowd. Before the game, as the Miami team took slap shots directly in front of us, warming up their goalie, the Ohio supporters baited him without restraint.

"Hey, number fourteen," some deep-throated guy yelled out from the student section on our left. "I had your mother last night, and she sucked."

Janir glanced at me, and I managed a frown. Both he and Matt knew they could say anything at my house, but in public it was a different story. We sat in the rink's general-admission section along with local hockey enthusiasts and a few other parents and children. In the row directly in front of us sat a father and his young daughter. He wore polished wingtips and an overcoat, and she a pink ski parka. She was cute, a bit younger than Janir, perhaps seven or eight. She sat up straight and still, staring intently at the whirling skaters, at the sticks and flying pucks. The innuendoes about the goalie's mother may have gone over her head, but no one could have ignored the alternating chant that started up just before the game from the two student sections on the northwest and southeast corners of the rink. "Miami U!" sang out the students on one side, and the others answered, "Fuck sheep!" Quickly the chant picked up steam. "Miami U! . . . Fuck sheep! Miami U! . . . Fuck sheep!" It went on and on.

Janir and Matt were cracking up. Me too. The father and his daughter sat perfectly still, not touching, not moving, not responding in any way. Matt was laughing so hard he dropped his Frito chips and melted cheese on the floor beneath the stands. Janir was in an ecstasy of wickedness and transgression. He didn't say anything, but I could feel his body moving to the words. He watched the two student sections like a tennis match, his head swiveling back and forth as the refrain continued.

●   ●   ●

Though swearwords were common currency in my house, I insisted on points of grammar. It was partly a joke—but only partly—when I leapt up in outrage after hearing Janir say, "I laid on the floor," or "There's two cartons of milk."

"I *lay* on the floor," I intoned. "There *are* two cartons of milk."

It was a game of theatrics. "If I was captain," he said—and I staggered to the couch, clutching my heart and grieving for the sad state of the language. "I've raised a barbarian," I moaned.

"All right," he said, "if I *were* captain."

Language was a game. It was fun. "Dear Dad," read a note he left me one day after school. It was written in cursive and contained all the formal elements he'd learned in class: date, salutation, main body, complimentary close. "I have gone to Todd Perkins's house," he wrote, "and I'll be back at a reasonable hour. Love, Janir."

His signature was full of schoolboy flourishes, and there was a postscript: "I'll clean my room later, I promise."

I joked with him about the formality of the note—and a few days later found another on the kitchen counter, written in the same decorous style.

"Dear Dad," it announced. "I'm at Thaden's and I'll be back whenever I Goddamn please."

By nine or ten he knew the rules about swearing better than I did. Each summer the Thorndikes gathered for a week at my dad's big house on Cape Cod, a house devoted to the pleasures of children and grandchildren. Janir had always loved his grandfather, and by now had thoroughly identified with the New England half of his heritage. Every year at my dad's he pored through a published genealogy of the family. He was related to all these people, and there was his name in print: Janir Daniel Thorndike. Having put up with his mother's irregularities for so long, he now gravitated to the stable Anglo side of his heritage—a world in which, not incidentally, families lived in many-roomed houses with pool tables, smooth lawns, badminton courts and motorboats.

After breakfast one morning, as Dad and I washed the dishes, I dropped a muffin tin on the floor. "Shit," I said, and bent to pick it up. But as I stood up I found Janir scowling at me fiercely. I wasn't supposed to say things like that at Grandfather's house.

Yet only two days later the restrictions were lifted as we headed back to Ohio and heard on the radio Randy Newman's catchy but insulting song about short people. The song may be a joke, as I've heard Newman claim, but Janir didn't like it one bit.

"Fuck him," he announced. "Short people are great!"

EACH YEAR THE VOLLEYBALL PLAYERS IN ATHENS HELD A coed tournament on my farm, the Trotsky Invitational. (In volleyball one spikes the ball, and we'd heard that Leon had been assassinated with an icepick. It turned out to have been an alpenstock.) We invited teams from three states, set up nets in the field behind my house and played from nine A.M. until the last light of dusk.

Clarisa called one year in the midst of the tournament. She was at the bus station in Athens, and would I come get her? She could not have chosen a busier day, and as I ran into town between matches I stewed at her assumption that whenever she pleased she could arrive without warning and move into my house for a one- or two-week stay. Yet it never occurred to me to put her up in a motel, since the point of her visits was for her and Janir to spend time together.

She was thinner and had lost some teeth—perhaps because of her car crash years ago. The damage to her cheekbone had turned out to be small, almost unnoticeable—perhaps she had been right about the wires—but she had a habit of tugging her hair down over the right side of her face, which called attention to the minor flaw. On our way out to the farm she lifted her suitcase onto her lap and opened it. It was filled with crazy clothes: worn velvet dresses, sequined sweaters, oversized satin pants and a crushed fedora. She put on the hat.

"How's Janir?" she asked.

"He's fine. He's getting bigger."

"Why didn't he come?"

"Today's the Trotsky and he's got some friends over."

In fact I'd invited him to come along, but he didn't want to. He'd been playing in the creekbed when I left, and by the time we got back he had disengaged himself from the other kids and was waiting for us on the front porch. He wore a cautious look, and when Clarisa hugged him he barely responded. He knew her capacity for bad behavior.

Shouts and calls drifted through the thick August air from the courts behind the house. "I've got to get back to my team," I told Clarisa. "Make yourself at home, there's plenty of food. Janir, are you playing in the creek?"

He nodded eagerly. I'd given him his escape, and he took off.

Only forty minutes later I heard the two of them shouting. I ran inside to find the house as hot as an oven and Janir on the edge of tears. Clarisa, wearing a pair of satin pants and a fringed scarf she had wrapped around her head and pulled down over the injured side of her face, was trying to fry some eggs in a pan on top of the woodstove. The eggs weren't cooking, but she was still feeding wads of newspaper into the big cast iron stove.

"For God's sake, Clarisa." I closed the door on the fire. "I try to keep the house cool in the summer, not heat it up."

"He looked in my suitcase," she said spitefully. "He thinks he's the boss around here."

I knew Janir was anxious about having his friends see her like this, with her fringed scarf and wild look. He stood in the middle of the room like an adult, his hands on his hips. "I told her to use the kitchen stove," he said.

"That uses gas," she complained. She pointed a bony finger at him. "Don't you know anything about ecology? Don't you want to help the earth? We all come out of the earth, you know. That's your real mother."

"It is not," he screamed.

"Janir," I said, "go play."

He ran out the door. I grabbed the pan with the eggs and slammed it down on the kitchen stove. "Damn it, Clarisa."

"You're raising him wrong," she said. She drew herself up in front of me. "You're spoiling him with all your money. You're too rich and white and he's getting to be a brat. He doesn't belong here. He ought to be in a city where there's all kinds of people."

There was clearly some justice to what she said, for Athens felt homogeneous after our life in Latin America. But I didn't want to argue it now. "He's not a brat," I said. "He's just . . . afraid of you."

She gave me a savage cold stare. Her dark eyes were ringed with heavy black liner, and her pupils were dancing. I was afraid of her myself.

"He's afraid you're going to do something weird," I said. "Kids hate that. He doesn't want his friends to come in and see you building a fire on a ninety-degree day with an old scarf wrapped around your head."

She watched me coldly. "He can't even speak Spanish," she said. "He pretends he doesn't understand."

"I tried, Clarisa. I still talk to him in Spanish sometimes. But his friends don't speak it so he's not interested."

"That's why he should be in California. He could learn there."

"Maybe he could."

"And I want him to live with me."

"Well," I said, "we'll have to see about that."

That was another lie. There wasn't a bunny's chance in Brooklyn I was going to let that happen. "Have you found a job?" I asked her.

A month ago her social worker had told me that if Clarisa wanted to get John Leslie back she had to find a job and keep it for six months. That was their only requirement.

"I'm looking," she said.

I imagined her showing up for a job interview wearing a mix of the clothes from her suitcase. Outside, my team was yelling for me: we didn't have any subs. "I have to go," I said. "Come out and watch if you want."

I feared she would. I was as self-conscious as Janir and didn't want everyone to see what a queer creature my ex-wife was. But instead of joining the crowd in the back meadow she disappeared into the woods east of the house, and I didn't see her for a couple of hours. My team made it to the semifinals, then lost, and ten minutes later I found her on the front porch talking with my friend Kathy Galt. Kathy's arm was looped through hers, Clarisa had taken off her scarf and tied back her hair, and she was telling Kathy about an argument she'd had with someone in San Francisco.

Kathy was interested, she was curious, she listened in a way that embraced Clarisa's anger and sense of deception instead of resisting them. I wish I'd been able to do the same. I knew enough. I knew how shy Clarisa could be here in the United States, especially when surrounded by people she didn't know. She was a small brown woman from another culture, of another race, and I had at least some inkling of how she had suffered from that. Yet in the ten days that followed I never once sat down and took her arm in mine, the way Kathy had, and asked how she was doing. I was too busy fending her off, keeping her at a distance, lest her eccentricities rub off on me or Janir.

How fragile I was, and how pitiful my fears seem now. Over and over, we fail those we love out of our own weakness.

•   •   •

A week into her stay Janir tugged at my sleeve, put his finger to his lips and drew me around the house into the junipers beside the porch. Clarisa was there, crouched on the concrete, focused and still. *Wham,* she smacked her palm down, picked something up and tossed it into her mouth. "Good ant," she said.

Janir and I glanced at each other, slipped away and ran down into the creekbed where we could burst out laughing.

"Your mom," I said finally.

"She *eats* them."

"She's a strange one. But then . . . *I* eat hairy caterpillars."

"Yeah, you do!"

That spring, on a dare from Janir, I'd eaten a pair of bagworms, in exchange for which he had washed the dishes for four nights. Of course Clarisa's ants, we knew, were altogether different. They were a sure mark of her craziness. How minuscule are the deviations in behavior that signal mental imbalance.

•   •   •

After ten days I bought Clarisa a ticket back to San Francisco, and the three of us drove up to the Columbus airport. Janir volunteered a hug as she was about to board her plane, then he and I climbed the stairs to an outdoor observation deck on the roof. We sat on a bench and waited. We were alone. A gusty wind pushed the clouds around, and a couple of jets roared up into the sky trailing plumes of dark exhaust. We didn't say anything. After Clarisa's plane taxied away from the building I put my arms around Janir and lifted him onto my lap as if he were five years old. He slumped back against my chest.

It was always the same: while she visited I was nervous, and after she left I was sad. My eyes were tearing in the wind. One of Janir's grandmothers was dead, and the other lived in El Salvador, a country now gripped by revolution. I wanted him to have a mother, a woman who would hold him like this and rock him in her arms. Clarisa was his only chance, and she had a long way to go before he'd let her get this close.

The plane turned at the far end of the runway, then blasted off to the west. We sat and watched it until it was too small to see. Even then we didn't move or say anything. We just went on sitting there, blown by the gusty wind and watching the sky where the plane had disappeared.

· · ·

As soon as Clarisa got home she started talking about having Janir visit her again in San Francisco. No matter that his last trip there had gone badly, and no matter that she'd been too unstable to keep custody of John Leslie: she began a campaign for a visit the next summer.

All fall she phoned every couple of weeks, and every time she told me she wanted Janir to come. Finally I agreed to consider it, and after Christmas I granted that if he wanted to make the trip, and if she stayed out of trouble until June, I'd go along with her plan. I thought that was a safe offer, because she had rarely made it through a full year without some disaster. In recent years she'd been arrested for drunkenness and public disturbance, and locked up twice at Napa State. No more of that, I told her, if she wanted to see Janir. No more raging fights with her Aunt Teresa, and no more waking me up with five-A.M. phone calls.

She surprised me by holding up her end of the bargain and avoiding all major crises. At the end of May I asked Janir if he wanted to go.

"Did you tell her I would?"

"I told her I'd let you. That doesn't mean you have to."

He thought it over for a few days, then said he would. I worried he might be doing it for me, because I'd made a deal with Clarisa. But surely it was more complex than that. Like any child, he wanted a mother. Clarisa was his, and he was willing to give her another chance—especially, I think, out of town, where none of his friends would see.

Everyone told me not to send him. Victor's levelheaded wife Jackie told me not to. Paquita and her sister Teresa told me not to. Even Clarisa's psychiatric social worker called to tell me it was a bad idea. Clarisa was living in a hotel, she said, and it was no place for a child.

Clarisa was furious when I told her I'd had second thoughts. Yet ultimately it was that outburst that convinced me to send him. Because she didn't fall apart, she just got mad like a normal person. After she calmed down she reminded me of our bargain, and of how she had stayed out of trouble all year. And while everyone had doubts about her, no one could point to anything she'd done recently that was dangerous or outright deranged.

Perhaps what swayed me in the end was my own Yankee sense of honor: I had made her a promise.

I thought as well of the hunger Janir must have had for a mother. I couldn't actually see that in him, but both logic and intuition told me it was there, buried within him.

On the day of the trip he wore a serious look. I put him on the plane with a small backpack filled with comic books, snacks and *James and the Giant Peach,* a book I'd once read to him and now he was reading on his own.

He'd been a slow starter with reading. Though I'd wanted him to learn—if only so he could entertain himself when I was busy—I never pushed him about it. I'd read dozens of liberal treatises on education, including all of John Holt's books, A. S. Neill's *Summerhill,* and *The Crack in the Cosmic Egg* by Joseph Chilton Pearce, a radical theorist who was convinced children would do best in school if they did not start reading until the age of twelve. That sounded extreme, but my approach with Janir was unchanged: I let him decide.

What finally goaded him to learn was entering public school. On the first day of classes he took a fifty-word reading test on which he recognized only two words, *yes* and *no.* After discovering that every other kid in his class could already read, he applied himself to the job and learned phonetics in a remedial lab. After six weeks he could read a simple book, and by the end of the year it was books without pictures.

Now he read the way I did when I was a child, completely absorbed. In the mornings I set his breakfast next to his book on the kitchen table, tied his shoes for him as he read, packed his lunch and carried it to the car as he followed behind, eyes still locked on the page. One morning, as we headed for the car, I veered off the path toward the creek and marched him to within a yard of the water before he looked up and said, "Hey!" He read all the way into town, got out of the car in front of West Elementary like a somnambulist and only then put down his book.

.   .   .

After sending him off on the plane for San Francisco I drove back to the farm and got in a couple of hours of work. Then I went inside and waited for him to call from the airport, as I'd asked him to. When he did, from an outdoor phone, he was already angry at his mother. I calmed him down and got the story: a bus had passed too close to them, and Clarisa had grabbed his *James and the Giant Peach* and hurled it against the rear window, cursing the oblivious driver and knocking the book out of its binding. When I talked to Clarisa I got a diatribe about how vehicles were defiling the earth.

After the call I sat on the porch of my empty house, my heart sinking. Not an hour had passed in a proposed three-week stay. I had made a terrible mistake.

I didn't go back to my crops. I didn't read or eat dinner. I just sat on the back porch and watched the afternoon fade into a cloudy dusk, then night. Restless heat lightning lit up the horizon. There was no thunder, just a silent flickering above the trees at the far end of the hollow, a jerky luminescence that kept me on edge.

At nine the phone rang. It was Teresa's daughter Cecilia, and she told me I should call Clarisa's hotel. "Talk to Curt," she said. "He's the manager. I just got off the phone with him."

"What's wrong?" I asked her.

"You better call."

"Is Janir all right?"

"I think he's safe for now."

Curt answered on the first ring. I told him who I was.

"Oh, Janir, sure," he said. He sounded too young to be running a hotel. "He's right here, I'll put him on."

He set the phone down with a bang. Voices filtered in, a clutter of other sounds. Janir picked up the phone and said, "Dad?"

"Janir, what's going on? What are you doing?"

"Watching television."

He was fighting not to cry. "Where are you?" I asked. "In the lobby?"

"Yeah."

"Is your mom there?"

"They took her away."

"Who?"

"The police."

At home he'd have been sobbing in my arms. Instead he was two thousand miles away, nine years old and alone in some transient hotel. "Janir, let me talk to the manager, okay?"

He turned me over without a word, and Curt told me what had happened. He sounded matter-of-fact, as if nine-year-old kids commonly hung out by themselves in his lobby. Clarisa, he said, had burned a letter in her room. Another resident had complained, the two women got into a fight and Clarisa called the cops. A couple of officers came, listened to both sides and removed Clarisa to a crisis center. Inexplicably, they left Janir alone at the hotel.

"Didn't they know about him?" I asked Curt. "Didn't you tell them?"

"I stepped out for a minute."

He was lying, I knew. The whole city sounded mad.

Teresa and Cecilia, bless them, picked Janir up and looked after him for two days, then put him on a plane to Columbus. It was the end of an era. There would be no more trips by Janir to visit his mother, and no more fantasies on my part that we could share in raising our son.

• • •

Only a few months later she sent Janir a letter. He opened it, sat down on the couch to read it, then brought me an index card included in the envelope. "What's this, Daddy?"

Taped to the card was a tiny piece of paper, barely a quarter inch square, printed with a likeness of Mickey Mouse. I'd heard of these but had never seen one. It was blotter acid, a full hit of LSD. On the card Clarisa had written, "Eat this, but don't tell your dad."

To this day, when I want to convince someone quickly that Clarisa was crazy, that's the story I tell.

E I G H T E E N

I SPENT UNTOLD HOURS LOOKING AFTER JANIR. OC-
casionally I griped about the job to friends, especially to single
mothers who were under the same gun. I found it a relentless duty
—yet I'm sure I had it easier than they did. Not because I did
any less work, but because I was recognized for doing something
uncommon.

"You're raising him yourself?" people said. "You do everything?
That's wonderful. That's really great."

Though I pretended to disregard such remarks, in fact I drank
them in. I'm sure if women got more attention and approval for
raising their children they would find it less of a burden. "Anything
can be endured," writes the novelist James Salter, "if all humanity
is watching. The martyrs prove it. We live in the attention of others."

Still, most of my life with Janir was ours alone. Year after year his
bedtime remained our daily bond. Though I no longer played "This
little piggy" with his fingers, and I sang him fewer songs, a story in
bed was our inviolable routine.

One December night we stayed up late baking my great-
grandmother's Christmas cookies, and by midnight we were still at
it. Janir brushed his teeth and got into his sleeping bag on the
couch. He was fading fast, but I still had to cut the last batch.

"Read to me after you're done," he said.

"What if you're asleep?"

"Read to me anyway."

I laughed, but said I would.

"You promise?" he said.

"I promise."

"Okay. And write me a note and tell me you did it. Put it on my
eyes so when I wake up I'll know."

•   •   •

I tried once to get out of reading him a story. Every Memorial Day weekend Bill Renz and I gave a famous bash at my house, the Spring Dance. A hundred people came, sometimes more, and usually I farmed Janir out for the night. But the year he was ten he announced he wanted to stay and be part of it. We tried to find one of his friends to spend the night, but they all had other plans.

I knew I wouldn't want to be interrupted once the party got going, so I warned him that this one night at home he would not get a story. All week I read him extra chapters to make up for it.

Sunday morning I mowed the meadow. Renz set up the stereo with a rented pair of five-foot speakers, we cleared the furniture out of the living room and made some plank tables for the potluck outside. The first guests arrived at three. We steamed ourselves in a sweat lodge over red-hot paving bricks, swam in the pond and ate dinner as the day began to cool. Then the dancing started, as it did every year, with the Isley Brothers' "Who's That Lady?"

We rocked the house. Everyone was drinking, Renz and I were dancing like fiends, two teenage bucks from out of town were putting the make on thirty-five-year-old June, and Alex and Aethelred did a dance that looked like a cross between the tango and the mashed potato.

Janir, all afternoon and evening, had been wonderfully independent. He corralled adults to play soccer with him, let a few of them climb up into his new tree house, ate a meal that was mostly desserts, then surveyed the dancing from his loft above the living room. I'd made up his mattress there so he could go to sleep, if he wished, in the middle of the action. But by eleven o'clock he was still awake—and he wanted me. I tried to pick him up and give him ten minutes of attention, the way I'd done that snowy night at the Shop Hop. But now that wasn't enough. He wanted his story.

"Janir, this is my party. It's only one night a year. Can't I have this one night on my own?"

He clung to me. He didn't say anything but wouldn't let go. I carried him outside and walked over the meadow with him across the damp mown grass. The house, from a distance, looked like a ship. Light poured out of every window, and from fifty yards off the big speakers made the ground thud.

"Okay," I said, "I'll read you a story."

I carried him through the crowd, upstairs and onto my bed. My whole body was resonating still to the rock and roll. Janir slipped off his shirt and pants and dove under the sheets. I stretched out beside him and picked up the book we were in the midst of, *The Little Prince*. It was an old copy, mine as a child, its cover worn and soft. I was just going to do my duty, read a few pages and get back to the dancing. Though the story was a good one, it could not compete with Eric Clapton.

Yet slowly, unexpectedly, it did. Janir lay against my chest as I read. We followed the drawings of the little prince with his simple round face and spiky hair, standing on his asteroid world. I read the chapter in which the fox explains how important it is to be tamed and cared for. The little prince, he says, must tend to his favorite rose. The fox is didactic but charming. "One must observe the proper rites," he says.

After a while I forgot about the party, and Janir and I wandered along together through the story. His breath fell on my neck, and his fingers, a bit grubby without his usual bath, kept hold of my ear.

"It is the time you have wasted for your rose," the fox explains, "that makes your rose so important."

When I came to the end of the chapter Janir reached out and closed the book. "You can go down now, Dad."

"You'll be okay?"

He nodded and flopped onto the pillow. I kissed him and got to my feet, emerging from the story as slowly as I'd come out of the dancing earlier. By now I was half reluctant to leave him and go downstairs.

The party had changed. Someone had turned the stereo off—I'd never even noticed—and the living room was almost dark. Randy Light set the beat with his guitar, while everyone else banged on pots, bongos, rhythm sticks, washboards and maracas. A few bare-foot dancers jumped up and down on the pine floor, and Michelle, always the wild one, had smeared her breasts with dark paint and stripped down to a fur loincloth. Before long I had rejoined the tribe, swaying shoulder to shoulder with them as I thumped on a cast-iron pan. Yet even there my mind was still half with Janir.

I had always assumed it would be a woman who would save me: who would hold and kiss me and give me the affection I hungered for. But women were not that interested in saving me. They had their own lives to worry about, and in the end it turned out to be my son—a child whose very conception I had resisted—who taught me the most about love.

•   •   •

Early one spring I drove down to South Carolina to visit some friends. Janir was sleepy and lay in back. He didn't feel good so I let him doze—but when I pulled into Charleston that night I could hardly rouse him, and when I touched his face he was burning with fever. I carried him into my friends' house and took his temperature: 105. We ran a cool bath for him and I got his clothes off, but he would not lie down in the water. I tried to rub him down with a wet towel, but he was delirious and hardly knew me. He stood in the tub screaming, "I *hate* you, I *hate* you." It scared me to see him so hysterical. But it didn't last. I wrestled him into the water, he collapsed into tears and soon I had him cooled down. Later I got some aspirin into him, and forty-eight hours later he had recovered.

I imagined how hurt I'd have been if Clarisa—sober, drunk or mad—had yelled at me like that. Probably I'd have turned and run. In fact, that's exactly what I *had* done. But such a dismaying scene was easier with Janir. When he howled and said he hated me I could shrug it off, because I didn't depend on him for reassurance and comfort. I just took the love he gave when he gave it. I wish I'd been that secure with Clarisa.

•   •   •

On the farm I had created a timeless world. Looking up the hollow from our back porch, the mown field was the only sign of human endeavor. The barbed-wire fences were all overgrown with blackberries and box elders, the gas wellhead was drowned in jewel-weed, and a tumbledown cabin by the creek had long since disappeared under the Virginia creeper. I liked the back of the farm like that, and only kept the field mowed for volleyball and baseball.

On summer evenings, when the sky remained light until nine, there was plenty of time to play ball after dinner. I threw down a shirt for home plate, took my mitt out to a little mound of grass clippings and started pitching to Janir. First underhand, then over. We had a collection of old balls: worn leather baseballs with scuffed covers and frayed red stitching, a few grass-stained softballs, mush balls, a Wiffle ball and a pair of indestructible hard rubber rockets.

Janir crouched over the plate with his official Little League aluminum bat. He connected easily with the first underhand pitches, hitting some grounders, a drive back to the mound and some long flies. After running through the dozen balls we rounded them up and started again. His hits were fewer when I pitched overhand. I kept the count in balls and strikes, calling them out like a radio announcer: "Two and two, we're in the bottom of the fifth. It's Harmon Killebrew at the plate, Jackie Robinson on deck, the pitcher's Nolan Ryan." My baseball history was weak, I just threw the names in at random.

Pow, Janir hit a long ball into the blackberry bushes beside the creek. Then a pop fly, a grounder and a ball. And then—it had to happen sometime—a foul tip that looped back into the window behind him. It went straight through one of the panes, knocking pieces of glass out onto the brick sill.

"Strike one," I said, as if I hadn't noticed.

"It wasn't my fault," Janir said.

I ignored him and called the radio play-by-play: "The old-timer's on the mound. He pulls on his hat, wipes his brow, spits out some quid. He toes the rubber, waits, looks off the runner on first. The count's one and one. Now the stretch. He kicks, pumps and delivers."

With that I winged one of the softballs as hard as I could against the brick wall of the house, ten feet away from the plate.

"Strike two!" I cried.

"No way," Janir said, and banged his bat on the plate, refusing to take it as a joke. "Two and one. Now throw me a real pitch."

I threw him a hundred pitches. I gave him some pointers on his stance and swing. Balls got lost and we searched for them in the long grass at the edge of the field. The first whippoorwill sang. It might have been a summer evening in Cooperstown, I thought, a hundred years ago, because aside from Janir's aluminum bat there was nothing to mark this as the twentieth century instead of the nineteenth. The house had a shingle roof, and the traditional brickwork was graced by corbels, roll-locks and soldier courses. The electric service line was buried under the lawn. There was no vehicle in sight, no patio furniture, no plastic anywhere. It was a timeless scene: a brick house, a mown meadow, a man and his boy playing ball.

Yet I wasn't happy.

Janir was. He was an animal child, ten years old, he stood up to the plate and took fluid practice swings. He was totally engaged.

Sometimes I was there with him . . . and then my mind would drift. I pitched and chased balls, I poked around in the blackberries and scratched my arms. I had my son, yet I was lonely. A year ago I'd made a mistake and screwed everything up.

After three years in Yellow Springs Ellie had come back to Athens. Her boyfriend came too, but she told me it wasn't going to last, and we started flirting the first day I saw her. I must have been out of my mind, but I couldn't help it. I still felt as if the love we'd shared had been ripped away from me, and nothing had been resolved between us.

When I told Natalia I had to give it another try, her warning was perfectly clear. "If you leave," she said, "don't ever come back."

Only three months later I knew I'd made a mistake. I'd been hurt too badly with Ellie to open my heart to her again, and I didn't believe she would leave her boyfriend. Finally I backed off—and by then Natalia had started dating someone else and was through with me. I was an idiot, and Natalia the ideal woman: saucy, beautiful and wholesome. All that was clear once I lost her.

I'd made a foolish choice and now, on those lonely baseball nights, I was paying for it. Dusk fell into the hollow, and the longing for a woman overwhelmed me. Janir and I kept playing until I could hardly see the plate.

"Five more pitches, Dad."

"Two."

"Three," he said.

I pitched the first one, he swung at it and lined a ball I never saw until it hit my shoulder. I dropped my glove and sank to my knees. Janir ran out to the mound. We left the balls until morning, and inside he made me lie down on the couch so he could rub my bruised shoulder. Perhaps I'd disguised my mood from him before, but he sensed it now.

After his story I lay alone on my bed upstairs, gazing out over the empty hollow. The fireflies were flashing and a pair of whippoorwills singing in earnest. Their piercing cries—one in the woods and the other closer to the house—were loud and shrill. Was ever a court- ship so repetitive? The insistent calls kept me awake for thirty min- utes, forty, an hour. There was never the slightest variation. I could have been listening to a recording: a loud intransigent loop being played outside my window. Finally I leapt out of bed, ran downstairs and out of the house. I found one of the mush balls and threw it into the trees by the river, and the birds went silent. But I hadn't gone back into the house before they started up again. I stood on the lawn, naked and violent. If I'd had a shotgun I'd have blasted away at them.

I trudged back upstairs and lay down in the dark. I was unhappy. I didn't have a woman and I wasn't giving anyone my best, including Janir.

•   •   •

Though I longed for a woman, when one showed up I didn't know what to do with her. The following year Annie Cole stopped by the farm one November afternoon when I was laying up bricks on the back wall of the woodshed. It was the warmest part of the day, and Annie wore only jeans and a T-shirt. She was the kind of girl one meets in a college town: twenty-two, fed up with school, living for free in someone's half-finished solar house. She was thin, taller than I, full of ideals and plans to save the world. She hunkered down on the ground beside me, folding her elbows over her knees the way men do in Arab countries. She had traveled in Egypt.

"Keep working," she said. "I want to see this."

I was laying on a line from post to post, the simplest kind of bricklaying. "What've you been up to?" I asked her.

"I'm gonna freeze in my house. The panels aren't even connected. But the hell with it. I'm going to Baja for a month."

She was leaving in a week with some friends to camp by the Sea of Cortez. They had a van. They would lie in the sun, go fishing and watch the whales. "We thought about taking a canoe," she said.

"Funny about that," I said, and glanced over my shoulder at the red canoe that hung at the far end of the shed. "I've got one of those."

"You want to come?" she said.

"You can borrow it if you want."

"No. Do you want to come?"

I set down my trowel. I'd known Annie for about a year. Last summer we'd traded vegetables for baked goods at the farmer's market, and only a month ago we'd gone roller-skating at the Doanville rink with some of her friends. Coming home we'd even kissed a little in the backseat of their car. Now she was making me smile.

"Would we be . . . sharing the same tent?" I asked.

"Yeah." She took my sleeve in her fingers and tugged on it. She laughed. "Don't you think we'd get along?"

"I think we would."

I was charmed. For a moment I yielded to the fantasy of the two of us on a Mexican beach, naked in the sun, the waves lapping our toes.

Annie reached out for my trowel. "Can I lay one?"

"Sure."

She plopped down too much mortar, smoothed it out and set a brick on it. She was instantly serious. When her long hair got in the way she wrapped it up on top of her head. I showed her how to tap the brick down and level it to the line. She laid a second, then a third.

"You know I have a kid?" I said.

"Sure, Janir. I met him at the market. He's a great kid."

"And I look after him. All the time."

"What about his mother?"

"She's kind of crazy."

Annie stood up. "We're all kind of crazy, don't you think?"

I told her the story about the blotter acid.

"Wow," she said. "That is weird. But isn't there someone who could take him for a while?"

"For a month?"

She looked at me, nodded slowly and set the trowel on the wall. It wasn't going to work, she could see. I leaned forward and kissed her on the cheek, but that buoyant moment had passed, when a pretty girl makes a daring suggestion and you can see yourself headed south with some people you hardly know, rolling down the highway toward the sunlight and warm water, sipping wine and kissing Annie Cole on the bed in back of the van as someone else drives and someone else makes avocado sandwiches.

•   •   •

The year Janir turned twelve I drove him and his friend Jesse Dewees to Vermont, where they would spend a month at a summer camp. Somewhere in rural New York we stopped at a market for sodas and road snacks, and as we got back in the car the two boys hunched together, suppressing their laughter.

"What?" I asked.

They wouldn't say.

"Something inside?"

They looked at each other with exaggerated open eyes, then laughed.

"What was it?" I insisted.

Finally Janir blurted out a one-word answer: *"Penthouse."*

"You guys had a look?"

"Buy one," Janir said. "Yeah," Jesse said.

"You really want me to?"

They nodded eagerly.

This tested my liberal theories. I remembered being twelve myself, and secreting in my closet a little stash of pornography torn from a copy of *Esquire.* Though plenty arousing at the time, those photos of women in one-piece swimsuits were mighty tame compared with what *Penthouse* now published. But I went back into the store and bought the magazine for them, and for the next hour we drove in silence, the boys' heads bent over the glossy pages, their snacks uneaten and sodas unopened.

Later, over the years, I bought and left around my house *The Joy of Sex,* a book for adolescents called *Changing Bodies, Changing Lives,* and Sheila Kitzinger's great book, *A Woman's Experience of Sex.* These were certainly more-enlightened volumes on the topic—but I doubt that any of them had quite the same impact as that first magazine.

•   •   •

That fall after camp Janir went to his first dance at the Athens Middle School. I dropped him off at the gym, did my weekly shopping at the supermarket and drove back uptown for a Mexican dinner at the *Casa Que Pasa?* I was dawdling over dessert, still killing time, when an old friend, Rose Dikas, slid into my booth. Rose and her husband had a young daughter, cute as a cricket, and for them this romance thing was still years away. But when Rose heard where Janir was she jumped to her feet. "I have to see this," she said. "Come on."

"No way, Rose. I can't go into that dance. Nothing in the world would embarrass Janir more."

"I'll go in and bring you the report. He'll never know."

We walked to the school, and I hung back in the shadows while

Rose ambled up to the gym and stepped inside. Ten minutes later she came flying down the path, her hands in the air, her voice barely contained. "You have *got* to see this! It is pure raw sex in there."

"Rose, don't do this to me."

"You have to go. It's your responsibility as a parent."

"If Janir sees me he'll die."

"He won't see you, it's much too dark. Just slip in the door and stand next to the wall."

She was right. It was so dark I could hardly make out the clumps of kids gathered by the tables at the far end of the gym. The music was piercing but slow, as if Black Sabbath had recorded a ballad, and out on the floor three couples rotated slowly like hams on a hook. Each boy pressed his palms against the top of his girl's buttocks, and their hips ground together. It was hard to believe these kids were anywhere near Janir's age.

"So?" Rose asked when I got back to her.

"Pure raw sex," I agreed.

•   •   •

After ten years in Athens I was an old hand at the farmers' market and sold two other days a week to restaurants and supermarkets. My organic fields were producing well, I worked hard and efficiently, I knew every produce buyer in town—and I still couldn't make more than five or six dollars an hour.

I knew plenty of people around Athens who'd made small fortunes growing marijuana, and some thought I was a fool to go on tending what a friend called "dollar plants instead of thousand-dollar plants." But even though the county was filled with dope, I was never tempted to grow any. I hadn't smoked the stuff in years, and I was a single father who couldn't risk a stay in prison.

In the last year I'd made almost as much money from three magazine articles as I had from six months of farm work. I'd been working on my novel for six years and thought I could finish it in a concentrated burst. I wanted to write full time, and to live in a town where I would meet more women. I told Janir I wanted to move to Boulder.

He was loath to leave his friends, his school and his soccer team, on which he was now a starter. He argued with me but never dug in his heels. Though I was asking a lot of him, he was old enough to know I'd also given him a lot. We were in this together, and finally he agreed to go. For my part I made a vow: I would move him once, but not again before he finished high school.

My friend Bruce flew out from Colorado to help. We loaded up both car and truck with books, clothes, bikes, the canoe, my computer and all my files. It was 1984. We completely filled both vehicles, and on a humid August morning drove away from the farm, leaving a life that had been everything, and not enough. I rented the house to a friend: I couldn't imagine selling it. The fields, in a single untilled season, had gone back to timothy, ironweed and wild carrot. The air was blue, and the creek dry under the bony sycamores. Janir, as we pulled out of the drive, was reading. I couldn't believe it: he had his nose in a book as we left.

"Janir," I said, "this is it. We're going."

He looked around briefly, took hold of my ear with his fingers and said, "Yeah."

He'd made his adjustment months ago. Though he was leaving his friends and the house he'd grown up in, we were moving to Colorado where he could ski. I turned onto the paved state road and headed west, and Janir went back to his Stephen King. Bruce drove the truck behind us. I was crushed. I couldn't believe I was forsaking Athens after ten years: that I'd given up farming, that I still didn't have a woman, that I was forty-one and on the move again.

IN BOULDER WE LIVED UPSTAIRS FROM BRUCE AND HIS girlfriend Susy in a house at the edge of the greenbelt, a small duplex surrounded by wild plums, hackberries and lilacs, with a rent unchanged from the early fifties. The one hitch was the apartment's single bedroom. I took it for myself so I could write there, and built a canopied bed for Janir at one end of the living room and a chest-high room divider to give him some privacy.

Though we had scarcely a third as much room now as on the farm in Ohio, we invented new games to fit the house. Janir came home from junior high, threw his books on his bed, grabbed the volleyball and dragged me away from the computer. He didn't even go into the kitchen for something to eat. "Let's go," he said. "Stop writing, I'm ready."

"Shoot-on-Goal" was a fast violent game played between the couch and the room divider. He knelt on the carpet with his back to the wall, and I tried to kick a volleyball past him to score a point. The rules were simple: no high kicks, the ball could glance off the couch or the divider, rebounds were fair game and could be attacked at will.

Janir was fearless. He took a few shots to the face—unavoidable in the heat of the game—but never flinched on my next try. One afternoon the ball caromed off his shoulder into the window and blew out the glass.

"Whoa," he said.

"Strike one!" I cried.

We cleaned up and went on playing. The next day I brought home a pane of double-strength glass, replaced the window and cut a piece of plywood to protect it while we played.

Eventually that contest was supplanted by a wonderfully violent game played in the same small space, but with a beach ball. We faced off only a few yards apart and whaled on the eighteen-inch ball, trying to ricochet it off the ceiling or walls onto the floor of the other's court. Over the months every rule was adjusted to a nuance. The sharp corners of the space heater and dresser were festooned with squares of duct tape to protect the balls from puncture, and still we went through one a week.

As a member of the counterculture I had tried to get excited by the New Games in which no one loses. I thought they were boring. I was drawn, as always, to vigorous competitive sports. On television I watched football, rugby and hockey, using Janir's fascination with these games to sanction my own. Though true violence was only a vicarious interest for me—I'd never been in a brawl and I liked my teeth the way they were—when one hockey player slammed another into the boards and they ripped off their gloves to trade punches, I watched intently. There was plenty of raw emotion behind such fights.

I also liked Janir's teeth the way they were, coming along nicely in his new braces. But he was intrigued, I knew, by the after-school showdowns at Casey Junior High. Rumors usually preceded these bare-knuckle fights, and Janir always went to watch.

"How about you?" I asked him one day. "You ever going to get in a fight like that?"

"Dad, wake up. These guys are idiots. They just fight 'cause they like to."

"You ever been in a fight?"

"Sure. Back in Athens."

"When?"

"In the seventh grade."

"Who with?"

"We had a little gang," he said. "We rivaled Scott Dunphy and Shane Sullivan. One time we chased Scott around because he was alone, then Shane showed up. He wasn't big but he was a scrapper, and he backed us all down. Then I told him he sucked donkey dicks, and he shoved me into a trash can and knocked Matt into a tree. Matt hurt his hand but I was okay."

"And you never told me," I said.

"Nah."

"Any other fights?"

"With Shane, I guess. A few."

He watched for my response. I hadn't listened with glee to his story—but I wasn't sorry to hear he'd done some fighting, or at least that he'd stood up for himself. Janir was small, just as I had been at fourteen and fifteen, and it was at that age, partly because I was afraid, that I'd run into trouble at school.

I'd always been small as a child. While growing up in my protective family that scarcely mattered, but in the ninth grade I went away to Deerfield Academy and had to stand on my own. My first year, out of all five hundred students I was the smallest boy. I stood four-eleven and weighed ninety-two pounds, and was suddenly acutely aware of it. From my first week at Deerfield I sensed a danger I'd never felt in elementary or junior high school.

My first defense was to make myself invisible. I walked the way everybody else did, tucked my books under my arm the same way, adopted every school custom of dress and demeanor. I didn't want to be singled out for what so clearly distinguished me, my diminutive size, or for what I feared would be discovered, my timidity.

Deerfield in the late fifties was a conservative school steeped in tradition. We had fourteen check-ins a day, classes in Latin, a vigorous program of athletics and every night a study hall. Coats and ties were required at all meals and classes. On Sundays there was a morning service in the village church and an evening hymn-sing in the auditorium. Each weeknight the entire student body met to hear general announcements and the homilies of Frank Boyden, who had been headmaster of the school for almost fifty years. Mr. Boyden urged us to "play fair," to "keep things on a high level" and to "be worthy of your heritage." There was a moral tone to the school, an assumption of rectitude and honor I swallowed from the very start.

Beneath that principled veneer students were hammering out the usual adolescent pecking order. Halfway through my freshman year one of the more popular kids in the class, Tony Barlow, took to wandering into my room to badger me after study hall. At first he was almost friendly.

"Hi there, Klondike. Got your little life arranged?"

He'd tweak my ears, sit down at my orderly desk and rummage through the drawers, open one of my notebooks from class and scribble some message next to my notes: "Thorny's a dike," or "Teacher's Little Pet." He'd jab me in the kidneys, then lock me in a half nelson. One night he assumed a fighter's stance and said, "Come on, baby, let's go a few rounds."

He knew I was afraid. I hadn't grown up fighting and didn't know how.

"Come on," he said. "Gimme a shot. I'll just stand here. I won't even move. You just hit me."

"I'm not going to hit you."

"What, you gonna hurt your hand?"

"Get somebody else to hit you."

He worked me over. He pushed me onto the bed, then twisted my arm behind my back and pushed my face down into the pillow until I couldn't breathe. Panicked, I bucked off the bed—but then exploded into tears. Tony let me go. I think it scared him. I was fourteen, far past the age when a boy could cry. I turned away and stumbled into my closet to sob, burying myself among the woolen suit coats.

At breakfast the next morning I glanced at the other boys, wondering how many of them had already heard about the incident. I had cried. There could be no greater disgrace.

I never told the proctor or the dorm master or my parents, for ratting on another student would have been spineless and reprehensible, and I was trying to be worthy of my heritage.

Things got worse my sophomore year, when I was still the smallest kid in the school and more self-conscious about it than ever. Though I turned fifteen that fall, I had yet to enter puberty. I had a child's high voice, a little boy's penis, no pubic or armpit hair. All this was on display daily when we showered at the gym.

All the old-boy sophomores—those of us who had come to the school as freshmen—lived in Chapin Hall. Most of the jocks, thugs and class heroes lived downstairs, while the more studious and mild-mannered kids were assigned to the second floor. My small single room, near the end of the corridor, had a bed, a desk, a dresser and a door with no lock. Radios, phonographs and pinups were forbidden. Chapin Hall, like the rest of the campus, was a monastic preserve into which girls did not intrude. In 1958 Deerfield was still thirty years away from going coed.

That year two of the tougher kids, Drew Desmond and Matt Lockridge, had somehow been assigned to the dorm's second floor. Resenting this exile, I think, they took out their animosity on the weaker students they'd been housed with. After study hall at night I heard the first bad signs: a scuffle a few doors down, then low voices in the corridor. Matt appeared at the door of my room, dragging my friend Nick by the ear, bending him almost double. Nick was a skinny kid who ran cross-country, and neither of us weighed more than a hundred pounds.

"My glasses," Nick said, his voice high with pain. Matt pulled him into the room, plucked off his glasses and shoved him onto the bed.

Drew sauntered in behind them, the man in charge. In a fight, I think, Matt could have taken Drew—but it wasn't as simple as that. Drew was smarter, more inventive and sadistic. He usually appeared with a smile, an amused and unruffled air. He took hold of my shirt, lifted me off my chair and announced cheerfully, "Mouse fight! Get ready for a mouse fight!"

First they prepped us for the combat. Matt put me in a leg lock and clamped down until I feared my tibia would snap. Drew grabbed Nick's hair and made passes with him as if Drew were a toreador and Nick a bull with no horns. They pinched us and goosed us and ground their knuckles into our scalps. They banged us together, then held me down and used Nick's hand to slap me in the face. I didn't say anything and I didn't cry—I was *never* going to cry again —but it was close.

A few kids looked on from the doorway. The corridor master was never around. Nick and I shot a conspiratorial look at each other: this time we would refuse to fight. We were friends, on Sunday afternoons we went running in the lower meadows. This time we would not give in, we would take the pain and suffer in silence.

But they kept it up until they broke me. They pinched my face. They called me "pussy." They poked and punched me until the tears started rising—and instead of crying I exploded. I flung myself against Nick, and instantly we were flailing across the bed onto the floor as the pain and frustration boiled over. Every fight was the same. We didn't want to hurt each other and never used our fists, but gripped each other in frantic headlocks, my arm around his neck and his around mine. Locked side by side we squeezed fiercely, our sweaty temples jammed together, each trying to crush the other into submission. We gasped for breath and fought off the pain, desperate not to lose.

This time I was the one to give in. I didn't have to say anything, I just relaxed my grip and it was over. In an instant I was the school's worst weenie, and this time it was Nick who earned the spurious cheers from Matt and Drew as they paraded him around the room, his thin arms lifted between them in mock triumph.

Nick and I avoided each other's eyes. The next day we would talk—but not about the fight. We always pretended it had never happened.

After everyone left I closed my door. No one ever knocked or came in after a mouse fight. My legs trembled and my arms felt as limp as cloth. Shame filled the air like motes of dust. I closed my eyes and breathed it in. I lay on the torn-up bed and let myself sink to within an inch of crying, but didn't.

•   •   •

Though I didn't want Janir to be a brawler, I'm sure I'd been giving him the same subliminal message for years: Don't be a wimp, it doesn't work, stand up when you have to. And clearly he had taken the point, for though always one of the smaller kids, he was quick to defend himself, quick to wrestle with friends of any size, quick to join a row on the soccer field, quick to hurtle down the steepest ski slopes.

Over Christmas break one year I chaperoned his ski team on a five-day downhill at Powderhorn. There the kids dressed in helmets and skin-tight suits to compete in a race measured—and sometimes decided—by hundredths of a second. At night, back at the motel, they played a more primitive game called "Battle Royale," in which Janir was always an instigator. He would tackle Ian, who grabbed Randy, who fell on Matt, who called on Dave for help. Soon every boy on the team had thrown himself onto the thrashing pile between the room's two beds. They pushed and pummeled each other, disappeared under the roiling mass of limbs and torsos, emerged half crushed, shook themselves and rolled across one of the beds onto the pile again. This primeval rite sometimes continued for forty minutes.

Most boys get tested physically. If they want to be part of the team they have to join the fray. They have to fight or show they're not afraid to. They have to jump off a six-foot ledge on skis, then a ten-foot ledge, then fifteen. At summer camp in Vermont they have to dive into dark water from the lip of a granite quarry. They have to ride a motorcycle, then a bigger motorcycle. They have to bungee-jump and sky-dive and paddle out into the dangerous surf. The pressure is always on.

As a teenager I'd sometimes been crushed by that pressure—but Janir was better at it. Completely at ease in his body, he welcomed every physical challenge. Skiing was perfect for him, both the technical demands of slalom and the thrill of downhill. The Lake Eldora Racing Team, which started dry-land training in September and didn't finish racing until the middle of April, became the center of his social and athletic life.

Though I'd grown up skiing myself, years ago I'd lost interest in the sport. It was too stylish, too elite, too expensive. Now, because Janir got so involved, I started again. It was even more expensive: in addition to coaching fees there were motel and travel costs, lift tickets and reams of equipment. Janir had slalom, giant slalom and downhill skis, all top-of-the-line models replaced every year or two. He had boots, bindings, poles, ski bags, gloves, hats, helmets, goggles, edge sharpeners, wax kits, parkas, padded sweaters, downhill suits and warmups. I was moaning about the cost one day to Don Gini, whose four kids had all gone through the Lake Eldora program.

"Think about it," he said. "You want to spend ten thousand dollars on skiing, or you want to spend it on a lawyer?"

He was probably right, for our kids were much too busy to think about drugs or larceny. They trained hard—four days a week in junior high and six in high school—and ski racing was a major part of their identity. They were a crew, a posse, they knew all the moves, the lingo, the trails at every area, the stars on the World Cup circuit. Many of the kids on the team, Janir included, earned international FIS ratings. Though thousands of rungs below Marc Ghirardelli or Alberto Tomba, they were ranked on the same computerized list.

Each year the Lake Eldora team staged a dual slalom between parents and racers. I beat Janir his first year on the team, and the second year it was close. The third year I pushed through the starting wand, and after the first few gates I seemed to be in the lead. I was winning, I was winning!

Only, however, because at the starting gate Ian Gini had reached down at the last instant and snapped Janir out of his bindings. It took him a moment to step back in, so he didn't catch me until halfway down the course. I heard him drawing closer, his turns biting the packed snow. In a flash he drove by, cross-blocking every gate and stretching out for the electronic beam at the finish line.

How good it was to be beaten: how great for both of us. I pulled up at the bottom of the course, leaned on my poles and gasped for breath. I could still hear the echo of Janir's crisp turns. He skated over and put a consoling hand around my back. "Pretty good, Dad. Gotta square those shoulders, though. Maybe next year."

•   •   •

For better or worse, it's ingrained in our culture: kids need to be good at something. They need to stand out and be acknowledged. It might be for sports or music or computers or the study of lizards, but they need to be recognized.

Janir chose skiing, which like so many sports was laced with posturing and attitude and ostentatious display. But I never resisted that, I got behind it. When he and his friends used skiing to pump up their egos I encouraged them. I loved their vaunts and vainglory: their audacity, their bragging boisterous language, their raps cribbed from the black stars on MTV who sang about how rich and sexy and powerful they were. I think kids need that.

And there was a poetry to their language. Janir and his friend Randy Curtis invented a boastful rhyming dialect called "Messin'," and Janir often spoke it around the house. One evening after I criticized the haphazard look of his math homework he sprang up on a chair and told me to back it off:

"Back it eef, Snake, 'cause it's para-geet. Take it from Bester, Lester. This is your beeg-time mess master talkin', the best of all, you mess wit me and you take a great fall. I pull some air, I get very tall, then it's hangreta and over the knoll. I always deal and I never squeal. I'm always one-up so never forget, you mess wit me and you gonna fret. I'm de best, de best around, I mess everyone up in this whole damn town. So back it eef and do as I say, or you gonna get messed in a beeg beeg way."

What a prodigious hunk of muscle and good humor! Some of those phrases, like "pulling air" and doing "hangretas" were esoteric ski jargon. "Always deal, never squeal" was vital dogma. The impromptu rhymes were accompanied by urban black gestures, and the rap finished with a flying leap off the chair onto the couch.

"Just one more thing," Janir announced twenty minutes later, after brushing his teeth, "and that's hug in bet. You mess wit me and I bust your het."

Such bravado. That was "hug in bed" and "bust your head" he was talking about. He was bad to the bone, all right, and I'd be in serious trouble if I didn't get over there soon and give him his hug in bed.

Save for the hour, his bedtime had hardly changed over the years. I still read to him every night, though now it was *Papillon,* Maya Angelou, Peter Freuchen's *Vagrant Viking,* Roger Angell on baseball, mysteries by Susan Dunlap and thrillers by Thomas Harris. Later, in his junior year in high school, we lay side by side on his bed at night but read separate books: Nelson DeMille for him and Ellen Gilchrist for me.

As a young boy Janir had often appeared after a bad dream and climbed into my bed to sleep. Even in high school a nightmare sometimes shook him awake, and he stumbled into my room in the dark.

"Bad dream," he murmured.

I woke up and made room for him, gave him a hug and lay beside him as he drifted off to sleep. I was aware of his size, his bulk. I thought of the long string of bedtimes that had joined our lives. That was changing, of course, as everything did. By his last year in high school we still read before sleep but apart now, each in his bed. He was growing up and getting ready to go into the world, and I was getting ready to let him.

• • •

When Janir was younger, scores of parents had warned me about the harrowing years to come. Most people regarded adolescence as some kind of Armageddon, a battle one was sure to lose. But when those years arrived I found them delightful. I told everyone how much easier it was than when Janir was four or five, and how much fun we were having.

"Sure," they said, weaseling out of it. "Because you've got a boy. Boys are a picnic compared to girls."

Life would certainly have been different with a daughter. I doubt if we'd have wrestled or played as many games—but perhaps we'd have talked more. Though Janir and I were close, we rarely discussed our emotional lives. Sex and romance were especially difficult to talk about, and I sometimes worried that my own troubled history with women had predisposed him to avoid the subject.

One Thanksgiving, instead of accepting an offer to an adult dinner I knew would bore him, we drove up to the Red Lion for our holiday meal. Though I cooked at home every night, I wasn't much good with big birds or roasts. We sat in one of the restaurant's wood-paneled rooms a few miles up Boulder Canyon, the windows radiating an icy cold as an early night spilled down from the mountains. One big lively party was drinking and making toasts at a table in the middle of the room, having so much fun they made the rest of us feel left out.

I told Janir the well-worn tale of how much his uncle Al and I had endured as boys, suffering through prim, coat-and-tie Thanksgiving dinners at my aunt and uncle's. "That was back when kids had to behave," I said. "Back when they were seen and not heard. Back before video games, before ten-speed bikes, before the hula hoop."

"Yeah, yeah," he said, "when you had to walk five miles to school every day through the blowing snow, uphill both ways."

"Yes, in the wilderness of Connecticut."

"You're such a cornball, Dad."

The meal arrived, two great platters of food, and for a while we ate in silence. Then, over the last of the turkey, I tried to draw him out about how school was going, and his friendships. The bent of my questions was predictable: I wanted to know how he felt.

"Fine," was all he said. "Everything's fine."

I pressed him. "And girls? Any girls you like?"

"Dad," he hissed, "can't you see I don't want to talk about my feelings?"

I retreated into a sulk. The party at the noisy table had moved on to champagne, and the waiter brought them two more bottles. Finally Janir took pity on me. "It's just the way I am," he said.

More than once that year he had performed a humorous rap on this subject written with his friend Randy, which included the lines,

> Now I don't like broken hearts, emotions or feelings,
> But in the game of love that's part of the dealings.

Perhaps, I thought, he was just shy about the topic, the same as I had been around my parents. Still I was disappointed. I'd spent twenty years learning how to talk about emotions, and now my son wasn't interested. I had assumed this was a progression, that after my struggles it would all come easier to him.

"It's amazing," I said. "I've got a son and a father who are exactly the same."

"Yeah," he said matter-of-factly. "And my son will probably be just like you."

• • •

My first novel had been published in 1989, and by now I was deep into my second, *The Potato Baron*. Though I hardly seemed qualified to write a book about a twenty-year marriage, the novel came easily. I think this was because of Janir, for our life together, especially as he got older, called for the same give-and-take as in a marriage, the same juggling of needs and demands. There were galling restrictions on both parties, and sometimes we flew into a quarrel, even screamed at each other.

One of my grievances was the laundry. I'd never liked doing it, and as Janir got older I tried to push some of the work off on him. "You're in high school," I said. "You're old enough to do your own laundry."

"Did you do your laundry," he asked, "when you went to that ritzy prep school? Besides, I've got homework. You want me to get into college, don't you?"

He was always the scammer. And he knew I was a soft touch, that I did most of the housework so he could be free. I understand a man who waits on his wife, or a woman on her husband.

Sometimes I do. One day I washed four loads of clothes, hung them to dry on the porch, brought them back in and divided them up. I put mine away and left Janir's pile on the couch.

"They're clean," I said when he came home from soccer. "Now put them away."

He was busy, he had homework. His clothes lay in a lump at the far end of the couch. After he left for school the next morning they were still there. It annoyed me, and when he came home I jumped in his face. "I washed and dried the damn things, now you put 'em away."

Silently, nonchalantly, he picked up his clothes and dropped them at the foot of his bed. There they stayed for two more days. We had an agreement about his bed: he didn't have to make it, but he had to spread the quilt over it so I didn't see it wasn't made. The clothes were out of sight, but I knew they were there. On the third day I told him, "Put those damn clothes away. I'm fed up with this."

He leapt up from the couch, already primed. "That's my bed and those are my clothes, so get off my back about it."

"How can you live like this? You're such a slob."

"You call me a slob?" He grabbed my arm and pulled me into

the kitchen. "Look at this," he said, and took a fork from the drainer. The first one was clean, but the next had bits of food stuck to it. He found flecks on a cup as well, then on a plate. I admit to being a shoddy dishwasher: I'm fast but flawed. Janir held the plate up in front of my face, pointing to a spot on it. "Look at this."

"Okay," I told him, "then you start washing the dishes. You never do anything around here. I do all the work."

He dropped the plate on the floor. Just released it and let it fall. It was Corelle, he knew it wouldn't break. But it pissed me off and I kicked the plate aside. "Tomorrow we're starting a new regime around here and *you* can be the peon. You can scrub the damn toilet and vacuum the floors."

"I vacuum the floor. I do it better than you do. This place is a dump. I don't even have my own bedroom."

"Okay, you want to live in a bigger place? Quit skiing and we'll spend the money on a house. What the hell, we'll get maid service."

He took a half step back. "Can I say what I want?"

His face was dark. I knew what was coming. I hesitated, but finally nodded.

"Fuck you," he said. Then he turned and left the kitchen.

Well, I thought, he did ask first.

●　　●　　●

Only a couple of weeks later, one Saturday night, I took him and a friend to the movies, they ran into two more friends from tenth grade, and I sat across the aisle to stay out of their hair. After the lights went down Janir stood up from his seat, three in from the aisle, and scooted over to whisper, "Dad, I feel bad you're all alone over here. You can sit with us if you want."

I didn't, but I cherished the offer.

●　　●　　●

His junior year at Boulder High I went to all his home soccer games. By now he was a quick and decisive player, a force to be reckoned with at center half. Yet on his JV team he not only didn't start, the coach rarely played him. I couldn't figure it out, because Janir looked as good as anyone on the field. Sometimes, if the game wasn't close either way, the coach put him in for three or four minutes at the end.

I did my best to stay out of the politics. One Wednesday in October, halfway through the season, they played Fairview, Boulder's other high school. Janir got in at the end, but they lost 6–2. After the game he joined his teammates in a long line as they slapped hands with their opponents. He was still breathing hard from his few minutes of play, but his face looked like stone.

Afterward the coach called the team in for a meeting. Janir, instead of joining them, picked up his bag and passed me without a glance, his cleats striking the concrete walk. He threw his bag into our car and sat down with a rigid expression.

"Aren't you going to the meeting?" I asked.

No response. I got in, started the car and headed home.

"It wasn't that bad a game," I said. "Half of it was the goalie's fault."

Janir stared straight ahead. But I persisted. "I don't think you're going to get very far with your coach if you just walk away. Everyone else went to the meeting."

"He's an asshole."

"Yeah, he probably is. But if you want to play you have to put up with him. Even if you don't feel like it you've got to look enthusiastic. I watched you on the bench, and you were pissed the whole time. If I were a coach and wanted to make a substitution, I'd pick someone who looked eager. It might not be fair, but that's the way it works. How else are you going to prove yourself?"

"Yeah, great. Take his side."

I was divided myself. I was trying to convince Janir of how the world worked, of how competition was inevitable—and at the same time I hated that there was only one JV team and half the kids never got off the bench. When I went to the affluent Deerfield Academy, though I suffered humiliations in the dorm, there were almost a dozen soccer teams, and even as a timid and diminutive freshman I got to play on a team with a coach, uniforms and a full schedule of home and away games. Win or lose, I love competitive sports, and I didn't want Janir to be shut out.

At home he dropped onto the couch and stripped off his cleats, socks and shin guards.

"I'm quitting," he said.

"Janir, you can't. How many more games have you got?"

"We never win and he's a lousy coach. He doesn't know anything about soccer. He thinks I should play forward. I'm a halfback, I told him. The first game I scored *two* goals from halfback. And when I come out all he says is, 'You missed some opportunities.' The next game he subs me out, and now I never get in at all.''

I couldn't understand it myself. Was it only in my imagination that the coach played the Anglo kids more, while the darker players stayed on the bench? Yet one of the standouts was a black kid, a friend of Janir's who played all of both halves. There were Mexicans on the team, Vietnamese and Cambodians. It was hard to tell.

"If you want to play varsity next year," I said, "you can't quit JVs."

Janir stood up and flung his shin guards into the corner. "Fuck next year. I've gone to every single practice and busted my ass for two minutes a game. I play better than half the guys out there and I'm sick of it.''

"But aren't you going to stick it out? You can't just quit."

"Yes I can." He stood in front of me, his hands on his hips, his chin raised. "You know why? Because I do what I feel like.''

•   •   •

A couple of months later I had some bumper stickers printed up. There's one now on the back of my truck:

I Do What I Feel Like
—JANIR

I N OUR FIRST YEAR IN BOULDER, JANIR AND I STUMBLED across a show on television about schizophrenics. *Schizophrenia* was not a word I tossed around about Clarisa, though I knew that was what she suffered from. She'd been diagnosed, medicated, occasionally confined by the state of California. She was bipolar as well: up and down, fidgety and despondent. I didn't mention her as Janir and I watched the show, but during an ad, after several interviews with street people, institutionalized patients and lost souls who couldn't follow a topic for more than ten seconds, Janir said, "These guys are like Mom, aren't they?"

"Some of them. Some seem a lot worse."

"What is schizophrenia?"

I brought my dictionary back to the couch. "A psychotic disorder, it says."

"What's that mean?"

"I don't know. I think it's what you see when your mom gets weird."

"I hate it when she does that."

"It's probably some chemical imbalance in the brain. Doctors study this all the time and they still haven't figured it out. There are drugs for it, but I don't know how well they work."

"Does she take them?"

"Sometimes. I think other times she sells them and buys LSD on the street. That's the worst thing she could do—but who's going to stop her? The only way is to lock her up, and she hates that. After a month she gets out and there's no one to control her."

Janir sat on the couch, staring at another homeless person on the TV. "I wish she'd get better."

I put my arm around his shoulder. "She loves you, you know. She just has trouble showing it. She calls you, she writes you, she comes to see you. She does her best.''

"Yeah, I know. Don't worry, Dad. I deal with it.''

•   •   •

Now that we lived closer to San Francisco, Clarisa visited us more often. One May morning I woke to find someone slipping through my room into the bathroom. I sat up in bed, still half asleep. "Clarisa?'' I said.

"I came on the Amtrak.'' She closed the door, then turned on the faucets in the tub.

She always arrived the same way, without the least warning. She just appeared and moved in with the clear conviction that we were still a family. And in some way we were. I got up that morning, went into the living room and woke Janir.

"Your mom's here,'' I said.

He sat upright fast. "Where?''

"In the bathroom.''

He listened to the running water. "What's she doing?''

He got out of bed and tiptoed to the door to listen. Then he led me into the kitchen.

"Don't tell her where my school is,'' he whispered.

No one can embarrass a fifteen-year-old boy like his parents. I was bad enough myself—clueless, out of it, obsolete—but Clarisa was a terror.

"Don't worry,'' I whispered back. "I won't tell her.''

When she emerged from the bathroom her wet hair lay on the shoulders of yet another old velvet dress. She greeted Janir mildly, with a small hug—but he had seen all this before and didn't trust her. The usual pattern was calm, then a storm.

As he ate breakfast she puttered about the stove. This too was typical. She had brought her own tortillas and now she toasted one directly over the gas flame, then ate it standing up.

"Clarisa,'' I said, "what happened to your teeth?''

She gave a little laugh. "I lost them. I've got dentures but I don't like 'em.''

Janir went on eating, hunched stiffly over his bowl of cereal. He finished, washed the bowl, put his books in his knapsack and went outside to unlock his bike. Clarisa followed him.

"Where are you going, son?''

"School."

"Where's that?"

He ignored her and threw a hard look at me: I better not tell. I shook my head minutely. He slung himself onto his mountain bike, said "Gotta go, I'm late," and started to ride off. Then he braked, turned around and told Clarisa, "Don't touch any of my stuff."

She didn't say anything, and he left. Afterward I sat in the kitchen with her over a cup of coffee. Except for her teeth she looked okay. She still had her thick dark hair, and she had put on some weight, which suited her. It was amazing, I thought, what the body could withstand: alcohol, drugs, bad food, days on the street. I asked how long she had come for.

"Three weeks."

"Well," I said, "we'll see." I knew we'd never make it through that long a visit.

Clarisa lit the stove again—I'd turned the burner off when we followed Janir outside—and scrambled a couple of eggs. Over the space of five or ten minutes her face grew furrowed and her movements jerky. She was coming unhinged as I watched. Finally she blurted out, "How long can I stay?"

I knew I wouldn't get any work done while she was in the house. "How about a week or ten days?"

She stared at me angrily. "Just because you have money," she snarled, "just because my face is brown you think he's *your* son. Where were you when I gave birth to him? You weren't even there."

"I wanted to be. They wouldn't let me."

"I'm his mother." She struck her fist against her chest. *"Soy yo la mamá."*

"Yeah, and I'm his father."

She knocked a cup off the table and broke its handle. Each time she came she cracked things, chipped things, left a trail of damage behind her.

"Quit acting so crazy," I told her. "You want to win Janir over, don't throw these fits around him."

This never worked, but I did it every time: tried to talk her out of her irrational ways. She stormed into the living room, gave me a contorted look, picked up her bag and abruptly left the house. The door slammed behind her. She was headed for the bus station, I thought, and from there back to the Amtrak station in Denver.

I sank onto the couch. How bitter this was for all of us: for Clarisa who couldn't stop herself, for Janir who'd been given such an unruly mother, and for me who could neither find another woman nor cut loose of this heartache that never ended. I tried to calm down with some chores. I washed the dishes and took a Brillo pad to the stove. Then I stopped. It was too sad. I put on my jacket and ran out of the house. Maybe I could intercept her before she got to the bus.

I was backing down the drive when I caught sight of something white among the mountain mahogany that lined the irrigation ditch above the house. I stopped, climbed the bank and found Clarisa rinsing out a dress in the flowing water. Her suitcase was open and some wet clothes were spread out on the bushes.

I nodded, parked the car and went back inside. I'd been sad, imagining she had gone, and now I was unhappy she was still here. I turned on the computer but couldn't write. After a while Clarisa came back in with her bag and made a nest for herself on the couch. She was quiet, she looked chastened. She watched television, ate more eggs and tortillas, and after lunch went out for a walk.

In the late afternoon I came back from a run on the Mesa Trail to find Janir fuming. He had come home from school and discovered that his poster autographed by the skier Phil Mahre was no longer on the wall beside his bed. Clarisa denied she had taken it, but when he looked in the garbage can outside there it was, ripped into pieces.

"What the hell is this?" he'd demanded, sticking the pieces in her face.

"You don't need that poster," she said. "You don't even know those people."

That night I cooked dinner and we ate in front of the television. We hardly talked. After dinner Janir did his homework, then stacked his books on his desk and took his nightly shower. While he was in the bathroom Clarisa examined the books. They were all clearly labeled: Boulder High School.

By the time he finished showering Clarisa had bedded down on the couch.

"Give me a hug," she said, and he did. "See you in the morning," she said.

"See you in the morning," he responded.

Though it was only nine-thirty he went to bed. Normally we'd have talked, told stories, played a game of Boggle at the kitchen table. But I think neither one of us wanted to wound Clarisa with our easy affection.

The next morning after he left for school she told me she was going to the library. Good, I thought. I could do some work, and she wouldn't get into much trouble there, for the staff was used to the homeless and to odd behavior. Clarisa borrowed my daypack and left the house wearing two of my shirts over her blouse.

Here's what happened.

Just before noon she walked into the high school, went to the office and asked where she could find Janir. In spite of her billowing satin pants, her three shirts, the exaggerated circles of rouge on her cheeks and a single false eyelash that stood out like a bristly rake above her left eye, they told her. Luckily for Janir he was between two classes and caught sight of her in the corridor before she found his room. He took her by the arm and marched her down the stairs and out of the school, away from everyone he knew. He walked her to the bike path, then all the way back to our house.

When Janir told me what had happened I said we could ask her to go. He nodded in quick agreement. She had done the unforgivable, and now we closed ranks against her. That night after dinner I told her she had to leave. She didn't put up a fight, which only made it sadder. Once again she bedded down early, and the next morning I drove her down to Union Station in Denver and put her on the train back to San Francisco.

•   •   •

Schizophrenia is genetically linked, and Janir was now entering, at least statistically, the ten most dangerous years for the adult onset of the disease. I watched him constantly: his small depressions, his explosions of anger, his occasional retreat from friends or school. It looked normal to me. Remembering my own adolescence, he seemed a much better balanced kid.

In the fall Clarisa returned. I came home from the supermarket one Saturday morning to find her by the irrigation ditch, again washing some clothes. She had come "just for a week," she said. I let that stand, took her on some errands and kept an eye on her. She seemed okay. When Janir came back from dry-land training he took her presence in stride. The older he got the easier it was on him.

That night we went out to dinner, then a movie. Clarisa sat between us in the dark theater. I spent part of the movie wondering if some day she might simply grow out of her troubles. It did happen, for her aunt Meches had come around after thirty erratic years. But when we got in the car to drive home from the movie, Clarisa began to mumble from the passenger seat and give me strange looks. She talked in Spanish, then English, then a jumble of the two.

"You can't do that," she said. "*No puedes*. Not to me when I know. You know, but it's my face. *Nada, no saben*. Shit pieces. You don't listen. You just look in the river."

Here it comes, I thought. She grumbled on, growing less and less coherent, her forehead wrinkling and twisting. I glanced at Janir in the backseat. He turned away and looked out the window. He hated this more than anything.

"No reason," she said. "*Son pendejos y no hay porqué*. Morning, morning he says and night, they got drugs in cups and big cars. Big *idiota* cars and smelly and *you* don't know. *You fucking never know*."

I sped up. We were only ten blocks from home and I thought we could make it back in time to defuse the squall. But it was too late. She sat rigidly upright, her seat belt pushed off her shoulder, her hands gripping the dash. She screamed and swore, and for a moment I feared she might jump out of the car. I turned onto University Avenue and drove on through the barrage of her words. There was no escape, they engulfed us in a furious torrent as Clarisa jerked her body and pulled at one side of her hair.

I slowed down and turned to Janir in the backseat. His face was a mask. "She can't help it," I said.

Clarisa was still erupting beside me like lava, but my concern was all for Janir. "It's nothing we did," I told him. "It's just something inside her."

He gave me a tiny nod. We let her rage on—and by the time we pulled up next to the house it was over. We got out of the car, walked past the lilacs and went inside. We'd gone out to dinner and a movie, Clarisa had lost it and now we were home. I took out some chocolate ice cream and scooped it into three bowls, and we sat in front of the television and ate it. No one said a word until after Janir went to bed. He lay on the other side of the room divider, his light turned off.

"I better go home tomorrow," Clarisa said.

I didn't say anything, and neither did Janir. I wanted her to go, and I'm sure he did too—yet how dismal this was. She had made a thirty-six-hour train ride to get here, and now faced the same trip back, all for a one-day visit: one chaotic day in which she and Janir had barely talked. It wrung my heart.

I wanted to think it was her own fault. Every time she came she made us all miserable. But that didn't make me feel better. She sat on the couch without her teeth, her hands clasping her knees, looking small and pathetic.

I went to bed but left the door ajar, and for almost an hour I heard her rustling around, cooking something, moving papers, opening and closing Janir's dresser. She was looking, I knew, for something of his to take with her, preferably something he had worn. She did that always, often leaving in trade some mad hat or useless article of clothing. I didn't care. She could have whatever she wanted. I'd buy him a new shirt or sweater when we figured out what was missing. Probably she would lose it in a week, but so be it. I lay in bed feeling sad.

The next morning we ate breakfast together, the three of us quiet and circumspect. It was Sunday, one of those bright Boulder October mornings with the dahlias still in bloom, the trees just turning, the air windless and mild. We drove to Denver almost without speaking, walked through Union Station and waited beside the tracks for the train to roll in. The distant peaks of the Rockies were covered with snow, but here in the city it barely seemed like fall. The station dated from an earlier era, and the dry air was free of smog. We waited, soaking up the brilliant sunlight.

The train pulled in with a great rumble and a blast of hot air. The cars were dusty after their long passage across the plains. In the fifteen-minute wait, while another locomotive was added for the climb into the mountains, we settled Clarisa into a near-empty car. I was so unhappy I could hardly look at her. She wore almost ordinary clothes—a blouse, a sweater and a loose pair of pants—and all morning she had behaved so well I'd thought about taking her back to Boulder to see if we couldn't spend a few simple days together.

The conductors came and went on the platform outside, and a few more passengers boarded. Clarisa turned to Janir. "Keep your grades up," she said. "And get plenty of fresh air, this mountain air is good for you."

It was such normal motherly advice that he looked at her, I thought, with a kind of longing. But it was time to go. The new locomotive had been attached. Clarisa held out her arms to me and I gave her a hug. In the twenty-four hours she had been with us, I realized, she and Janir had never touched. But now the way was prepared. She turned to him.

"Dame un abrazo, hijo," she said.

And he did, taking her in his muscled arms and giving her a solid, ten-second hug. As she leaned into him I watched her face. Her eyes were closed and her forehead finally smooth. She had made this entire trip just to touch her son, to embrace him for an instant. That's how important he was to her.

She led such a painful life. She drank, she took drugs, she slept in parks or in the backs of cars, she got into an argument with someone in a bar, broke a bottle and ate some pieces of glass. An ambulance came and took her to the hospital's locked ward, and for three or four weeks they kept her medicated. But she hated being locked up. She behaved well, and eventually they released her.

She needed a dictator, I thought, a round-the-clock attendant who could step in and control her, make sure she didn't sell her meds and buy LSD, get her a place to live and make her stay there. The state had tried but couldn't do it. They found her an apartment, a shelter or a hotel—but then she broke the rules and the manager kicked her out. Year after year no one could deal with her. I wasn't going to move to San Francisco to look after her, or take her into my house to live. Not while Janir was there. She had worn out her mother, her aunt Teresa and her cousin Cecilia. She had burned through a string of psychiatric social workers. Even her brother Victor, who had carried the entire family on his back through the long Salvadoran nightmare of the eighties, could do nothing for her. Over the years she had lost her teeth, her looks, the rights to her second son. But she had never stopped loving Janir.

I stepped down off the train, wiping my tears so he wouldn't see. We stood on the platform side by side, staring up at the car's smoked windows. We waved, but couldn't see in. Finally there was a whoosh of air, a pause and a clank as the silver cars inched forward. Conductors closed the doors and the train slowly accelerated. The last car left the cool air swirling behind it. Janir and I stood for a moment on the empty platform, then I put my arm around his shoulders and we headed back through the station.

A WOMAN IN BOULDER TOLD ME THIS STORY ABOUT HER son:

She couldn't touch him. He had started pulling back in early adolescence, and by fourteen he no longer wanted to be held or rubbed or even poked. Not by her, anyway. She couldn't put her arm through his or run her fingers through his hair. All that had ended from one year to the next. He grew up, went off to college, lived his own life.

"He's twenty-three now," she told me. "Last Christmas when he came home I took him to a party and I was staring at him from across the room. You know how it is with your kids, they're so beautiful you just want to inhale them. In the middle of the party he came up to me and said, 'Mom, why are you always *looking* at me?' Even that was too much for him, so now all I can do is watch him out of the corner of my eye."

I was lucky with Janir. Though he didn't want me to drape my arm around him outside Boulder High where his friends might see, we still found ways to be close. We read together at night, and we had lots of rough-and-tumble. Sometimes he'd tackle me as I walked into my room, crying "Administer the hit!" as he hurled me onto the bed, a linebacker taking down a running back. We'd wrestle and pin each other against the wall and then—funny how these things happen—we'd stop wrestling and simply lie there arm in arm, sometimes talking and sometimes not.

Once, when I tackled him in return and flung him onto the couch, he gave a small yelp as he landed. I jumped up with an exaggerated look. "What was *that?*" I cried. "A squeal! A squeal!"

"No way," he said. He drew himself up and assumed his most dignified expression. "That was a manly cry of pain."

•   •   •

Finding a woman in Boulder had not gone well. First there was one who wanted me, then a different one I wanted. Leslie Thorpe was adventurous and attractive and a single parent, and only weeks after we met I fell in love with her. It was the simplest thing in the world. But she had some secrets and an old boyfriend. Eventually she left me to go back to him, and I went into a tailspin.

Nothing, I found, had changed about heartache: I lay again on the living room floor and wept, listening to the Rolling Stones, not getting what I wanted. Some months later, chastened and cautious, I stepped back into the arena. But I was leery, I knew the perils of the heart. There were women I might have opened up to completely, but didn't.

Elisabeth.

Nora.

Maybe it was sharing my life with Janir that precluded sharing it with anyone else. He got along fine with the women I dated, but he was never very interested in them. He was easygoing, he chatted with them, he didn't seem to begrudge the time I spent with them. Yet sometimes I had the feeling he was simply waiting until they left.

A Saturday night in darkest winter. As I cleaned up after dinner Janir got ready for the next day's skiing. He sharpened the edges of his slalom skis, then waxed them at the kitchen table, running an old electric iron over the bottoms and filling the house with the sweet smell of wax. Though it was only eight, night had fallen hours before. He had skied that day, and he would wake at six-thirty the next morning to catch the team van up to Eldora to run more gates. On those winter weekend nights he didn't date and rarely went out with his pals.

But I, on this twenty-below night, had to circulate. I had to go out into the city and look for women. I had called around to friends, but no one knew of a party. In the paper I read that the city's original good-time band, the 4 Nikators, were playing at the Boulder Theater. I finished the dishes, gave the sink a cursory scrub and changed into a polo shirt and a pair of light slacks. I slipped my thin-soled dancing shoes into the pockets of my heavy coat, picked up my gloves and hat and stopped to give Janir a hug.

"Go get 'em, Dad."

He had finished his skis and was laying everything out for tomorrow's early departure. "Don't wait up for me," I said.

"Give me 'hug in bet' when you come in. Even if I'm asleep."

"How will you know?"

"I'll know."

"You won't remember it in the morning."

"Do it anyway."

"Sometimes you wake up enough to play with my ears," I told him. "Do you ever remember that?"

"No. But give me a hug anyway."

"You want some ice cream before I go?"

I felt guilty leaving him alone in the house. But he hardly cared. He was sixteen. "I'll get some later," he said.

Though the windowpanes were coated with rime, he was dressed as usual in shorts and a T-shirt. Before I left he wrapped himself in his old Sears sleeping bag and settled down on some blankets in front of the TV.

Why was I doing this? I could have just stayed home with my boy and watched a basketball game on the tube and gone to bed early. But something drove me out into the arctic night. I knew what it was. I had to prove something, if only to myself: that I had not given up on finding a mate. This was not an idle gesture, for giving up was a serious matter. I'd seen people do it—both men and women— occasionally with dire consequences.

Frank, for example, the guy who had lived in this very apartment before Janir and I moved in. I'd met him on several visits when I still lived in Ohio, and Bruce and I had taken to calling him The Loneliest Man in the World. Frank was depressed. He had a boring job reading meters in a giant Denver warehouse, he had no woman, and his ex-wife controlled his visits with his two kids.

Bruce was concerned, and one Saturday night he took me upstairs to try to shake Frank out of his doldrums. "There are women out there," Bruce assured him. "You just have to go out and find them."

"Come on out with us," I said.

"At least we'll be talking to them," Bruce said. "Even that makes you feel better."

Frank shook his head. "I don't think so."

"What are you going to do? Just sit around at home?"

"My kids are coming over tomorrow."

"Frank," we urged him, "it's Saturday night. This is the time to get out there."

We worried about him. He did want a woman, he had confessed to that. But now he only shook his head. Bruce and I jumped up and down in his living room, laughing and talking, a couple of jocular guys. "The town is full of pussy!" we cried. "Beautiful women who want to talk to you."

That was a stretch, considering how dejected he looked. But no approach had any effect. He stayed home that night the same as always, and when we returned from the Walrus at one A.M. we saw his lonely light burning in the upstairs apartment.

Frank never escaped his depression. One March afternoon he drove up to Brainard Lake, walked into the woods and hung himself from the branch of a tree. That's how I got his apartment.

•   •   •

I left Janir in front of the TV and stepped outside, flinching under the cold. The car felt stiff and the seat brittle, but the Toyota turned over as dependably as ever. I let it warm up, scraped the windows clear, then started down the drive. The tires squeaked on the packed snow. The streets were almost empty, and until I got downtown I saw not one person afoot.

I found a parking space almost in front of the theater—a sign I'd come too early. The paper said nine o'clock, but I should have remembered the bands never started on time. Inside I changed into my dancing shoes, stored my boots and coat with the hat-check guy and strolled through the converted movie theater. I didn't see anyone I knew, and the crowd was thin. I felt awkward, as I always did in a bar alone. A couple of White Russians helped: after those I stopped feeling like everyone was looking at me, pegging me for a loner and a loser.

A few more people drifted in, and finally the band came on. The lead singer had an amazing voice and threw her miniskirted body all over the stage. That got things going. I danced with a few women, but didn't meet anyone I could talk to easily. The band took a break.

I'd been there for a couple of hours. I might have stayed for the second set, but in the slack smoky moments after the band left the stage I only wanted to go home. Maybe Janir would still be up, watching the end of a game.

I carried my boots out to the car, not bothering to change out of my dapper shoes. I was too steamed up to feel the cold. The drive was less than a mile, and I stayed in second gear the whole way, aware of the two White Russians and of setting a bad example. All I wanted now was to catch Janir before he went to sleep.

I didn't. The house was dark. I let myself in, hung up my coat and crouched on the rug beside his bed. He lay there among the blankets, breathing peacefully and sweating. He'd forgotten to turn down the heat. I put my head on his chest, and after a while his hand came up and groped around until it found my ear.

"Cold ear," he murmured.

That was his favorite, he didn't like them warm. He rubbed one, then the other, then drifted back to sleep. I knelt beside him with my chin against his arm. I'd wasted another night in a dance hall where I didn't know anyone and hadn't met anyone. Now my clothes and hair reeked of cigarette smoke, and in the morning I'd feel the two drinks. I was a fool. I should have just stayed home with my son.

The space heater hissed at the far end of the room, and the brittle maples scratched against the outside walls of the house. Year after year, as I shared my life with Janir, my friends had all gotten married. Ellie had married, Natalia had married, Bill Renz and Claudia, Bruce and Susy, Jane and Brad, Beth and David, Val and Ron. My brother and Ellen had been married forever. Maybe my life with Janir was the barrier. Maybe there was only so much room in the human heart, and I had filled it up with my son.

Or maybe I was good with Janir and not so good with women. Living with a child is a separate skill. It's easier to give your life to a child, to humble and devote yourself without expecting anything back, because a child is not going to take care of you or answer your needs. A child is going to be perfectly self-centered. And how liberating that is for both of you.

· · ·

In the spring of 1987 I finished *The Potato Baron,* and my father flew out to Boulder to look after Janir for six weeks so I could do some research in Mexico for the next book. What a granddad. He cooked for Janir, helped with his homework, drove him all over town, even coped with Clarisa when she showed up on one of her surprise visits. As my sister-in-law says, "On the grandfather scale of one to a hundred, we give him one hundred."

I thought about them, my father and son, as I drove through the deserts of Chihuahua and Sonora. I knew my dad would not be stretching out beside Janir at night to read him a story, nor would he ask him the embarrassing personal questions I was inclined to. Janir would miss me, I knew: he wouldn't trade me in for anyone. But in some ways he might have found life with my father more restful than it was with me.

Recently I'd been goading Janir about his schoolwork. To get into the University of Colorado he had to stay in the top twenty-eight percent of his high school class. CU was only one option, but I was convinced he'd be happier in Boulder than at one of the smaller state colleges in Gunnison or Durango. I felt I knew what was best for him, and made him a deal: something between a deal and an ultimatum. I would keep up the pressure on his schoolwork until halfway through his senior year. By then college admissions would be decided, and he could do as he pleased. Once in college his only rule would be not to flunk out.

For two years I twisted his arm: "When's that English paper due? Have you finished your history? What are you planning for your science project?" It was coercion—but sometimes you have to be coercive.

Night after night we did our homework together. One night I sat at my computer writing a book review for the local paper, then the newsletter for his ski team, a monthly project someone had to write, print, copy, fold, staple and mail. From Janir, struggling with his algebra at the kitchen table, I could hear the telltale signs of frustration: small grunts and exhalations, then a sheet of paper balled up and thrown on the floor. Then another, then a curse as he slammed down his book. He slouched into the living room, fell onto the couch and lay there with his arms folded.

I stood up and ambled in. "Troubles with that math?" I asked.

No answer.

"What are you working on?"

"The book is fucked up. You can't figure it out."

"Did you go over it in class?"

He looked at me as if I'd offered him a bowl of dog shit for dessert. My implication was that his teacher had explained it, and Janir hadn't paid attention. He turned his gaze to the blank screen of the television. I went into the kitchen and opened his book.

"What are you working on?" I asked.

"It's stupid. You can't get it."

"Let me give it a try."

I'd done this plenty over the years, relearning lots of Algebra I and Geometry. But Algebra II was much harder. I'd only gone that far in math myself, and seemed to have forgotten all of it. Janir came in reluctantly and showed me the problems. I sat down and read the page he was on, then went back to the previous page, then the one before that. Janir stood next to me, his arms folded, his posture announcing his own failure and mine to come.

"Let me work on it," I told him. "Take a break, watch some TV."

I went back to the start of the chapter. It was baffling. I didn't know the terms, I looked at the examples but couldn't figure out how to apply them to other problems. I learned a few things, but altogether it was impenetrable. Who wrote these damn textbooks, anyway? I wrestled with it for an hour before giving up.

"I can't get it," I admitted. Janir lay stretched out in front of the television, watching some sitcom. He nodded but didn't say anything.

I went back to the newsletter, and Janir turned off the TV. He had other homework, and I figured he was working on that. I forgot about him. We were both busy. Then a snatch of song. A whistle even. He was having fun with something. And ten minutes later: "Hey Dad, come here."

I went into the kitchen.

"It's easy once you get it." He was steaming along, filling up the pages of his ring binder. "See, you just have to construct a triangle inside the nonagon with these two end points and the center of a circle. Then you divide three hundred and sixty degrees by nine to get the angle at the center vertex. Then you make a right triangle and figure out the sine."

"Well, great. You make it look simple."

•   •   •

I was better at English. I rewrote half his papers with him, then his college essay, going over his drafts sentence by sentence. Considering how the schools had given up on teaching students to write, I never thought it was unethical to help him. Besides, my parents had done the same for me: that was how I learned to write in elementary school and junior high.

Janir and I spent hours on SAT preparation books, both math and English. He kept his grades up and got into CU, and we celebrated at the Red Lion. Next year he would live in Sewall Hall, only ten blocks from our house on University Avenue. But big changes were coming, for now he would be on his own, and so would I. Since the day he was born my life had revolved around his. I wasn't tired of that exactly, but I'd done a lot of child care in the last eighteen years.

Many kids choose a college away from home, in part to make a break from their parents and the friends they grew up with. In our case I was the one who left town. I had never connected to Boulder the way I had to Athens: it was too big, too impersonal. Though I was now a twice-published novelist, I'd found few friendly writers in town. The faculty at Naropa Institute's Jack Kerouac School of Disembodied Poetics seemed as pompous as their department title, and I'd made some diehard enemies at CU's creative writing department by reviewing their novels—and actually criticizing them—in the *Daily Camera*.

I had a couple of friends in Santa Fe, and had stopped to visit them on my way to Mexico and back. I liked the mix of cultures: Spanish, Anglo and Pueblo Indian. It was an older, slower and more engaging town. So in September, the week Janir moved into Sewall Hall, I moved to New Mexico. I found a small adobe house in the barrio, bought a couch and a table at the local flea market, built a bed and some bookshelves, settled in and started writing in one of my small white rooms. I joined a writers' group and made some friends through volleyball . . . but I missed my son.

Over the years we'd spent plenty of time apart. Each summer, starting when he was twelve, he had gone to Camp Sangamon in Pittsford, Vermont, first as a camper, then as a counselor. After his first season there I asked him if he had missed me. He thought about it, then shook his head. "Not really."

Nor had I. When apart we had always enjoyed what Nana called "a good miss."

It was different in Santa Fe, for this was more than a vacation. There were pleasures to living alone, of course: I kept my house tidy and came and went as I pleased. In the evenings I cooked a simple meal and ate it to "All Things Considered." I'd left the television in Boulder and sat after dinner beneath a crook-neck lamp reading the book review section of the *Times*. At night, before sleep, I lay in the only bed, staring at the dark branches of the apricot tree outside my window.

Janir's childhood was over, and all our years together. It was logical, it was inevitable, I had known it was coming. Yet I was bluer than I'd been in years. I limped around the house with a sprained ankle from volleyball. I sat down at my desk each morning and worked long hours on my next book. On Sunday nights I went out to a movie. That was the one night I couldn't stay in the house, for on Sunday nights in Boulder Janir and I had often watched a movie together at home. Which movie hardly mattered: it was the end of the week, we lay on the carpeted floor with our backs against the couch, ate chocolate sundaes and watched whatever film came on. It is the time you have wasted for your rose that makes your rose so important.

Janir, I'm sure, gave little thought to our old life. He had started the great adventure—just as I had at his age. Whenever I called he sounded lively and excited. I was glad, of course. That's what I wanted.

Still, my days felt empty. Alone in my silent house I unconsciously kept to the same schedule we had shared for years. I got up at quarter to seven and had breakfast. I worked, I went for a walk past the train station, I fixed dinner. I went to bed at eleven.

When my ankle got better I played some ball. The rains of autumn swept in and brought down the apricot leaves, all in an hour. I went to a party and made some friends. I would manage on my own, of course.

In early November I drove up to Boulder for a visit. A half-dozen stereos blared through Janir's coed dorm, and skateboarders rolled down the halls past giant posters of Michael Jordan, the CU football team and assorted babes and hunks. I picked up the faint but unmistakable scent of dope.

Janir loved his dorm, loved college, even liked his classes. As we left the dorm he held the door open for three girls coming in, all blonds, all ponytailed. "Hi Janir," said the first with a lilt. "Hi Janir," said the next, and "Hi Janir," the third.

"I've got a ton of friends," he told me.

•   •   •

We spent Christmas in Vermont with my brother's family, then flew back to Boulder. I'd kept control of my old apartment there by subletting it to a friend who agreed to let me have it whenever I came to visit. That way Janir and I still had something of a home together. We stayed there until his dorm opened after New Year's, watching television, reading together at night and sleeping in our old beds.

In March I drove up to see him again—but this time he couldn't stay over. He was pledging a fraternity and had to sleep there every night. My kid was joining a fraternity! I suppose there was some logic to it. Because Sewall was a freshmen-only dorm, Janir had to go somewhere the next year and many of his friends were pledging. Still, it surprised me after all the times we'd talked about "those stupid frat boys."

"Dad," he said, "how long ago was that?"

"I don't know. Last year, maybe a couple of years ago."

"Think about it. Those might have been all your ideas."

Indeed. After dinner I dropped him off at Sigma Chi. I would have liked to go back to our house and talk some more, but he had work to do for the brothers, cleaning their bathrooms with a toothbrush. It seemed a thin line between maintenance work and hazing.

The next morning we went skiing at Lake Eldora. On an empty back slope he came to a biting stop and sprayed me to the waist with snow. I growled and he laughed. We stood for a while in the cold sunlight watching a couple of camp robbers as they looped across the slope from spruce to spruce. He pulled off his glove and took hold of my ear.

"Very cold ear," he said.

That night he had to help cook dinner at the fraternity, and the next morning he was leaving at six for a race at Winter Park. I hadn't seen enough of him, hadn't had enough contact with him, and today was the end of it. At home after showering, in his last half hour free, we stretched out on the rug in front of the TV and watched a hockey game. Television had long been our excuse to lie shoulder to shoulder without doing anything. After a while I slid my arm behind his neck. I wanted to tell him something: how glad I was we had gotten these few minutes together.

It was an awkward declaration, but I made it. "I'd hate to come up," I said, "and not get to lie around like this the way we used to. At least for a few minutes. I know you're busy and you're growing up, but I still love to hold you."

The game droned on in front of us. For a moment I thought he wasn't going to say anything. Then he shifted his weight closer and said, "Always hold me."

•   •   •

He didn't get into Sigma Chi. After ten weeks of scrubbing their bathrooms and running errands for them they blackballed him and one other pledge. They didn't give a reason.

How could this be? Janir got along with everyone. Now he was angry and hurt and didn't want to talk about it. "They are stupid frat boys," he said.

When I called a week later he sounded reasonably cheerful. I asked, "You're not stuffing those emotions and feelings, are you?"

"I got over it. Yeah, I was hurt for a few days. But I've got other things to do."

"Where you going to live next year?"

"Toku and Jiro are getting a condo. I already talked to them about living there. Dad, don't worry, I'll be fine."

"Always deal?" I said.

"Never squeal."

Janir at 18

A COLLEGE KID NEEDS MONEY: FOR TUITION, FOR RENT, for clothes, for movies, for an old computer and an older car, for road trips to Malibu and Mardi Gras. I know Janir could get by with less, but I don't want him to. Money, I believe, can do a lot for your spirit. Besides, I've been making more recently, with checks coming in from Hollywood: someone has optioned my second novel.

His junior year, Janir decides to spend a semester in Spain. He makes the application and takes care of all the details, and I move some cash into his account to pay for it. His choice of country makes me happy, for he'll be studying the language he learned first and the one I'm fluent in. He's headed for Seville on a program sponsored by the University of Wisconsin. He won't know anyone there, but that doesn't worry him. He makes friends easily.

On a frosty day in January I drive him to the Denver airport and we check in with the airline an hour and a half early as requested. Janir's new luggage bulges with his clothes and gear, and he carries his passport, ticket and traveler's checks in a separate pouch—but not, we discover, his Eurailpass or his program acceptance letter.

"You may need that to get your visa," the airline attendant tells us.

"Where is it?" I ask him.

He looks at the floor, finally remembers. "In my file cabinet. In a red envelope."

"Goddamn it, Janir."

The attendant stands poised behind her keyboard. I don't care, I'm pissed. Only yesterday I locked the cabinet in the brick shed next to our old apartment. I asked him three or four times if he had everything he needed. I listed some items—but I too forgot about his Eurailpass and the letter. So mainly, of course, I'm mad at myself.

He's silent, cowed by my outburst. I glance at the clock. "Maybe I can get them." It's a seventy-mile round trip, and I've got less than ninety minutes. It would be close.

"You can do it, Dad."

"All right, I'll try. If I don't make it back, get on the plane anyway. Go and we'll work it out. Probably you can talk your way through."

I give him a hug in case I don't get back in time, then turn and run: through the lobby, up the escalator and out across the pedestrian bridge to the parking lot. I run all the way to my truck, jump in completely out of breath, start the engine, wheel down the circular ramp to ground level, pay the parking fee and take off for Boulder, pushing my four-cylinder pickup to its limits. On the highway I get into fifth gear and put it up to eighty. The speed limit's fifty-five. I watch for cops. One passes me headed the other way, but we're separated by a long concrete divider, so the hell with him. I lose speed going up a few hills, but pass everyone on the last long descent into Boulder.

Another cop, but this one's parked with his lights on, giving someone a ticket. I pass him doing seventy and he never looks up. I'm tense, I'm alert, every few minutes I calculate the time. I don't want Janir to fly off to Spain thinking I'm still angry with him. That passed in a minute, and after today I won't see him for six months.

I cross Boulder to our old apartment, run across the snow, open the padlock on the steel door and toss things out of the way so I can get the file cabinet open. Quickly I find the red envelope with the pass and letter inside. I close the door and sprint back to the truck.

It's going to be close. I tear back down the highway to Denver, get off at the airport, do sixty-five on Quebec Street and zip up onto the departures ramp at 11:40, the exact minute the plane is supposed to leave. I abandon the truck in a no-standing zone and run up to the automatic doors, pushing them apart as they open. I hurry through the metal detectors, then try not to look like a terrorist as I speed-walk the last few yards to Janir's gate.

There's no one there: no passengers and no attendants. The door to the jetway is closed, and I can't see if the plane has left. I feel sick.

Suddenly the door swings open and two people come out: a woman in high heels and a dark airline suit, and a guy with a clipboard and a radio. I run up to them. "Has it gone?" Of course it hasn't gone, they just came from there. "I've got something for my son," I tell them, and hold out the red envelope. "He's got to have it."

The guy with the clipboard considers me for a moment, then picks up his radio and keys the mike. "Hey, Jack, you close the door yet? Yeah . . . well, open it up. I've got somethin' goes on board."

Yes! I follow the guy into the jetway, then run ahead of him, my knees wobbling on the shaky floor. Just as I round the last corner the plane's door moves out and over. I step inside and hand the envelope to the flight attendant.

"You can't go in," he says. "Who's it for?"

I peer past him into the body of the plane. "Janir Thorndike," I say. "His name's on it. There! There he is in back!"

At the far end of the cabin Janir has seen me and stood up. He's smiling. I can see his white teeth from ninety feet off, and his arms are raised above the people in the next row.

I got it! I mouth to him, and point to the envelope in the attendant's hand. Janir looks handsome, he looks beautiful. *Good-bye,* I mouth. *I love you.*

He's waving with both hands. The attendant gives me a nudge. "Gotta close the door," he says.

I step out into the jetway, and the door swings into place. "Thanks," I tell the man with the radio, and put my arm around his shoulder. "He's going to Spain!" The guy consults his clipboard: this is more than he bargained for. Finally he nods. "I have a son too," he says.

I'm too selfish to talk about his son, and float out through the lobby back to my truck. Though unlocked, nothing's missing. There isn't even a ticket on the windshield. I sit down behind the wheel and collapse. How close it was: only a minute later would have been too late. But now we've had a great good-bye. I've seen Janir's smiling face, and he's seen mine.

•   •   •

He calls me every week, twice as often as he used to from Boulder. On the phone he calls me Snake, Daddy-O, Johnny. He tells me Spanish women are gorgeous. He says flamenco is exciting and *la Sevillana,* another dance, is even better, and that in all of Spain Seville is the place to be. There are thirty-nine guys in his program and 112 girls. He lives with a family, and his Spanish improves by the day.

He makes plenty of friends, both Americans and Spaniards. He explores the narrow streets of the old town and eats standing up at Los Gallegos, a cramped restaurant where the waiters bellow their orders back to the kitchen. He drinks wine in the Patio San Eloy with a gypsy woman who sings off-key and plays the guitar worse than I do.

After six weeks he asks me to come for a visit. "Dad," he says, "you've got to see my life."

I find this request so engaging I immediately start making plans, and by the end of March I follow him across the Atlantic.

I haven't been to Europe since 1965. Too boring, I've always thought: not as dramatic and raw as South America. Perhaps not—but from the minute I get there I'm completely engrossed. The Madrid sanitation collectors are all on strike, and the terminal is piled high with trash. Everyone smokes. They crush their butts on the marble floor with an elegant turn of the heel, directly beneath signs announcing *No Fumar*. Though at home I hate smokers, here I hardly care. I'm on vacation, I'm in Spain, I'm going to see my son. The women are all beauties, just as he promised, and from their splendid lips the accent of Madrid seems delightfully artful: *la thona,* they say for "zone," and *el thapato* for "shoe."

Twenty hours after leaving home I finally reach Seville. Janir waits on the other side of customs, looking completely relaxed in his running shoes, jeans and Camp Sangamon T-shirt. How miraculous it seems to find him here, far across the ocean. We embrace each other, a long hug coming easily in a foreign country. Then we catch a bus into town. I let him show me the ropes.

He's completely relaxed about being an American—not at all the way I was when I first went to El Salvador as a Peace Corps volunteer. There, none of us wanted to stick out as gringos or act like the embassy or AID people: wealthy, loud and insensitive to the local culture. We tried to dress like Salvadorans, and to speak Spanish whenever in public, or at least mute our English.

Not Janir. He talks on the bus as if we were in Denver. He's an American in Spain and doesn't care who knows it. But he also speaks some in Spanish: *"Primero vamos al hotel. Es en el centro."*

"Está en el centro," I correct him.

He makes other mistakes in tense and agreement, and I correct them all. Finally he gives me a look and falls silent.

God, I'm a prig. Instead of celebrating his new Spanish I have to ram the grammar down his throat and try to teach him everything I know in a day. We ride the bus without talking. I hardly slept on the all-night flight and now I'm exhausted. The bus empties out slowly as it approaches the center of town. At a traffic light Janir lifts his hand and wordlessly takes hold of my ear. I am forgiven.

He has reserved a room for me in the old quarter of town, where the tight streets wind past flower shops, ornate doorways and small parks dotted with lime trees. The hotel is old, cool and dimly lit, my room an irregular trapezoid with only a tiny window near the ceiling. It's as austere as a monk's cell, but I don't care. I just need to sleep.

Janir goes off to his family for dinner, and I crawl under the blankets. The next thing I know someone's tapping at the door. I struggle up and let him in.

"On your *feet*," he barks. "It's Thursday night, almost the week-end!"

By nine o'clock the first restaurants start opening their doors. We walk to Los Gallegos, stand at the long zinc bar and ask for two swordfish plates. The waiter roars back to the kitchen, *"Dame do' pe' e'pada,"* swallowing all his *s*'s and *z*'s in an accent I can barely follow. He marks what we owe in chalk on the bar.

The swordfish arrives in two minutes. It's packed with garlic and hardly the delicacy we eat at my father's on Cape Cod. I doubt its character altogether, but no matter: I'm hungry, the fish is dense and salty and comes piled with French fries and a salad. We eat standing up among workmen and older couples, the city's thrifty diners.

"Cheapest place in Seville," Janir says proudly.

After dinner we walk the streets of the Barrio Santa Cruz, where customers fill the bars and spill out onto the narrow sidewalks and tiny plazas. The Spanish boys look urbane, and the girls dazzling. Most of them are in their teens, and almost no one is over thirty. By that age they must all be busy with families. The boys roam from bar to bar in small groups, or pull up on thunderous motor-cycles in smooth leather jackets with their hair slicked back, never a helmet. The girls wear heels and little eighteen-inch skirts, or tailored shorts over pale white hose and loafers. Though the atmo-sphere is carnal, the youngest revelers look no older than four-teen. Clearly this is a safe city: the girls go in pairs, but they go anywhere.

We wander from bar to bar ordering *tintos de verano,* a summery drink of red wine and soda. Everywhere Janir knows people: mainly American friends from his program, but also young Spaniards. The barrio is thronged. Drinks spill and glasses break constantly, but no one pays any attention. By dawn the entire neighborhood will be swept clean by a crew of workers in orange jumpsuits.

Inside the Patio San Eloy, as Janir sings with the off-key gypsy woman, I meet an older couple who instantly win me over by refusing to believe I'm Janir's father. We must be brothers, they insist. Of course I soak that up.

Then, after they've been so flattering, I'm surprised to discover they're younger than I am, only forty-three and forty-one. The man has a paunch and jowls. The woman is dark-eyed, pale, perhaps once a great beauty but now worn.

"You Americans all look so young," the man says, without the least rancor. As we talk he and his woman indulge in continuous cigarettes, *tintos* and sandwiches of *jamón serrano,* the country ham that hangs from hooks behind the bar. The couple runs a small publishing business together. They have three kids apiece and are separated from their spouses. They've been lovers for two years.

"Will you marry?" I ask them.

The woman shakes her head. "In Spain you do that once."

"We don't care," he tells me. "We're happy."

"Feliz en la cama," she adds with a sly smile: happy in bed.

In this bar full of kids I must seem the ideal confidant. They tell me secrets. They let me know that now, in their forties, they are living out the great sexual adventure of their lives. I love to hear this. I'm happy for them. We drink and tell stories.

Midnight comes and goes. Janir checks up on me to see if I'm still entertained. I am, I'm having a great time. I've rediscovered the thrill of travel, and I drink freely, as I rarely do at home. We move on with a pack of his friends to a Caribbean bar, an African bar, several others. I'm tipsy but starting to fade. The men in orange jumpsuits have begun to sweep the streets. Before I leave I get detailed instructions from Janir on how to find my hotel within the maze of the barrio. We'll meet tomorrow at noon after his morning classes.

"Will you make it to your classes?" I ask.

"I always make it to my classes."

"A little hung over?"

He smiles. "Always dee, never squee."

•   •   •

For a couple of days in the middle of the next week, while Janir studies, I take a bus into the country west of Seville to see the old Spain. In the hill town of Aracena, surrounded by cork trees and olives, I sit in the tenuous spring sunshine and talk to old men in black wool suits, half deaf, their fingers blunt and horny, their ears bristling with white hairs. They know all the bullfighters Hemingway wrote about in the twenties and thirties: Joselito, Chicuelo, El Cagancho. One old guy once walked the forty miles to Seville to watch Juan Belmonte fight.

Janir and his friends, though they've come to study Iberian culture, care little about the old ways. They're having too much fun in the current fiesta. Upon my return to Seville he and his friend Tawnya invite me out dancing. She's kind of his girlfriend, I suppose —though it's hard to tell exactly what that means these days, given how their whole crew hangs out together, makes weekend trips to Portugal and Morocco and spends the night in hotel room configurations I'd like to hear about but am too diplomatic to ask.

Janir, Tawnya and I wander around town from bar to bar and eventually wind up at the Salsodramo. There the big floor is jammed, the sound system is bumped—and my kid can dance! This is new, or new to me. He leaps up on a bench against the wall and shows me some rap moves, some Latin palm-on-the-stomach moves. Tawnya, blond and irrepressible, joins right in. I join in myself.

•   •   •

One night at one A.M. Janir and I sit down at a marble table inside a small café. Outside it's drizzling. A bored waiter brings our pastries and espressos, then leans against the chrome cooler. We're the only three people in the room.

I've brought along a list of questions. Janir likes to be interviewed about his life, and in the past I've queried him about camp and college, sometimes with a tape recorder. Now I have only a notebook and pen.

"I've been thinking about writing a book," I tell him. "About you."

"You mean a novel?"

"No, a memoir. About raising you, what it was like."

"Okay," he says.

"So I want to ask you some questions."

"Ask me."

We talk about his childhood. I ask him a hundred questions and search through his memories. I have my own but am aware of their mutability. He reminds me of incidents I had forgotten, and tells me stories I never heard from junior high and high school, his bad-boy exploits. I write everything down. Eventually I come around to Clarisa.

"Has growing up with her been a great handicap?"

"It's not like an ordeal or anything. But it's a hassle when people ask about her. I never say she's a schizophrenic. I can deal with her better now that I'm older, but it still makes me uncomfortable."

"How about being a single child? What do you think about that?"

He hesitates for the first time tonight. He pushes his empty cup around in its saucer. All the rest of his answers have tumbled out.

"Sometimes I wish you and Mom didn't get divorced and had another kid. So I could have had a brother or sister. I think it'd be easier to deal with her if I did, because I could relate to another kid easier than I could relate to you about it."

I focus on my notebook as I write this down—but underneath I'm stunned by his wish that Clarisa and I had stayed together. Has he thought about this possibility all these years? I did want him to have a sibling, but I gave up the idea of doing that with Clarisa when he was three. Was that a terrible mistake? Something I haven't wanted to face?

I signal the waiter for two more espressos. "Do you have any fond memories of your mom?" I ask Janir.

He thinks about it. "Not really."

"None?"

He shakes his head.

"Not one?"

My incredulity presses on him. He glances around the room, studies the ornate mirror on the far wall, the stiff black chairs and checkered floor tiles. Outside, the rain is still falling. Finally he says, "She made me a salad one time."

"When was that?"

"In Athens. On one of her visits. I had to take some green food to school, everyone in the class did, so she made me a salad from the garden. I don't know why I remember that."

A wave of sadness sweeps over me. This is the fondest memory he can come up with about his mother? That she made him a salad? I feel like crying. Janir watches me, then stares out the window.

The waiter brings the espressos. At home, if I had any hope of getting to sleep before dawn, I could never drink coffee this late at night. Here it doesn't seem to matter. I pick up the tiny white cup and focus on it, trying to get past the surge in my chest. I blow on the dark liquid but still burn my lips.

"I wasn't very good with your mom," I say finally. "I was too young, too insecure."

"You were a weenie," he says. He knows all my stories from Deerfield.

We have come around, I realize, to talk like two adults about broken hearts, emotions and feelings. Yet surely Janir will have to struggle with his parents' history the same as I have done, the same as we all do. In some ways my parents were a mismatch, and for thirty years I've been reflecting on their story and trying to use my own life to heal the rift in their relationship. It's a common ambition, and no matter how Janir and I talk he will probably do the same.

"How about you?" I ask him. "Do you think you'll get married and have kids?"

"Not right away. You taught me that. You should think it over, not just jump in. But sure, I'll get married. I like the idea of a big family, maybe three kids. I'd look after them as much as my wife. Of course it would take an ideal job to make enough money and also have free time."

"What if I had another child?" I ask him. "What would you think of that?"

"That's cool." He stretches his feet out beside the table. "He wouldn't be like a brother, but I could still hang out with him and teach him things."

"Like what?"

He flashes me his smile. "I could teach him to be as sweet as me."

•   •   •

My two weeks in Spain are almost up. We've been sitting in the Parque Maria Luisa, talking and reading, and we're about to part for a couple of hours: Janir to eat dinner with his family, and I to sit under the rhododendrons and write in my journal.

I walk him to the edge of the park. There he gives me five and sets out across the Plaza España. It's warm, the sun has come out after two days of rain and once again Janir looks thoroughly American. He wears a Colorado Buffaloes sweatshirt, a baggy pair of shorts and his cherished Cal Bears baseball hat, the one he threw into a bullring a month ago. The matador wiped it on his bloodstained suit, and his assistant threw it back to Janir in the stands. As usual he wears it backwards. He strides without a sidewise glance past the great curving plaza, one of the architectural triumphs of Spain.

I watch him go. It's two hundred yards to the Avenida Borbolla along a street closed to cars, and Janir is alone on the sunny wide pavement. A gust of wind lifts a cluster of dried leaves from the park and swirls them along behind him, but he doesn't seem to notice. He's probably thinking about something. Sometimes he hums a tune as he walks. He wears his springy nylon river sandals over a pair of white socks. He doesn't mind standing out: I think he likes it. He's at ease with his dark skin. Being Latin, he told me the other night, is "better than being an average white guy."

Yet suddenly, on this empty street in Seville, I see him as exposed and unprotected. Against all logic my eyes fill with tears. Maybe it's only the majestic plaza that makes him look so alone. I know he's healthy and happy, that he has plenty of friends and is doing fine. Yet now I'm crying. Maybe it's his mother. Maybe it's the memory of my own lonely years in prep school and college—a time no one, not even Janir, can help me reclaim. He reaches the Avenida Borbolla, crosses the street and joins the strangers on the distant sidewalk. I watch him until he disappears. This, I think, is what I've done with *my* life.

FOR THE BEST IN PAPERBACKS, LOOK FOR THE

In every corner of the world, on every subject under the sun, Penguin represents quality and variety—the very best in publishing today.

For complete information about books available from Penguin—including Puffins, Penguin Classics, and Arkana—and how to order them, write to us at the appropriate address below. Please note that for copyright reasons the selection of books varies from country to country.

In the United Kingdom: Please write to *Dept. JC, Penguin Books Ltd, FREEPOST, West Drayton, Middlesex UB7 0BR.*

If you have any difficulty in obtaining a title, please send your order with the correct money, plus ten percent for postage and packaging, to *P.O. Box No. 11, West Drayton, Middlesex UB7 0BR*

In the United States: Please write to *Consumer Sales, Penguin USA, P.O. Box 999, Dept. 17109, Bergenfield, New Jersey 07621-0120.* VISA and MasterCard holders call 1-800-253-6476 to order all Penguin titles

In Canada: Please write to *Penguin Books Canada Ltd, 10 Alcorn Avenue, Suite 300, Toronto, Ontario M4V 3B2*

In Australia: Please write to *Penguin Books Australia Ltd, P.O. Box 257, Ringwood, Victoria 3134*

In New Zealand: Please write to *Penguin Books (NZ) Ltd, Private Bag 102902, North Shore Mail Centre, Auckland 10*

In India: Please write to *Penguin Books India Pvt Ltd, 706 Eros Apartments, 56 Nehru Place, New Delhi 110 019*

In the Netherlands: Please write to *Penguin Books Netherlands bv, Postbus 3507, NL-1001 AH Amsterdam*

In Germany: Please write to *Penguin Books Deutschland GmbH, Metzlerstrasse 26, 60594 Frankfurt am Main*

In Spain: Please write to *Penguin Books S. A., Bravo Murillo 19, 1° B, 28015 Madrid*

In Italy: Please write to *Penguin Italia s.r.l., Via Felice Casati 20, I-20124 Milano*

In France: Please write to *Penguin France S. A., 17 rue Lejeune, F−31000 Toulouse*

In Japan: Please write to *Penguin Books Japan, Ishikiribashi Building, 2−5−4, Suido, Bunkyo-ku, Tokyo 112*

In Greece: Please write to *Penguin Hellas Ltd, Dimocritou 3, GR−106 71 Athens*

In South Africa: Please write to *Longman Penguin Southern Africa (Pty) Ltd, Private Bag X08, Bertsham 2013*